CONTRACT

GREENS CONCISE SCOTS LAW

CONTRACT

By

Stephen Woolman, Advocate

W. GREEN/Sweet & Maxwell
EDINBURGH
1994

First published 1987
Reprinted 1989
Reprinted 1990
Reprinted 1991

Second edition published 1994
Reprinted 1995
Reprinted 1998
Reprinted 1999

ISBN O 414 01058 2

Printed in Great Britain by
Headway Press Ltd, Reading

Preface to First Edition

Contract is a large and complex branch of law. In my view it is also a fascinating one. This short book is aimed at those approaching the subject for the first time. I hope it may serve to key readers into the major principles and issues involved. Because this is an introductory work, I have tried to avoid overburdening the text with too much detail. Fuller citation of authority is to be found in the books and articles mentioned in the select bibliography.

This book was conceived at the University of Melbourne. I am grateful to the members of the Law School there for their hospitality and encouragement. Various parts of the book have been read and commented on by John Blackie, Frank Maher and Colin Tyre. My thanks are due to them. I owe my deepest debt to Hector MacQueen with whom I have debated contract problems over several years and who read and commented on the final draft. The labours of typing and retyping were skilfully undertaken by Mrs Lorna Paterson.

The Old College
August 1987

S.E.W.

PREFACE TO SECOND EDITION

The river of contract law flows on. I have been tempted to add much of the new material which has swelled the casebooks since 1987. However, I have resisted that temptation. I have only added those cases which appear to me to be of significance. The philosophy of this work remains the same. It aims to be a short, understandable introduction to the subject. It is not a treatise. In this edition, I have attempted to recast some of the discussion to make it clearer or more accurate.

Advocates' Library
February 1994

STEPHEN WOOLMAN

CONTENTS

TABLE OF CASES

Table of Cases

TABLE OF STATUTES

CHAPTER 1

INTRODUCTION

CONTRACTS feature in many areas of our lives. Each day we may be involved in a variety of different contracts: buying goods, travelling by bus, going to the cinema or arranging for a washing machine to be repaired. Some of our most important long-term relationships—those concerning how we earn a living and where we reside—are based upon contracts. Nor can we fail to be aware that the business world is rooted in contract. Auctions, share-dealing, insurance and commercial leasing are just a few examples. The list could be extended almost indefinitely. What links these many different types of contract? Let us consider a few explanations in turn.

One answer that suggests itself is that every contract effects an exchange. The exchange may be goods for money, as in the case of sale of goods; or services for money, for example where a client instructs a solicitor to draw up a will; or goods for goods—the contract of barter. The exchange may take place at the time the contract is made or it may be postponed to sometime in the future. Most contracts possess this element of exchange. Exchange, however, cannot be the whole answer because in some contracts no such element is present. An aunt may draw up a contract under which she is to pay £500 each year to assist her niece through university. The contract is valid even though the aunt receives nothing from her niece in return. Similarly there is no legal objection to an agreement whereby a sportsman consents to refrain from writing newspaper articles about his team. The agreement can be enforced despite the fact that the sportsman does not get paid or receive any other benefit for signing the agreement. So while exchange is a common factor in most contracts it is not a necessary ingredient.

A second potential link between the different types of contract is the concept of promise. It is possible to reduce every contract to the form "X promises the following" and "Y promises the following." In the case of the contract of employment, the employee's main promise is to carry out the work he is instructed to do. The employer's main promise is to pay the employee's wages. Promise is useful because it emphasises the obligatory nature of contract. The moral precept that we must abide by our promises enables us to accept readily that people who break their legal promises must face

1

the consequences. So if the employee breaks his promise and does not perform his duties, the employer has the option of terminating the contract of employment. Equally if the employer breaks his promise, the employee is entitled to sue to recover the wages.

There are, however, two reasons why it is inappropriate to define contract in terms of promise. The first is that, as we have seen, the great majority of contracts actually do involve an element of exchange. One thing is given in return for another. The concept of promise does not truly explain this reciprocity which is at the core of most contracts. Viewing a contract as a promise distorts the picture by failing to reflect that the promises are the counterparts of one another. A look at a simple contract of sale of goods may help to illustrate this point. The customer who purchases a newspaper can be viewed as promising to pay the price. Similarly the news-agent can be seen as promising to transfer the newspaper. Such an analysis, however, seems artificial: it does not square with the reciprocal nature of the purchaser's and seller's acts.

The second reason for not defining contracts in terms of promise is because in Scots law there is a separate category of obligation which is actually called promise. This category is distinct from that of contract. A promise is an obligation where only one party undertakes to be legally bound and the obligation arises by an act on his part alone. Suppose a newspaper runs a promotional cam-paign in which it states that £50,000 will be paid to the first person to paddle around the Scottish coastline in a kayak. A person who performed this feat might enforce this obligation as a promise. The newspaper would be bound to pay over the sum to anyone who satisfied this condition. In Chapter 4 we shall see that the dividing line between contract and promise is very narrow. Nonetheless it is preferable to avoid defining the one, contract, in terms of the other, promise.

The discussion so far shows how difficult it is to find a definition of contract which will overcome all objections. Some jurists have given up the search as a lost cause. Most, however, have come to the conclusion that a definition can best be framed in terms of the notion of agreement. All contracts involve the parties acting in concert to achieve a particular end. It may involve the construction of an oil tanker, the provision of an overdraft, or the purchase of a bar of chocolate. In each case the parties agree on the nature and the goal of their particular contract. Accordingly a contract can be said to be a legally enforceable agreement. Two points need to be made about this definition. First the term "enforceable" is used here in a special sense. Most agreements are not enforced in the sense that the parties are made to fulfil their contractual obliga-tions. Instead each party is accorded remedies in the event of the other's failure to perform as agreed. If a builder fails to turn up on the due date to erect an extension to a house, the owner will not litigate to make the builder come and actually build the extension. Instead he will claim damages. Secondly, agreement may be more apparent than real. Does an individual really "agree" to the terms of a car-hire contract? The customer usually signs the form put in front of him without attending in any detail to its terms. If he does read the small print, he may not understand its meaning. Even the most battle-hardened solicitor may sign such an agreement on the footing that he is in no position to negotiate more favourable terms. Defining contract as an enforceable agreement therefore may not satisfy the jurist, but it does provide a working definition.

A query may be put. Even if agreement does link all the different types of contract, surely the truth is that the principles relating to each contract form a separate branch of law? There are, for example, special rules relating to marine insurance which are not mirrored in other types of insurance contract, far less in contracts of lease or partnership. Why do lawyers not speak of a law of contracts rather than a law of contract? Paradoxically, the answer to this question stems precisely from the great variety of contracts which exist. The range of contractual arrangements which people can enter into is so vast that it is not possible to lay down specific rules to cover every situation that might arise. Accordingly when a contractual dispute arises, there is often no special rule to resolve the issue. Recourse must then be made to the law of contract, because it has general principles rather than particular rules. A new or unusual situation can be resolved by reference to a principle even where the special rules are silent. So in looking at a particular legal problem, it is always necessary to have in mind both the general principles and the special rules relating to the contract in question.

The interaction of the special rules and the general principles is illustrated by the contract of employment. Over the past three decades there has been a great deal of employment legislation. Questions concerning, for example, discrimination, maternity leave and the right to an itemised pay statement are the province of this modern law of employment. But that has not eclipsed the role of the law of contract entirely. Questions concerning whether the contract has been formed and, if so, on what terms, remain within the province of the law of contract. Likewise questions relating to who can sue on the contract and what the measure of damages for breach ought to be. In some rare instances different solutions may be provided. An employee who is sacked may seek a remedy by raising an action of unfair dismissal in an industrial tribunal. That is a statutory remedy of the law of employment. But it is still open to an employee to bring the older contractual action of wrongful dismissal in the sheriff court or the Court of Session. This might be advantageous to the employee who has not worked for a sufficient length of time to claim unfair dismissal, or who feels that the financial limits on the awards made by industrial tribunals are too low compared with awards in the courts.

In this book we shall discuss the general law of contract. In passing, we shall also consider the law of promise. The principles of contract law will be illustrated by reference to the many different varieties of contract. As is demonstrated by the example of employment, the law of contract provides a framework of principles into which each individual contract fits. We begin by looking at the development of contract and shall then consider some aspects of contract theory.

DEVELOPMENT

In primitive societies with fixed social and economic positions there is no great need for a law of contract. Contracts will be relatively simple and will usually involve simultaneous exchange—barter or sale. There is not a great deal of scope for disputes to arise. Both parties can see and touch the commodities with which they are dealing, whether they be gold or grain or animals. Ownership usually depends on an individual's status—as chief, slave or child—rather than on the contracts which he makes. The role of custom is more important in individuals' lives than their ability to make contracts. So whether a person owns a particular parcel of land will depend on several factors: can land be owned by an individual in that community; does that person have right to the land by virtue of inheritance or marriage? Ownership will not, however, depend upon purchase of the land from the previous owner. A law of contract comes to be required when there is a development from simultaneous to future exchange. Sometimes this is referred to as the change from "executed" to "executory" contracts.

The Romans were the first to work out in detail the legal consequences of contractual obligations. As Rome developed in commercial as well as in political importance, there was a need to devise laws to regulate the great increase in business transactions which occurred. Originally it was a rather rigid system. Contracts could in general only be enforced if they were real or formal. Real contracts were those which required something more than mere agreement. At first some ceremony would have to be gone through. Later what was required was transfer of the item in question. The transfer could be actual or symbolic. So far as formal contracts were concerned, a set of formalities had to be complied with for the transaction to be effective. Instead of two parties merely agreeing that A should sell B a share, or that X would lease a room in the urbs from Y, formal contracts required that some set pattern of words had to be gone through, or some special writing used. In the later period the jurists succeeded in making the law much more flexible, but it remained a law of contracts rather than contract. This meant that if a dispute occurred, it would be resolved by reference to the rules of the particular contract in question, not by reference to some general body of principles.

The continental jurist Grotius is generally regarded as the author of the modern law of contract. His achievement was to take the principles laid down by the Romans in their several species of contract and to bind them together into a coherent body of law, animated by the general notion that all obligations should be binding. In other words when persons make agreements, it should bind them, notwithstanding that no formal or real requirements are complied with.

The architect of modern Scots law, Viscount Stair, borrowed from a number of sources when writing his magisterial work, the *Institutions of the Law of Scotland*. As well as drawing heavily on Roman law, Grotius and other continental writers, Stair relied on the canon law and the common law of Scotland as it existed in his time. There are two important points to note about Stair's treatment of contract and its related obligations. The first is that his account is a much more substantial, developed treatment than that found in contemporaneous English works. Blackstone, for example, hardly devoted any pages to contract law and it can be fairly said that the English did not have a law of contract until the nineteenth century. The second point is that Stair was even more radical than Grotius in his desire to remove formal and real impediments from the law. He adopted the maxim of the canon law: "every paction produceth action." Loosely translated, this means that every seriously intended engagement is binding on the parties, irrespective of the form in which it is couched.

The eighteenth and nineteenth centuries were periods of great social and economic change. The shift from agriculture to industry and the urbanisation of the population saw a large increase in the number and range of transactions which took place. Manufacturers bought materials, hired workers, subcontracted work and sold the goods produced: all on a scale hitherto unknown. Law was not immune from this change. Courts had to attempt to deal with a variety of new types of transaction. They responded by fashioning new law to meet the new conditions.

Two interlinked ideas came into prominence: freedom of contract and sanctity of contract. Freedom of contract is the notion that everyone, unless insane or under age, can exercise choice. They can choose (a) whether or not to enter a particular contract and (b) to determine the terms on which it is made. Sanctity of contract is the corollary of freedom of contract. It simply means that all contracts freely entered into are binding upon the parties. In an age of expansion, when Britain's pre-eminence in many spheres—military, economic and scientific—was at its height, there was a natural reluctance to tamper with the established order of things. While things were going so well for the country as a whole, the argument ran, any intervention might seriously hamper continued prosperity and development. In economic matters this led the government to pursue a *laissez-faire* policy. It did not attempt to regulate markets or manufacturers except in the case of extreme abuse. In the legal context the courts were unwilling to interfere with the contracts coming before them. Workers were bound by their contracts, however long their working hours or poor their remuneration. It was not for the judges to relieve someone of a bad bargain. Freedom of contract was an application of the utilitarian philosophy that everyone was the best judge of their own interests. Bentham stated that "no man of ripe years and of sound mind, acting freely, and with his eyes open, ought to be hindered, with a view to his advantage, from making such bargain, in the way of obtaining money as he thinks fit, nor . . . anybody hindered from supplying him, upon any terms he thinks proper to accede to."[1]

Freedom of contract should not be overemphasised in the Scottish context. A study of the contract cases decided by the courts presided over by the greatest Scottish judge of the nineteenth century, John Inglis, successively Lord Justice-Clerk and Lord President of the Court of Session, suggests that the concept never reached the same zenith in Scotland as it did in England. The courts did in general seem more willing than their English counterparts to step in to correct obvious unfairness when circumstances warranted it. However, freedom of contract was and remains an important strand in contract thinking.. If the parties are of equal bargaining strength and want to tailor a contract to their individual wishes, the law has always given them wide scope to accomplish their aim. A recording star, for example, might negotiate a contract with a promoter of rock concerts. It may allow for a very high fee to be paid and contain a variety of unusual terms and conditions. Perhaps it is stipulated that champagne will be available in the star's dressing room or that a masseur will be provided.

---

[1] *Jeremy Bentham's Economic Writings*, ed. Stark (London, 1952), i. 129.

If the nineteenth century can be viewed as a century of *laissez-faire* then the twentieth century can be seen as one of the intervention. Even in the nineteenth century the notion of freedom of contract was largely a juristic abstraction rather than a reality of everyday life. A traveller from Edinburgh to London would have to go by train, by coach or by ship. By the end of the century the train would almost certainly be his preferred mode of travel. As only one company operated the railway line between the two capitals, the traveller had no choice about the party with whom he contracted. Moreover when he went to the booking desk to buy his ticket, the opportunities for negotiating the terms of travel were non-existent. He either bought the ticket on the railway company's terms or he did not travel. Freedom of contract in such a situation is a myth.

With the growth of monopolies in various fields, whether governmental or private, freedom of choice in deciding with whom to enter contracts has been eroded. Likewise the opportunity to negotiate terms. Many businesses fix their contractual terms in advance by the use of printed forms. To rent a television, hire a car or borrow money from the bank an individual normally has to sign a printed form which already has the terms of the contract embossed upon it. There is no opportunity to vary the terms; they must be taken as they stand or left. French lawyers refer to such a contract as a *contrat d'adhésion*: one either adheres completely or not at all. The recognition that all contracts were not freely entered into and freely negotiated led to the development of new doctrines and new principles. But these developments have occurred in the context of a widely held belief that an important feature of the law of contract is its tendency to promote stability by having certain legal rules. People must be able to predict how their contracts will be enforced. And what they themselves have agreed will usually determine their legal rights. So the presumption is to enforce the arrangements that the parties themselves have arrived at. Interference by the courts will only occur in strictly defined circumstances.

CONTRACTUAL THEORY

It is helpful to obtain a mental fix on the place of the law of contract relative to other areas of law. On page 8 a broad division of the law is given.

Public Law and Private Law

It is possible to think of law regulating two different forms of relationship. Public law is that area of law which concerns the

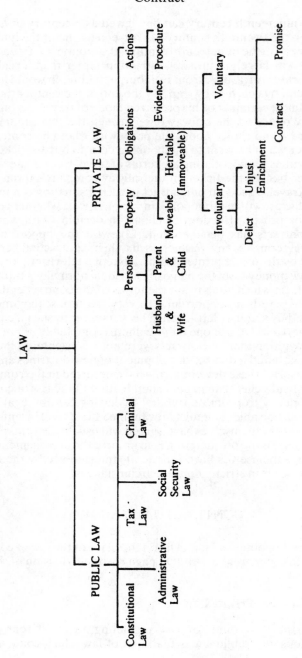

relationship of the state with private persons, or of different organs of the state with one other. Thus taxation is part of public law because in matters relating to income or corporation tax the revenue authorities are always involved. Disputes arise between private persons and H.M. Inspectors of Taxes as to the amount of tax due. Similarly, in matters relating to Value Added Tax (V.A.T.), the two parties will be the person subject to the tax and the Commissioners of Customs and Excise. In administrative law, a government department or local authority is usually one side of the equation. In criminal cases the state, in the guise of the Lord Advocate or procurator fiscal prosecutes those who have transgressed the provisions of the criminal law.

Private law is that body of law dealing with the relationships of private persons. A person can be an individual, a partnership, a voluntary association, or a company. So when two neighbours have a dispute about an overhanging branch, or a customer queries the quality of an item he has bought in a shop, or a shareholder wishes to take action against the directors of a company, these are all within the sphere of private law.

This distinction is much more important in English law than in Scots law. The history of Scots law indicates that the courts have been reluctant to differentiate between the two forms of relationship. The same principles apply to each.[2] In any event the boundaries between the two forms of relationship often dissolve. It is still possible for a private individual to raise a prosecution in the civil courts. Public authorities are subject to private law. A contract made by a local health authority to build a hospital or to be supplied with laundry is just as much governed by private law as any similar contract made by a private person. Sometimes, a contractual dispute may have profound political and social consequences. An example is provided by *British Coal Corporation* v. *South of Scotland Electricity Board*[3]:

In the early 1960s, the South of Scotland Electricity Board resolved to build a new power station in Scotland. The British Coal Corporation (then the National Coal Board) were aware that unless the station was coal-fired, it would have a significant and adverse effect on the mining industry in Scotland. After much discussion and negotiation, S.S.E.B. determined to build a coal-fired station at Longannet in West Fife. The

[2] see in respect of judicial review *West* v. *Secretary of State for Scotland*, 1992 S.L.T. 636.
[3] 1991 S.L.T. 302.

station was to be supplied from a local seam—the Hirst seam. Extensive works were required to provide the mining capacity to supply the new station. The station itself required special furnaces to burn the type of coal supplied from the Hirst seam. The agreement between S.S.E.B. and B.C.C. was recorded in a number of letters which passed between the parties in 1963. One feature of the agreement was that B.C.C. undertook to supply all the station's requirements during its lifetime (which was expected to be about 25 years). The parties concluded various further agreements in the succeeding years, mainly concerned with pricing. In 1988, when the last of these agreements expired, S.S.E.B. decided to issue an open invitation for the supply of coal to the station. B.C.C. raised an action of declarator, seeking an order that S.S.E.B. were bound to take all their coal from them. Lord Dervaird upheld B.C.C.'s contention that S.S.E.B. were bound "to take exclusively from B.C.C. such supplies of coal as were required for the operation of the power station at Longannet . . . "[4]

This case may have a significant bearing upon the local economy of West Fife.

Property and Obligations

More detailed consideration must be given to the relationship between the law of property and the law of obligations. These two branches of private law often interact, because property is often transferred or affected by a contract such as sale or lease. Property is concerned with ownership, which gives rise to a real right (*jus in re*) on the part of the owner. Obligations, on the other hand, only give rise to a personal right (*jus in personam* or *jus ad rem*). The difference between real and personal rights can best be explained by an example:

> When a house is sold in Scotland, the first step is for the purchaser and seller to complete missives. This is the contractual stage of the process. The missives are the letters exchanged between the parties' respective solicitors setting out the property to be sold, the purchase price, the date of entry and so on. Subsequently, the seller grants the purchaser a document known as a disposition in return for the price.

---

[4] *Ibid.* p.321E; the case was continued to allow argument on what price was to be paid for the coal.

Once the missives are completed, the purchaser has a personal right against a particular person, the seller. Should the seller default in transferring the house, the purchaser can sue him for delivery of a valid title. But if the seller goes bankrupt or sells the house to someone else, the purchaser's right to the house may be defeated. His only remedy may be to attempt to recover damages from the seller. When the purchaser receives the disposition and his title to the property is registered in the appropriate land register, however, he becomes the owner. As owner he has a right to the property, a right which is "good against the whole world." He can prevent anyone from defeating his title. A real right involves the idea of a right to a thing, whereas a personal right connotes a right against a person.

A personal right can only exist if someone has a correlative duty or obligation. Although we term this branch of the law the law of obligations, it would be equally possible to call it the law of personal rights. Stair explained the relationship between rights and obligations as follows:[5]

> "Obligation is a legal tie by which we may be necessitate or constrained to pay or perform something. This tie lieth upon the debtor; and the power of making use of it in the creditor is the personal right itself, which is a power given by the law, to exact from persons that which they are due."

Accordingly the feature of an obligation is that there is always a correlative right.

Obediential Obligations

Some obligations arise by force of law and are termed obediential obligations. There are two types of obediential obligation: delict and unjust enrichment. The law of delict is concerned with the obligation to make reparation for harm done. If a pedestrian is negligently knocked down by a car, or a politician is defamed, any court action which is subsequently brought is an attempt by the person injured to satisfy a personal right. He seeks a court decree requiring the other person to fulfil the obligation of compensation which the law has placed upon him. The second class of obediential obligation, unjust enrichment, relates to situations where one person has benefited at the expense of another. Here the obligation is to restore the parties to the position where neither can be said to be "unjustly enriched". This obligation comes into play, for

[5] *Institutions*, I.iii.1.

example, where one person is paid money by mistake, or builds a house on another's property believing it to be his own. Here the respective obligations which arise are for the recipient to repay the money and for the owner of the ground to pay to the extent to which he is enriched. From these examples it can be seen that unjust enrichment is based on equitable considerations.

Voluntary Obligations

There are two types of voluntary obligation: promise and contract. Voluntary obligations, by contrast to obediential obligations, arise through choice. Unless a monopoly exists, a person can choose with whom to contract. He is not bound to buy cheese in a particular shop or to take out insurance with a particular company. Any contract entered into is the choice of the parties concerned. It arises out of the parties' own volition. So the difference between the two types of obligation is the difference between imposition and assumption. Obediential obligations are imposed, voluntary obligations are assumed. Stair suggested that voluntary (or conventional) obligations arose through the exercise of will. In the case of unilateral promise it is the will of the person making the promise. In the case on contracts it is the will of both parties to the transaction. For this purpose Stair divided acts of the will into three categories: desire, resolution and engagement.[6] One might conceive a desire, and even resolve to carry it out, but neither of these states of mind gave rise to a legal obligation. It was only when there was some determinate purpose to do something, manifested by words or actings, that there could be said to be engagement and consequently that legal rights and duties arose.

This notion of voluntary obligation resting on the idea of will plays an important role in contract law and ties in very closely with freedom of contract. It is no surprise that in England, will-theory had its heyday in the nineteenth century. The basic rationale is fairly straightforward. A person has free-will and can do what he likes so far as he is not restrained by law. By choosing to engage with someone he voluntarily relinquishes his independence by granting that person a right against him. As he has chosen to assume this obligation he should be bound by it.

There are powerful objections to this theory. Adam Smith was one of the first writers to criticise the idea that obligations sprung purely from the exercise of the will. He noted that if someone engaged to do something in the future and subsequently changed his mind then the logical consequence, according to will-theory,

[6] *Institutions*, I.x.2.

should be that he was relieved of his obligation. Yet this was not the case. A person who made a contract could not slip out of it by changing his mind. It was therefore not, Smith suggested, the will of the person engaging which gave rise to the obligation but rather "the expectation and dependence which was excited in him to whom the contract was made."[7] This difference of theoretical approach is of considerable importance. Smith's view is that the law is really concerned with protecting the person to whom the undertaking is made, rather than binding the other person to his statement. It is erroneous to consider the two views as opposite sides of the same coin. If the foundation of the law of contract is the inquiry, "Has a declaration of will been made?" that is very different from the inquiry, "Should we protect the interest of the person who relied upon the other's statement?" In our discussion of the various topics of contract law we shall see that there is a continuous interplay between the consensual approach of Stair and the reliance approach of Smith. We shall see that, in general, the reliance view prevails, but occasionally it is the consensual view which is emphasised.

SCOTS LAW AND ENGLISH LAW

In many areas of contract law the Scots and English approach is broadly similar. Sometimes, however, the detailed rules differ markedly north and south of the border. Examples are the law relating to formalities, illegality, collateral contracts, capacity, frustration and assignation. A well-known example relates to house purchase agreements. In Scotland the parties are bound at an early stage on completion of the missives. In England the stage at which the parties are bound comes later, when formal documents are exchanged. That is why the practice of "gazumping" is virtually unknown north of the border. Two other major points of difference are privity of contract and consideration. Both these doctrines are part of English but not Scots law. Privity of contract means a rigid adherence to the principle that only the parties to the contract acquire rights under the contract. Consideration is a requirement that a contract is only binding if there is some element of bargain or reciprocity in the arrangement. These ideas will be considered more fully in the appropriate chapters of this book.

This does not mean that the solutions to problems which arise differ. It would be odd if a large retailer trading in both England

---

[7] *Lectures on Jurisprudence*, ed. Meek, Raphael & Stein (Oxford, 1978), ii. 56.

and Scotland found that its ordinary contracts were dealt with in a completely different fashion by the two legal systems. Rather, the solutions are often the same but arrived at by a different route. English authorities must accordingly be used with care. It is as if one is translating from one language into another. The elegance of French poetry can never be matched by a translation into German. So with Scots and English law. A sentence of the great legislative draftsman Sir M. D. Chalmers seems apposite. In relation to the English Statute of Frauds 1677 he noted "it has . . . never applied to Scotland and Scotsmen never appear to have felt the want of it."[8] The contortions which English law has found necessary to get round the more unhappy applications of that Act and of other doctrines such as privity of contract would likewise not be welcomed in Scotland. One other point about the difference between the two legal systems concerns procedure. Until the late nineteenth century, the Common Law courts administered different remedies from the Chancery courts. Despite the nineteenth century reforms, English lawyers persist in talking about "common law" and "equitable" rules and remedies. Our courts have always had an inherent equitable jurisdiction (with a small "e") and the different procedural approaches find no counterpart in our law.

Nevertheless the greater size of England and the fact that London is the commercial hub of the United Kingdom means inevitably that there are a far higher number of reported decisions on contractual issues there. Many English decisions have either been accepted into Scots law or are of high persuasive value. Accordingly we shall advert to a number of English cases in this book. Differences between the two systems will be pointed out where appropriate.

[8] Chalmers, *Sale of Goods Act* (12th ed., 1945), p. 26.

CHAPTER 2

FORMATION OF CONTRACT

WHEN does a contract come into existence? Often the answer will be clear. By their conduct, or by means of the written or spoken word, or by a combination of these methods, the parties will make it plain that a binding contract exists between them. At the newsagent contracts are commonly made without any words being exchanged. The customer tenders his money, together with the newspaper he wishes to purchase. This money is accepted by the vendor and placed in the till. Verbal bargains may be struck at second-hand car showrooms. The seller indicates a price. The prospective purchaser suggests a different price. After haggling about this and the other terms of the contract—whether, for example, road tax or a full tank of petrol is included—the purchaser pays the price which is finally agreed and drives the car out of the showroom. Setting out contract terms in writing to which the parties append their respective signatures is of course the clearest method of concluding a contract.

Sometimes, however, it may be difficult to determine with precision when a contract has been concluded. Suppose Valerie is interested in going on holiday to Denmark. She telephones a travel company and discovers that a package holiday is available departing on a particular date. She rings off to discuss matters with her proposed travel companion. The next day she sends a booking form to the company. Is the contract complete when the booking form is signed, when it is sent, when it arrives at the company's offices or when a deposit on the price of the holiday is paid? No clear-cut answer can be given. It will depend on the wording of the booking form, the method by which the parties communicate, their subsequent actions and the context in which these occur. In this chapter we shall consider the relevant principles which apply to these issues.

AGREEMENT

As was discussed in Chapter 1, contract is usually analysed in terms of agreement. Formation occurs when the parties to the contract reach agreement as to the essential features of their transaction. This is sometimes referred to as *consensus in idem* (meeting of the minds). Agreement does not mean that the parties' minds have coincided on every point. A person cannot know the inner thought-processes of the other party. Accordingly it is not necessary that there is full subjective agreement. Suppose a musician flags down a taxi in the street and is carried to the desired destination. At the end of the journey he refuses to pay the fare unless the taxi driver carries his heavy instrument up three flights of stairs. The taxi driver refuses on the basis that their agreement concerned carriage by vehicle alone. The driver's approach would be preferred. The law adopts an objective approach in testing agreement, one which is concerned with the "external indicia of agreement". Instead of looking at what the parties to the contract were actually thinking at the time of contracting, the law looks for those outward indications which evince *consensus*. The question is, would it appear to a neutral third party that agreement had been reached? In other words, would such a person infer from the contracting parties' words and deeds that a proposal had been assented to?

Sometimes, parties may have different beliefs at the relevant time. In *Muirhead and Turnbull* v. *Dickson*[1]:

> The manager of a Glasgow piano shop called on Dickson and his wife at their home. Dickson agreed to take a piano from the shop at the price of £26, payment to be made by way of monthly instalments. No written document was signed. A few days later the piano was delivered. Dickson began paying the instalments but after five months stopped paying. The piano shop raised an action to recover the piano from him. It argued that Dickson had received the piano under a contract of hire-purchase. Under such a contract, ownership of the piano did not pass until all the instalments were paid. Alternatively, the shop contended that the parties had never reached agreement at all, so there was no contract and the shop was entitled to return of the piano. Dickson maintained that he had bought the piano on credit sale. A credit sale contract would have made Dickson owner of the piano and left the piano shop to attempt to recover the balance of the price.

It was held that, viewed objectively, the evidence disclosed that a contract of credit sale had been entered into. A factor of some importance in the case was the relative novelty of hire-purchase. The court thought that the onus was on the piano shop to make it plain that it was this new arrangement which had been entered into.

[1] (1905) 7 F. 686; 13 S.L.T. 151.

But the point to emphasise is that the parties had not agreed as a matter of psychological fact about the terms of the contract they had entered into. Nevertheless they were bound, for even where "parties honestly differed, the commercial contracts cannot be arranged by what people think in their inmost minds. Commercial contracts are arranged according to what people say."[2] Accordingly Dickson was the owner of the piano and the shop could not recover it from him. The shop's remedy was to seek payment of the outstanding instalments.

However, even if parties have proceeded with performance of the contract in the belief that it is binding, the courts will not enforce the contract if they find that agreement has never been concluded:

> "It is not enough for the parties to agree in saying there was a concluded contract if there was none, and then to ask for a judicial decision as to what the contract in fact was. That would be the same thing as asking us to make the bargain when our sole function is to interpret it."[3]

In the case in which that statement was made, work was carried out on a garden pond. When the contractors asked for payment for the work the householder refused, claiming that the work was defective. Both in the sheriff court and in the Court of Session the contractors' claim for damages for breach of contract was successful. Nevertheless, on appeal it was decided by the House of Lords that in truth there was no contract between the parties. The contract documents showed that the contractors had offered to hire the equipment. But the householder had purported to accept an offer to hire the equipment *and* to operate the equipment to clear the pond. As the offer and the acceptance had not met, there was no *consensus*. Accordingly, the contractors had no contractual claim to recover the cost of the work done on the pond. Instead, their remedy lay in the law of unjust enrichment. This decision is perhaps an extreme application of the objective approach. Where work or performance has followed on an apparent contract which the parties themselves believe to be binding, the courts will normally give effect to that intention.

Most contracts can be analysed in terms of offer and acceptance:

---

[2] *per* Lord President Dunedin at p. 694.
[3] *Mathieson Gee (Ayrshire) Ltd.* v. *Quigley*, 1952 S.C. (H.L.) 38; 1952 S.L.T. 239.

"an offer accepted is a contract."[4] The person making the offer is known as the offeror. The offeree is the person to whom the offer is made, while the acceptor is the person who accepts the offer. In a simple case the offeree and the acceptor will be the same person. But where the parties negotiate over a period, there will often be a series of offers and counter-offers before agreement is finally reached. In such cases, the person who was the original offeror may become the eventual acceptor. For instance, A offers to hire B's discotheque for one night at a price of £500: B replies that he is prepared to hire out the discotheque to A for two nights at a price of £750: A accepts this suggestion. On this scenario, A is the acceptor as well as being the original offeror.

OFFER

The Distinction between Offers and Invitations to Treat

The key feature of an offer is that it contemplates acceptance. As soon as it is accepted a contract is formed. No further negotiation is contemplated. An offer may be express—"I offer you £50 for your old lawnmower"—or implied, for example handing over money for a theatre ticket. Sometimes there is no intention to be bound by the other party's acceptance. Instead the person is merely indicating his bargaining position. In effect, he is saying "these are the terms upon which I am willing to negotiate further." Statements of this second type are known as invitations to treat. It is not always easy to distinguish invitations to treat from offers. Suppose in talking to a friend X says: "I am interested in selling my car for £2,000." Normally that would be regarded as an invitation to treat. No clear intention to be bound by acceptance is evinced by X. But if there had been prior negotiations between X and his friend it might amount to an offer. Perhaps they had discussed the possibility of a sale and all that remained to be settled was the price. If it could be shown that X had indicated that he would be bound by his friend's acceptance, the statement would be an offer. In several common situations English law has adopted presumptions as to whether some statement or action amounts to an offer or an invitation to treat. Scots law has fewer authorities on this branch of the law, but it is probable that in most instances we would approach the matter in the same way. These are only presumptions, not rules of law. Accordingly they can be displaced if the contrary intention is proved.

[4] Stair, *Institutions*, I.x.3.

Shop displays

Is an item on display in a shop window or on a supermarket shelf an offer or merely an invitation to treat? If such displays are offers then the shop is bound by the acceptance of the customer. It could not refuse to sell the item to a customer who tendered the correct price, subject to any statutory provisions which apply (for example regarding the sale of cigarettes to persons under sixteen years of age). If on the other hand the shop is simply inviting offers, then it always retains a discretion to refuse to sell an item to a particular customer.

There is no recent Scottish authority in point on these matters. In one old case it was accepted that such displays were invitations to treat.[5] In England, the two leading authorities which analyse the issue are unusual. Each concerned prosecutions in respect of alleged offences by shopkeepers. Accordingly they were criminal rather than civil cases. The first case concerned the sale of drugs without the supervision of a qualified chemist;[6] the second, offering an offensive weapon for sale.[7] In each case the display was held to be an invitation to treat rather than an offer. A factor stressed by the court was that a shop is a place for bargaining, not for compulsory sales. However, the prospective purchaser may have been lured into the shop precisely because of the display. Imagine, for example, a display tag in a window which read "Special Offer, Fur Coat, one only, reduced from £7,500 to £1,500." It would be rather unfair if a prospective purchaser who had queued for several nights was told by the shop that they were not going to sell it to him because he was an animal rights campaigner. Yet that is the shop's right under the present law, even though the term "offer" is used. Of course shops normally want to dispose of items and most shopkeepers would be unwilling to have their goodwill damaged by the bad publicity that such behaviour would bring. The shop may even have committed an offence under the Trade Descriptions Act 1968. But so far as the prospective purchaser is concerned, he is not legally entitled to the coat simply by tendering the correct price.

The presumption that a display is an invitation to treat can be displaced. In one case an individual took a deckchair from a stack on the beach.[8] He was injured because it was defective. The display

---

[5] *Campbell* v. *Ker*, 24 Feb. 1810, F.C.
[6] *Pharmaceutical Society of Great Britain* v. *Boots Cash Chemists (Southern) Ltd.* [1953] 1 Q.B. 401; 1 All E.R. 482.
[7] *Fisher* v. *Bell* [1961] 1 Q.B. 394.
[8] *Chapelton* v. *Barry U.D.C.* [1940] 1 K.B. 532.

of deck chairs was held to constitute an offer and the man received damages as compensation for breach of contract. He had concluded the contract by removing the deckchair and sitting on it: that was the acceptance. It may be that the court was more inclined to reach this result because personal injury was involved.

Auction sales

The three stages of an auction sale can be analysed as follows:

    (a) the exposure of the item for sale   — invitation to treat
    (b) the bidding   — offer
    (c) the fall of the auctioneer's hammer   — acceptance

Until the hammer falls, the bidder is entitled to withdraw his bid. No contract exists until that moment. Individuals who feel nervous about making inadvertent gestures in salesrooms may be comforted by this knowledge. What of the seller? Like the buyer he too may wish to withdraw after the bidding has commenced. To accomplish this he may put a reserve price on the article to be auctioned. This ensures that the item is not sold below a certain sum.

> In *Fenwick* v. *Macdonald Fraser & Co.*, a man named Fenwick bid 42 guineas for a bull named "The Margrave of Ballindalloch" at Perth auction mart.[9] Although his was the highest bid, the auctioneer withdrew the bull from sale saying that it had a reserve price of 150 guineas placed upon it. There had been no notice that the sale was under reserve. Indeed, the conditions of sale expressly stated that: "The highest offeror on each lot will be preferred" and that it was "an unreserved sale." Nevertheless Fenwick lost the legal action which he subsequently brought. The Second Division based its decision on the ground of reciprocity: one party could not be bound while the other was free. As Fenwick remained free to withdraw his bid, it followed that the owner was likewise entitled to withdraw his bull.

In similar circumstances today, an action of damages for misrepresentation might well lie against the auctioneer in respect of the conditions of sale. But the bidder would still not be entitled to the bull, as he would be deemed to be making an offer which had not been accepted. Accordingly there would be no completed contract of sale.

[9] (1904) 6 F. 850.

Advertisements

Advertisements, whether on television, on hoardings, or in the press are presumed to be invitations to treat. The position is analogous to that of shop window displays. An advertiser is granted the right to determine the person with whom he contracts. If an advertisement was an offer, the advertiser might be contractually bound to persons which he was unable to supply. Suppose a company advertising solar units was faced with unusually heavy demand. It would be unfortunate if it were held liable in damages to all persons who sent cheques in response to the advertisement, irrespective of the availability of the units. In appropriate circumstances, however, the general presumption can be displaced. For this to occur, the advertisement must clearly indicate that the advertiser intends to be bound upon acceptance. An example is provided by *Carlill* v. *The Carbolic Smokeball Co. Ltd.*[10]:

> The Carbolic Smokeball Co. placed an advertisement in the Pall Mall Gazette in November 1891. It stated that the company would pay £100 if anyone caught one of a number of specified diseases after using one of their smokeballs in the prescribed manner for two weeks. The company claimed to have deposited £1,000 in the Alliance Bank to show its "sincerity in the matter." Mrs Carlill bought one of the balls and used it for two months. She caught influenza (one of the specified diseases) and requested payment of the £100 sum. The company refused to pay. Accordingly, an action was raised by Mrs Carlill.

The Smokeball company put up several arguments in its defence to the action. One argument was that the advertisement was merely an invitation to treat. This was rejected. The wording of the advertisement went beyond an indication of the company's bargaining position. As Bowen L.J. put it: "It is an offer to become liable to anyone who, before it is retracted, performs the conditions." The court awarded Mrs Carlill her £100 reward.

Tenders

A tender or quotation to carry out work is an offer. For example, a letter from a plumber which states that a new bathroom will be installed at a specified price is converted into a contract by simple acceptance. In some instances, for example in relation to car

[10] [1893] 1 Q.B. 256.

repairs, the repairer may be unwilling to give a definite quotation. Then the parties must reach some agreement as to the manner in which the price is to be fixed. It is common to stipulate that express authorisation is required for repairs beyond a certain maximum cash limit, or that the car owner will pay for all costs reasonably necessary to obtain an M.O.T. certificate.

Other Cases

Where no presumption exists, distinguishing offers from invitations to treat remains a question of interpretation. The touchstone, here as elsewhere in contract law, is that of intention. If the person's statements or actions disclose an intention to be bound, it is an offer. If not, it is an invitation to treat. Questions of intention provide the courts with difficult problems. Automatic vending machines are a case in point. Who makes the offer:, the machine or the customer? In one English case involving a ticket machine at the entrance to a car park, it was argued that the machine made a standing offer because it had to deliver the ticket to any person who put the correct money in the slot.[11] It had no discretion to accept or reject a particular person. This is probably the correct analysis, even if it may seem rather surreal to apply the concept of intention to machines. That point loses force when it is remembered that it is not the intention of the machine itself which is relevant, but rather that of the owner of the machine.

The intention of the alleged offeror must be gathered from the whole circumstances surrounding the parties' communications. In *Dawson International plc* v. *Coats Paton plc*[12]:

The defenders, a large Scottish textile company, thought that they were vulnerable to a hostile takeover. In early 1986, representatives of the board of directors met with the pursuers' board to discuss a possible offer from them. It was agreed by the defenders to recommend the pursuers' offer to their share-holders and this was done. Subsequently, the defenders withdrew their recommendation. The pursuers claimed there was a contract in terms of which the defenders would recommend their offer. They sought damages for the abortive costs of their takeover bid. It was held that no such contract existed.

Lord Prosser stated:

[11] *Thornton* v. *Shoe Lane Parking Ltd.* [1971] 2 Q.B. 163; 1 All E.R. 686.
[12] 1993 S.L.T. 80.

"Speaking generally, I would accept that when two parties are talking to one another about a matter which has commercial significance to both, a statement by one party that he will do some particular thing will normally be construed as obligatory, or as an offer, rather than a mere statement of intention, if the works and deeds of the other party indicate that the statement was so understood, and the obligation confirmed or the offer accepted so that parties appeared to regard the commercial 'deal' as concluded. But in considering whether there is indeed a contract between the parties, in any particular case, it will always be essential to look at the particular facts, with a view to discovering whether these facts, rather than some general rule of thumb, can be said to reveal consensus and an intention to conclude a contract."

Two further cases illustrate the narrow distinction between offers and invitations to treat. In the first case a dispute arose as to whether there was a concluded sale of a property in Jamaica called "Bumper Hall Pen".[13] A telegraphed to B: "Will you sell us BHP? Telegraph lowest cash price." B telegraphed in reply: "Lowest cash price for BHP £900." Following this, A telegraphed: "We agree to buy BHP for £900 asked by you. Please send us your title deed in order that we may get early possession." No further correspondence took place. It was held that no contract had been formed.

In the second case a merchant in Leith wrote to a firm in Largo, Fife as follows: "I am offering today Plate Linseed for Jan./Feb. shipment to Leith, and have pleasure in quoting you 100 tons at 41s. 3d., usual Plate terms. I shall be glad to hear if you are buyers, and await your esteemed reply."[14] The Largo firm purported to accept. The court decided that a contract had been formed.

The distinction to be drawn between the two cases is that in the first, the party was merely indicating the price at which he was prepared to contract; whereas in the second the word "offer" was actually used, a definite quantity and price were mentioned and the letter looked to the conclusion of the contract by reply.

Features of Offers

Who may accept

In some instances an offer is made to the world at large. Such offers are capable of acceptance by anyone who sees or hears the offer.

---

[13] *Harvey* v. *Facey* [1983] A.C. 552.
[14] *Philp* v. *Knoblauch*, 1907 S.C. 994; 15 S.L.T. 61.

The case of *Carlill* is a good example. The offer of reward was addressed to everyone who happened to read the advertisement. Normally, however, an offer is made to a particular person and the rule is that only that person can accept the offer. A purported acceptance by another person is accordingly invalid.

Communication

"An offer is nothing until it is communicated to the party to whom it is made."[15] This looks obvious. Imagine that a promoter had written out, but not posted, an offer to book a particular artiste for one of his venues. If the artiste surreptitiously found out about the offer he is not entitled to accept it. Exceptions can, however, occur where an offer has been communicated by another person. Whether or not a contract is formed will depend on principles of agency. In particular it will be important to find out whether the agent is authorised to make offers. If the artiste had been notified by the promoter's employee who normally arranged the bookings, a contract would be formed.

Revocation

An offer may be withdrawn at any time before acceptance. This is an important feature of offers and is known as *locus poenitentiae* (the opportunity of withdrawing). Right up to the moment the acceptance is given, the offeror can change his mind. The bidder at an auction has the right to withdraw his bid until the hammer falls. Apart from express revocation, an offer is impliedly withdrawn by the death, insanity or bankruptcy of the offeror.

Termination

Another method by which an offer comes to an end is termination. Where a time-limit for acceptance is attached, the offer automatically falls on the expiry of that time-limit. Of course the offeror can waive the time-limit if he so wishes. Where no time-limit is stated, an offer only remains open for a reasonable time. An early American case provided a good example.[16] In May 1837 an offer of reward for the "apprehension and conviction of incendiaries" was issued. Relevant information was given to the authorities in 1841. However, it was held that no obligation to pay the reward still remained, as the time lapse was unreasonably long. What amounts to a reasonable time will depend upon the circumstances of the case. Where the contract concerns the sale or supply of a commod-

---

[15] *Thomson* v. *James* (1855) 18 D. 1 *per* Lord President McNeill at p. 10.
[16] *Loring* v. *City of Boston* (1844) 7 Metcalf 409.

ity for which there is a ready market, acceptance will usually require to be by return of post. In *Wylie and Lochhead* v. *McElroy and Sons*,[17] a delay of five weeks in accepting an offer to carry out ironwork at new stables was held to be unreasonable. At the time the price of iron was fluctuating from day to day. To allow the client to wait and accept the offer when the price of iron changed in his favour would be unfair. It would allow him to speculate at the expense of the offeror.

It is possible in Scots law for a person to bind himself to keep an offer open for a specified period. Suppose X writes to Y on Monday stating: "I offer to sell you my house for £150,000 and will keep this offer open until Friday at 12 noon" X will be liable to damages to Y if he breaks this promise and sells to Z on Thursday. We shall discuss this situation in Chapter 3.

Referential bids

A fixed bid is one in which a definite price is mentioned. A "referential bid" is one where the bidder offers a certain sum in excess of any other bid made. An example is: "I offer £500 more than the highest bid you receive from any other party." Sometimes the two are combined, as in: "I offer £500,000 or whatever is offered by party B. plus £5,000, whichever is the greater." The House of Lords has held that such bids are only valid if reasonable notice is given to all parties that such bids may be used.[18] Otherwise the person making the referential bid would always succeed against a rival bidder making a conventional bid. This would be plainly unjust. A further problem which could arise if referential bids were widely used would be that it might lead to no valid bids being submitted. Because such bids depend upon at least one person using a fixed bid, then in the absence of such a bid there would be no reference point upon which the other bids could be based.

ACCEPTANCE

An acceptance is a final unqualified assent to an offer. Like offers, acceptances can be express or implied. The action of a check-out assistant in taking a customer's basket and ringing up the items on the till indicates implied acceptance of the customer's offer to buy. Silence does not constitute acceptance. A man who offers to sell

---

[17] (1873) 1 R. 41.
[18] *Harvela Investments Ltd.* v. *Royal Trust Co. of Canada (C.I.) Ltd.* [1985] 3 W.L.R. 276; 1 All E.R. 261.

beehives to a beekeeper cannot assume that a binding contract has been formed simply because he does not hear to the contrary. The neighbour's silence does not amount to acquiescence. Exceptionally, however, silence may amount to valid acceptance. This might happen where there is a history of dealing between the contracting parties, or where there have been prolonged negotiations. In our example, there may have been several prior transactions and on each occasion the neighbour has omitted to give any positive acceptance but has simply paid for the beehives when delivered. One must be careful to distinguish situations where the offeree is silent, from situations where an offer is followed by actings by the other party. An express offer followed by actions by the offeree consistent with acceptance is enough to infer the existence of a contract.

A purported acceptance which contains new terms, or materially alters the terms of the original offer is not an acceptance but rather a counter-offer. Further, such a qualified acceptance rejects the original offer. A neat illustration of these points is provided by the case of *Wolf and Wolf* v. *Forfar Potato Co. Ltd*[19]:

A Forfar company offered by telex to sell a quantity of Désirée potatoes to a firm of Amsterdam potato merchants. The offer was open for acceptance by 5 p.m. the following day. An "acceptance" was sent by telex the following morning. In this telex various new conditions were set out. When the Dutch merchants learned from a telephone call to Forfar that these new conditions were not acceptable, they sent a second telex. This second telex was also received before the time-limit had expired. It purported to accept the Forfar terms but reiterated that the Dutch merchants would be glad if their earlier conditions were given consideration by the Scottish company. No further communication was made by the Forfar company and no potatoes were sent. The Amsterdam merchants raised an action of damages for breach of contract. They argued that they had received an offer which they had accepted before the time-limit had expired.

It was held that no contract existed. The first acceptance amounted to a counter-offer which "killed" the original offer. It was, accordingly, no longer capable of acceptance. As the counter-offer had not been accepted by the Scottish company, there was no contract.

[19] 1984 S.L.T. 100.

Slightly different circumstances occurred in *Findlater* v. *Maan*[20]:

> Mr Maan advertised his house for sale. By letter dated 25
> March 1988, Mr and Mrs Findlater offered to purchase the
> property. A qualified acceptance was given by the seller on 28
> March 1988. By letter dated 29 March 1988 the purchasers
> accepted the conditions contained in the seller's qualified
> acceptance and inserted one further condition. On 30 March
> and without referring to the letter of 29 March, the seller
> intimated one further condition. On 6 April, the purchasers
> withdrew the condition contained in their letter of 29 March,
> accepted the condition specified in the seller's letter of 30
> March and purported to conclude the bargain. By this stage,
> the seller had changed his mind and did not wish to proceed
> with the sale. An action of declarator of contract was raised.
> The Second Division held unanimously that a contract existed.

In distinguishing the case from that of *Wolf and Wolf*, Lord Justice
Clerk Ross stated:

> "In my opinion the true approach to be made in the present
> case is as follows. The letter of 29 March and the letter of 30
> March were two offers which existed at the same time, one at
> the instance of the seller and the other at the instance of the
> purchaser. They were not written under reference to one
> another and neither of them superseded the other. They both
> co-existed. In that situation I am of opinion that it was open to
> the pursuers to accept the offer contained in the letter of 30
> March 1988."[21]

Whether or not an acceptance has been qualified is a question of
construction. The response may simply be hesitant or under reservation or a mere request for further information. In such instances
the acceptance will not amount to a counter-offer. Where an
acceptance contained the phrase "the usual conditions of acceptance apply" and there were no such usual conditions, the contract
was held binding and the phrase ignored as meaningless.[22] But if
new terms are being proposed then the purported acceptance will
amount to a counter-offer.

---

[20] 1990 S.L.T. 465; *cf. Rutterford* v. *Allied Breweries Ltd.*, 1990 S.L.T. 249.
[21] *Ibid.* p. 468.
[22] *Nicolene Ltd.* v. *Simmonds* [1953] 1 Q.B. 543.

Communication of Acceptance

The general principle is that no contract is formed until the acceptance is communicated to the offeror. The offeror cannot divine
when the offeree mentally assents to the offer. He requires communication of the acceptance before a binding contract exists.
Occasionally the offeror may waive the need for express communication of the acceptance. In *Carlill*, the contract was formed when
the smokeballs were purchased. Mrs Carlill did not require to write
to the company intimating that she accepted the company's offer of
reward should she succumb to one or other of the specified
diseases. The terms of the advertisement demonstrated that no
communication of acceptance was required.

Mode of Acceptance Prescribed

An offeror can prescribe the manner in which the acceptance is to
be communicated. He may stipulate that communication is to be
made by letter, by telex, by telephone or by facsimile. Where such a
stipulation is made, communication of the acceptance by other
means is invalid. In one case the exercise of an option to purchase a
piece of land was required to be "by notice in writing to the
intending vendor."[23] It was held that notification by telephone to
the vendor's solicitors did not satisfy this requirement. What was
required was written intimation to the vendor himself. Accordingly
the option was held not to have been validly exercised.

As we have seen, silence does not usually constitute acceptance.
Nor is it possible to prescribe that silence on the part of the offeree
is to be regarded as effective. An offeror cannot say: "I offer to
purchase your record collection for £400 and if I do not hear from
you by Wednesday I shall take it that you agree." To hold otherwise
would be to allow persons to have contracts imposed upon them
without their consent. Despite this principle, a practice grew up in
the 1960s whereby certain traders sent unsolicited items through
the post and then demanded payment if the goods were not
returned within a specified time. People who were unsure of their
legal rights thought they were bound to pay for these items. To deal
with this problem the Unsolicited Goods and Services Act 1971 was
enacted. It provides that recipients of unsolicited goods can treat
them as their own if they are not reclaimed by the sender within a
certain period. There is no obligation upon the recipient to return
them.

---

[23] *Holwell Securities Ltd.* v. *Hughes* [1974] 1 W.L.R. 155.

No Particular Mode of Acceptance Prescribed

If the offeror does not prescribe the mode of communication, the acceptance can be given in any competent manner. Normally it should be given in the same mode as the offer. Thus an offer made in writing should be accepted in writing. There is a measure of commonsense to be applied here. Whilst a telex acceptance to an offer posted by second class post is likely to be legally effective, the converse probably does not hold. This is because the inference to be drawn from a telex offer is that a speedy response is sought. By contrast, the use of second class post indicates a more leisurely mode of proceeding. In the case of instantaneous communications (oral, telephone, facsimile or telex) it is the offeree who must ensure that his words are heard and understood. Should, accordingly, a telephone line go dead during the course of negotiations, it is up to the offeree to ensure that his acceptance has been heard. The onus is on him to establish that a contract was concluded. If he does not telephone back to check matters, and any dispute arises, no contract will have been concluded.[24]

Postal Communications

Special rules apply to contracts made by post. Where a contract is made through the post the parties are not face to face. It is impossible for them to know simultaneously when assent is given to the proposed bargain. The general rule about communication of acceptance suggests that a postal acceptance should only take effect when it is received by the offeror. It is only when he receives the acceptance that it has been "communicated" to him. But in the earliest case to examine the issue, *Adams* v. *Lindsell*, it was pointed out that this led to circularity.[25] If the offeror was only bound when he had received the acceptance, then equally the offeree should be bound only when he knew that his acceptance had been received. And so on. The contract could never be concluded. In *Adams* the offeror had given his own address wrongly and the acceptance was thereby delayed in reaching him. On these facts the court decided that the contract had been formed when the acceptance was posted. The offeror was responsible for the late acceptance so he should bear the consequences of the delay.

Adams left open the question of the effect of a delay which was caused by the postal authorities rather than by the offeror. This

---

[24] See *Entores Ltd.* v. *Miles Far East Corpn.* [1955] 2 Q.B. 327.
[25] (1818) 1 B. & Ald. 681.

question was considered in *Dunlop* v. *Higgins*[26] where the House of Lords held that the ratio in *Adams* established the wider proposition that the acceptance was made when the offeree put it in the post: " . . . if the party accepting the offer puts his letter into the post on the correct day, has he not done everything he was bound to do?"[27] So it was held that acceptance takes effect on posting. In essence this rule of acceptance "effective on dispatch" is an arbitrary one. It means that in the interval of time between one party knowing that the contract is concluded and the other finding out, the law favours the acceptor. He can rely on the contract at the moment of posting. Once the letter of acceptance is put in the postbox a binding relationship is established. If, of course, the offeror does not wish this to occur, it is open to him to prescribe another method of communication. He can "contract out" of this consequence should it not suit him.

Consequences of the postal rule

The rule about postal acceptances being effective on dispatch is often termed the "postal rule". It is perhaps more accurate to say that there are a cluster of rules which apply to contracts made through the post.

Time limits
Where an offer is only open for a specified period, acceptance is effective when the acceptance is posted within the time limit even if it is not received until some days later. So where an offer to purchase goods stated: "This for reply by Monday, 6th inst."[28] a letter posted on the evening of the 6th, which only reached the offeror the following day, was held to be timeous acceptance. The man on the No. 23 bus might well be surprised by this result, but it remains the law.

An acceptance which never arrives
In one English case the rule that an acceptance is effective on dispatch was taken to its logical conclusion.[29] A contract for the sale of shares was held to have been concluded even though the acceptance went missing in the post and was never received. One Scottish judge, Lord Shand, doubted whether the same solution should be applied in Scotland.[30] His view is surely the better one. It

---

[26] (1848) 6 Bell's App. 195.
[27] *per* Lord Chancellor Cottenham at p. 207.
[28] *Jacobson, Sons & Co.* v. *Underwood & Son* (1894) 21 R. 654.
[29] *Household Fire Insurance Co.* v. *Grant* (1879) 4 Ex. D. 216.
[30] *Mason* v. *Benhar Coal Co.* (1882) 9 R. 883 at p. 890.

is one matter for an offeror to be contractually bound for a day or two before the offer is actually received, quite another when the acceptance is never received at all.

Revocation of the offer

We have seen that an offer can always be withdrawn before acceptance. When the parties conduct negotiations by post, notice of the revocation must actually reach the offeree. This can be done verbally.[31] Where, however, postal communication of the revocation is used, it takes effect on receipt. It is not necessary for the retraction of the offer to be actually brought to the attention of the offeree. Doing all that is reasonable to bring it to his notice, such as delivering it to his normal business address, is enough.[32] The reason for having different rules for postal acceptances and postal revocations of offers is as follows. Once the acceptance is posted, the offeree is entitled to rely on the contract. If the revocation of an offer were likewise effective on posting, the offeree could never know whether at the moment of posting the acceptance, a revocation was already speeding its way towards him. This would lead to uncertainty. However, this legal approach produces its own problems. A contract may be formed even though there is never a point in time when the parties have reached *consensus in idem.* In *Thomson* v. *James*, J made a written offer to purchase an estate.[33] Some days later T posted an acceptance to the offer. However, on the same day that the acceptance was posted, J had posted a retraction of his offer: J stated that his withdrawal was posted before the letter of acceptance. Both letters arrived the following day. Despite the apparent lack of *consensus* the court held the contract binding.

Revocation of the acceptance

Strict adherence to the postal rule should mean that an acceptance once posted is irrevocable. From the moment the acceptance is placed in the postbox the contract is binding on both parties. Surprisingly, in the only case upon the issue, *Countess of Dunmore* v. *Alexander*, it was held that the postal acceptance might be revoked.[34]

In reply to an inquiry from the Countess of Dunmore, Lady Agnew wrote a reference for one of her servants, Elizabeth

---

[31] *McMillan* v. *Caldwell*, 1991 S.L.T. 325, 329L *per* Lord Kirkwood.
[32] *Burnley* v. *Alford*, 1919 2 S.L.T. 123.
[33] (1855) 18 D. 1.
[34] (1830) 9 S. 190.

Alexander, whom the Countess was interested in taking into her service. The letter concluded: "If Lady Dunmore decides on taking Betty Alexander, perhaps she will have the goodness to mention whether she expects her at the new or the old term." The Countess answered this letter on 5 November requesting Lady Agnew to engage Alexander on her behalf commencing "at the new term, or as soon after as possible." On 6 November the Countess addressed another letter to Lady Agnew intimating that she no longer required Alexander's services. Both letters were sent on by Lady Agnew to Alexander, who received them by the same post.

Lord Craigie, in a dissenting judgment, thought that the Countess of Dunmore's letter was an acceptance which could not be retracted after it had reached Lady Agnew. The majority of the court, however, took the view that as the two letters arrived simultaneously they neutralised each other. No discussion of whether the letter of November 5 amounted to an acceptance or not was entered into. One suspects that the members of the court were not as alive to the legal niceties of the case as later jurists would have wished. A variety of explanations have been proffered for the decision:
  (a) that it was decided before the postal rule had finally been established;
  (b) that on a true construction it was a case of retraction of offer rather than of acceptance;
  (c) that it is a commonsense exception to the general rule.
View (a) would mean that the case has been impliedly overruled by subsequent authorities. This does not however appear to be the position. Although questioned, it is still cited as good authority. View (b) is tenable but does not square easily with the wording of Lady Agnew's letter, which does seem to be offering Alexander's services to the Countess. Accordingly the third view is probably correct. Although Alexander would naturally be disappointed on receiving the letters, she could hardly be said to have relied upon the contract. It is true that she lost the opportunity to enter the service of the Countess and her financial position was prejudiced in consequence. Against that argument, it must be noted that she had no time to alter her position on the strength of the Countess's offer. The second letter was "in effect, a postscript to the first."[35] We are not told which letter Alexander opened first. If she opened the acceptance letter first, then she had a few moments or minutes of

---

[35] Smith, *A Short Commentary on the Law of Scotland* (Edinburgh, 1962), p. 764.

expectation of the job. If she opened the retraction first then she cannot be said to have had any hopes of the job at all. In either case a legal remedy was probably not justifiable, partly at least on the *de minimis* principle (the law does not concern itself with trifles). This third view accords with an *obiter dictum* of Lawton L.J. who stated that the postal rule "probably does not operate if its application would produce manifest inconvenience and absurdity."[36] It might be suggested, for example, that a person who after posting an acceptance informed the offeror by facsimile communication to disregard the acceptance should not be bound. Similarly an acceptance posted on the eve of a well-publicised postal strike should not be effective.

The Future of the Postal Rule

Acceptance by telex
The postal rule does not apply to communication by telex and probably also by means of facsimile transmission (fax). These methods are treated in the same way as oral communications. A telex acceptance is effective when printed out at the offeror's end.[37] It follows that, depending on which method of communication is employed, an acceptance may have different legal consequences. In a transaction between a British and a foreign company, a telex acceptance presumes that the law to be applied to the transaction is that of the company receiving the telex. By contrast, a postal acceptance presumes it is the law of the company sending the acceptance letter.[38] Perhaps the distinction can be justified on the basis that the postal rule is an exception to the general principle of communicating acceptance and the ambit to that exception should not be widened. Moreover it is always open to the offeror to prescribe the mode of acceptance. If he wishes actual notice of acceptance to be brought to his attention, he should stipulate for that in his offer. Nevertheless it is curious that, depending upon the mode of communication employed, the legal consequences can so markedly differ.

International Sales
In the case of sales under the Uniform Laws on International Sales Act 1967, the postal rule is set aside in favour of the principle that acceptance is effective on receipt. Where, accordingly, a contract is made under the provisions of the Act and an order for goods is

---

[36] *Holwell Securities Ltd.* v. *Hughes* [1974] 1 W.L.R. 155 at p. 161.

[37] *Brinkibon Ltd.* v. *Stahag Stahl* [1983] 2 A.C. 34; [1982] 1 All E.R. 293.

[38] See Contracts (Applicable Law) Act 1990; Civil Jurisdiction and Judgments Act 1982 which deals however with jurisdiction rather than choice of law.

placed with a foreign company the contract will only be deemed to be concluded when an acceptance arrives at the ordering company's offices.

General Reform

The Scottish Law Commission has recently recommended that certain provisions of the United Nations Convention on Contracts for the International Sale of Goods (the "Vienna Convention") should be adopted as part of the domestic law of Scotland relating to the formation of contract.[39] In particular it is recommended that the postal rule be abolished: "An acceptance of offer becomes effective at the moment the indication of assent reaches the offer or."[40] Annexed to the report is a draft Bill, the "Formation of Contracts (Scotland) Bill". If and when the Bill reaches the statute book, it will have significant implications for this branch of the law.

LIMITS OF THE OFFER/ACCEPTANCE APPROACH

Although most agreements or apparent agreements can be analysed into a sequence of offer, counter-offer, acceptance, and so on, it is not always possible to do so. Hiring a taxi, buying a newspaper and many of the other common transactions of everyday life are, on one view, only capable of an offer/acceptance analysis by adopting an artificial approach. Few people think in terms of offers and acceptances when they make such agreements. It is only in relation to a small number of contracts, such as auction sales and written estimates for building work, that the offer/acceptance analysis is readily apparent. Some matters seem to defy the offer and acceptance approach. Consider the customer who presents a prescription to the chemist. She might be said to be exercising a statutory right to pharmaceuticals under the relevant provisions relating to the National Health Service, rather than entering into a contract.[41] But in general, a contractual analysis is helpful. It enables one to break down and isolate each component part of the transaction to determine what the respective rights and duties of the parties actually are at any particular stage. Some specific situations call for comment.

---

[39] *Report on Formation of Contract: Scottish Law and the United Nations Convention on Contracts for the International Sale of Goods*, Scot. Law Com. No. 144 (July 1993).

[40] Article 18 (2) of the Convention.

[41] see *Pfizer Corpn.* v. *Ministry of Health* [1965] A.C. 512.

Identical Cross Offers

If A writes to B offering to sell B his car for £500 and simultaneously B writes to A offering to purchase the car at the same price, then it would appear that consensus has been reached. The parties' minds are *ad idem* with regard to the essential features of the bargain. Normally of course, the parties will be delighted to go through with the bargain in such circumstances. However, if one of the contracting parties changes his mind and refuses to go through with the transaction, an offer/acceptance analysis suggests that there is no contract. Because neither has received an acceptance, neither can be bound. This may appear a rather rigid adherence to the requirement of offer and acceptance at the expense of the true issue in question, namely whether the parties are in agreement.

Members of a Club

When individuals join a club or society, no legal rights or duties will normally arise. Often the only obligation on members is to pay a subscription. But what is the position if individuals voluntarily submit to some legal liability in relation to other club members? It is difficult, applying an offer and acceptance analysis, to unravel the legal relationship of club members with one another. In one case, competitors in a yacht race agreed under club rules to pay full compensation to any other boat which they damaged during the event.[42] This waived the statutory rule which limited the liability of boats by reference to the tonnage of the yacht in question. While there was no doubt that the competitors had agreed to full liability, it was difficult to identify any process of offer and acceptance which had occurred between the individual entrants. The contract (if any) appeared to be between each competitor and the club. Nevertheless the court held that there was indeed an offer by one competitor to the next. It has been pointed out that, even if the analysis holds in relation to later competitors, it cannot logically explain the position of the first entrant who had not received any offer.

The Battle of the Forms

It has become increasingly common for businesses to contract on printed forms. These forms are prepared in advance by legal advisers and amount to "package contracts". When each party uses its own standard form and neither form refers to the other, it may appear that there is no consensus. If, however, performance fol-

---

[42] *The Satanita* [1895] P. 248, affd. *sub. nom. Clarke* v. *Dunraven* [1897] A.C. 59.

lows and a dispute arises it seems inappropriate to hold that there is no contract. Accordingly the trusty offer/acceptance analysis has been pressed into service in this arena as well, although it may not appear the most suitable approach. An example is provided by the case of *Continental Tyre and Rubber Co. Ltd* v. *Trunk Trailer Co. Ltd.*[43]

> Company T ordered a quantity of tyres from Company C. The order was placed on Company T's standard printed purchase form. No written acceptance was given, but Company C proceeded to supply tyres in a number of consignments. Each consignment was accompanied by a "delivery note" and several days after each delivery, Company C sent an invoice to Company T. Both the "delivery note" and the invoice sought to incorporate the sellers' terms into the contract. Those terms were materially different from the buyers' terms. A dispute arose regarding the quality of the tyres supplied. The sellers sought to rely on a term which operated in their favour and was included in their own standard form. It was held that the buyer's terms ought to prevail. The contract was complete when the first batch was delivered in response to the purchaser's order. The purchaser had made the offer which the seller had impliedly accepted. Accordingly, the delivery note and the invoice came too late to be the basis of the contract.

Whether, however, this is a useful analysis is a questionable proposition. In an earlier English case, Lord Denning M.R. had noted the difficulty of applying an offer, counter-offer, acceptance analysis and suggested that: "the better way is to look at all the documents passing between the parties and glean from them, or from the contract of the parties, whether they have reached agreement on all material points, even though there may be differences between the forms and conditions printed on the back of them."[44] Certainly we need to look carefully at such situations to see whether an alternative approach might be formulated.

---

[43] 1987 S.C.L.R. 58.
[44] *Butler Machine Tool Co. Ltd.* v. *Ex-cell-o Corpn.* [1979] 1 All E.R. 965; [1979] 1 W.L.R. 401.

INTENTION TO CREATE LEGAL RELATIONS

Not all agreements are contracts. Suppose V agrees to have dinner with a friend, or consents to a proposal made by a fellow member of a committee. Neither of these agreements amounts to a contract. In such cases the law deems that the parties did not intend to create legal relations. This is not an additional requirement for, as we have seen, a contract is only formed when a serious offer is accepted. If the offer is not serious, acceptance cannot create a contract. On grounds of policy, however, there are several categories of agreement which the law declines to enforce. In such cases there is a presumption that the parties did not intend to create binding relations. No legal rights and duties flow from such agreements and they cannot, accordingly, be enforced.

Social Agreements

In the host of everyday arrangements made by individuals, a large number are presumed not to create legal relations. An agreement to invite an acquaintance to a concert does not give rise to legal liability if broken. Of course one can figure exceptions. To request a neighbour to purchase expensive tickets for the opera on your behalf may well give cause for legal action if you fail to pay for them. The question in each case will be whether a reasonable person would have assumed that legal consequences would flow from the agreement.

Domestic Agreements

It is not desirable for one party to threaten the other with legal action in the event of a row in the home. Domestic harmony is ill-served when appeal can be made to courts of law over disputes arising between husband and wife, or parent and child.[45] Courts might find it difficult to disentangle the evidence led. Accordingly, the courts are reluctant to uphold domestic agreements as contracts. A wife who looks after her husband during an illness is presumed not to do so under an implied contract.[46] This is deemed to be part and parcel of their married relationship. But compensation in respect of such services is now available under statute.[47] In the past, agreements relating to maintenance between separated spouses were held to fall within this exception. But the great

---

[45] see *Balfour* v. *Balfour* [1919] 2 K.B. 571.
[46] *Edgar* v. *Lord Advocate*, 1965 S.C. 67.
[47] Administration of Justice Act 1982, s. 8.

incidence of such arrangements today has led to their more often being enforced than not. Indeed, it is always possible for the presumption to be displaced where it is clear that the parties intended to put their relationship on a legal footing.

Commercial Agreements Binding in Honour Only

Moral obligations do not always bring legal obligations in their train. A debtor compromised a sum which he owed by paying one half.[48] In granting a receipt, the creditors stated that it was "understood that [the debtor] will pay the balance of 10s. per pound whenever he is able to do so." On the same date the debtor wrote to the creditor and stated " . . . I beg to assure you that I will pay up the deficiency as soon as I am able to do so." It was held that the arrangement to make payment of the balance was an "honourable understanding" which did not import any legal obligation. Similarly, a "letter of comfort" from a parent company stating that it was their policy to ensure that one of their subsidiaries was in a position at all times to meet its liabilities did not render them liable for a £10 million bank loan when the subsidiary went into liquidation.[49]

The parties may stipulate that their agreement is not to be legally binding. Such arrangements are rare, because a party is unlikely to consent to a position whereby he cannot apply to the court for redress should the other party fail in his obligations. In the leading English case on the matter, *Rose and Frank* v. *Crompton Bros.*, a clause stating that the agreement was to be "binding in honour only, and not subject to the jurisdiction of the courts", was upheld.[50] Actual deliveries which had taken place under the agreement were, however, to be paid for on the basis that they formed individual contracts of sale. Clauses of this nature could enable parties to evade their normal legal liabilities. Happily the use of such clauses is rare. The cases that have come before the courts have shown that judges do not approve of these arrangements. In one case, an agreement was made in terms of which a government department agreed to make *ex gratia* payments in respect of harbour dues.[51] Although the Lord Ordinary recognised that

---

[48] *Ritchie* v. *Cowan & Kinghorn* (1901) 3 F. 1071.
[49] *Kleinwort Benson* v. *Malaysia Mining Corpn. Berhad* [1989] 1 W.L.R. 379; [1989] 1 All E.R. 785; see also *Avintair* v. *Ryder Airline Services Ltd.* 1993 S.C.L.R. 576.
[50] [1925] A.C. 445.
[51] *Wick Harbour Trs.* v. *The Admiralty*, 1921 S.L.R. 109, cf. *Edwards* v. *Skyways Ltd.*, [1964] 1 All E.R. 494.

agreements could be entered into which were not legally enforceable, he held that the department were bound to pay the dues. The words "*ex gratia*" were not in his view enough to remove the intention to effect legal relations.

Collective Agreements

Agreements between employers and trade unions are known as collective agreements. Often they are of great length and cover every aspect of pay, conditions and work practices. For a long time the status of such agreements was unclear, but in the late 1960s it was decided by an English court that collective agreements were not presumed to effect legal relations.[52] Breach of the terms of such an agreement could not therefore be remedied by litigation. This principle is now enshrined in the Trade Union and Labour Relations Act 1974. Unless the collective agreement is in writing and has an express stipulation that it is to have legal force, no action will lie if one side defaults in its obligation under the contract. The collective agreement is a statement of aspiration and an indication of good faith, rather than a legal document. Where a dispute occurs which cannot be resolved by agreement the sanctions are: strike action and work to rule on the part of the employees, lockouts and suspension on the part of the employers.

Voluntary Organisations

It is presumed that persons join clubs, whether sporting, political or recreational, for mutual association, not to assume legal rights or liabilities. So long as such bodies conduct their affairs according to the canons of natural justice and within the provisions of the race and sex discrimination legislation, no legal rights arise. The law will not intervene to say who is properly entitled to enter a particular competition or uphold the right of a sportsman to play a particular game. But the law will intervene when it is clear that the parties have intended legal relations, as in the case of the *Satanita*, where all the competitors had signed a carefully worded document. An intention to effect legal relations will also be deemed to be present where a member's financial (or "patrimonial") interest is affected by the action of the club or voluntary association.

A patrimonial interest is a property interest: one that can be valued in money terms. This question of patrimonial interest concerns persons who hold offices in voluntary associations and

---

[52] *Ford Motor Co. Ltd.* v. *A.E.F.* [1969] 2 Q.B. 303; 2 All E.R. 481.

in particular, ministers of religion. So far as the Church of Scotland is concerned, deprivation of office is a matter within the jurisdiction of the General Assembly of the Church. However, in non-established churches, the position is less clear. Where actual loss of office, or even loss of status, is concerned, the law has in the past intervened and adjudicated upon the rights and duties of the parties.[53] But the law steered clear of controversial theological matters. Thus a minister who claimed a change in his church's doctrine meant he would have to relinquish his post in accordance with his conscience had no redress.[54] Recently there have been two cases in England which deny that a minister has a contract.[55] The view seems to be that the spiritual nature of a clergyman's calling ousts the temporal. The practical consequence is that a clergyman is not entitled to sue for unfair dismissal in an industrial tribunal, because that right only exists if there is a contract of employment.

Gaming Contracts

Betting and other forms of gambling are considered too trivial to merit judicial attention. Courts, it is said, were not instituted to determine frivolous disputes. Thus the winner of a bet cannot enforce it against the loser or bookmaker.[56] Nor can a casino correct an error by a croupier in giving a customer too many chips after a win on the roulette wheel.[57] A written admission of the debt will not render a wager enforceable. Football pools fall within this category. Certain forms of gambling are strictly controlled or made illegal by statute.[58] Television plays and the seamier sort of novel suggest, however, that non-legal sanctions for the enforcement of such matters are a good deal more effective than the courts.

Social Work "Contracts"

It has recently become more common in the welfare field for social workers, parole officers and even headmasters to enter into written "contracts" with their clients and pupils. These agreements list the obligations that each party is supposed to fulfil but are clearly not legally enforceable. The fact that they are made at all perhaps

---

[53] see, e.g., *McMillan* v. *Free Church of Scotland* (1861) 23 D. 1314.

[54] *Forbes* v. *Eden* (1867) 5 M. (H.L.) 36.

[55] *Davies* v. *Presbyterian Church of Wales* [1986] 1 W.L.R. 323; [1986] 1 All E.R. 705; *President of the Methodist Conference* v. *Parfitt* [1984] Q.B. 368.

[56] *Wordsworth* v. *Pettigrew* (1977) Mor. 9524.

[57] *County Properties & Developments Ltd.* v. *Harper* 1989 S.C.L.R. 597.

[58] see, e.g., The Gaming Acts 1710, 1835 and 1968; Betting Gaming and Lotteries Acts 1963-71; Lotteries and Amusements Act 1976.

shows the potency of the idea of contract. Persons entering such arrangements regard themselves as morally bound to uphold the obligations to which they have agreed, even though there are no legal sanctions in the event of breach.

WHEN IS THE CONTRACT BROUGHT INTO OPERATION?

In some instances the parties to the contract may wish to postpone its legal enforceability. It is competent for the parties to provide that the contract shall not take effect until a particular date or event occurs.

> *Example*: A may agree to buy B's car provided that the car passes an M.O.T. test: A is not bound to buy the car unless and until the car passes the test.

Not all conditions have the effect of postponing or suspending the operation of the contract. The legal effect of a particular condition will depend on a number of factors. If the condition refers to a future certain event such as a particular date, or the death of a named individual, then the obligation is constituted immediately: "In truth such an obligation is a present obligation which is to be discharged in the future."[59] So if A agrees to pay a debt when A's grandfather dies, that obligation exists from the moment it is entered into. It is only performance which is postponed. But where the condition refers to a future uncertain event—that X will reach the age of 18, or that Y will swim the Channel—its effect will either be suspensive or resolutive: suspensive if the obligation only becomes enforceable when the uncertain event occurs; resolutive if the obligation exists immediately, but is to come to an end if and when the uncertain event happens. An example of a suspensive condition would be where a job is offered subject to a medical examination being passed. Only when a satisfactory medical report is received does a contract of employment arise. But an offer of employment subject to documentary proof that the individual held the academic qualifications which he claimed, would be a resolutive condition. The contract of employment would arise when the individual accepted the offer. If, however, he could not confirm his qualifications the employment would be deemed never to have arisen. These two examples demonstrate that determining which

---

[59] Smith, *A Short Commentary on the Law of Scotland* (Edinburgh, 1962), p. 617.

side of the divide a particular condition falls into is not always an easy matter.

A common expression in English law is that the agreement will be "subject to contract". Most agreements for house transfers in England include such a clause. Its effect is to suspend the operation of the contract until written documents are signed by the parties. This has led to the practice of "gazumping". A seller who has agreed to sell to a particular person may renege on his agreement and decide to sell to someone else. As there is no legally enforceable obligation the seller is entitled to do this. The different method of buying property in Scotland has prevented such a practice arising. Under Scots law there is no conclusive answer regarding the effect of a "subject to contract" clause.[60] It will always be a question of construction. Should it be clear that the parties did not intend to be bound until a formal writing is signed, then the contract does not come into existence until that condition is satisfied.

[60] *Erskine* v. *Glendinning* (1871) 9 M. 656; *Stobo* v. *Morrison's Gowns Ltd.*, 1949 S.C. 184.

CHAPTER 3

PROMISE

APART from contract, Scots law recognises a second type of voluntary obligation known as promise. Stair described a promise as "that which is simple and pure, and hath not implied as a condition the acceptance of another."[1] A clear case of promise is an undertaking to make a gift.

> *Example*: Rudolph, a wealthy philanthropist, visits an exhibition of watercolours by Zeke. Two days later Zeke receives a letter from Rudolph. It states that Rudolph is impressed by Zeke's paintings and that he promises to send Zeke £2,500 to assist him in his work.

Rudolph is legally bound to honour this obligation. He has incurred the obligation despite the fact that Zeke has done nothing. Indeed Zeke may be completely unaware of Rudolph's intention until he receives the letter. But once Rudolph declares his intention, Zeke acquires a personal right—a right to sue Rudolph for £2,500. Rudolph must fulfil his promise if required to do so by Zeke.

PROMISE OR CONTRACT

When is a particular obligation analysed as a promise rather than a contract. In particular, what are the differences between promise and offer? They can be listed as follows:

1. A contract arises out of the will of two parties. A promise is the product of one person's intention alone. No acceptance is required to create a binding obligation.
2. An offer is revocable until it is accepted. A promise is binding and irrevocable from the moment it is made.
3. A promise places an obligation on one person alone. By contrast, contracts place obligations on both parties to the contract. In theory this is true even of gratuitous contracts. For instance, if A offers to gift a statue to his local council and it accepts, the council is under an obligation to take the statue.

[1] *Institutions*, I.x.4.

In the case of a promise the council would always have a right to reject the statue.

The apparent simplicity of this account is belied by the problems which occur in practice in attempting to distinguish a promise from a contract. A person giving an undertaking will not normally have in mind the relevant legal rules. The words used will not be particularly precise or technical. In some instances there will be no words at all but simply acts or a mixture of words and acts. It is then necessary to analyse the circumstances to determine the exact nature of the obligation in question. This is not always an easy task. The problem of classification can be illustrated by reference to two cases. In the first, *Morton's Trs* v. *The Aged Christian Friend Society of Scotland*[2]:

> Morton wrote to a committee which was promoting a charitable society. He offered to pay the society £1,000 by 10 annual instalments of £100 if certain conditions regarding its constitution were observed. Morton's offer was accepted by the committee, the society was formed and the conditions in the offer complied with. During his lifetime Morton paid the instalments every year, but he died leaving two instalments unpaid. A dispute arose as to whether his estate was bound to pay the remaining instalments. It was held that the society were entitled to recover the outstanding sum from Morton's estate. There was a binding contract between Morton and the society.

By contrast in *Smith* v. *Oliver*[3]:

> During the course of her life Mrs Oliver had given money from time to time toward the cost of certain structural alterations to a church in Dalry, Edinburgh. After her death the trustees of the church raised an action against her executor, claiming that Mrs Oliver had promised to provide £7,000 in her will for the remainder of the outlay involved. No such provision in the will had been made. The trustees said that they had relied on the assurances that Mrs Oliver had given in arranging for the work to be undertaken.
>
> There was held to be no contract here, only a promise. As the trustees did not have the appropriate evidence to prove the promise, their action failed.

[2] (1899) 2 F. 82; 7 S.L.T. 220.
[3] 1911 S.C. 103; 1910 2 S.L.T. 304.

The substance of the transaction in each case was the same. Both Mr Morton and Mrs Oliver wished to make a gift, one to a charity, the other to a church. Can we explain why different legal analyses were applied? The answer lies in the circumstances in which the obligation was undertaken. Mr Morton had actually used the word "offer" several times in his letters to the committee. It was not disputed that they had accepted the offer. Mrs Oliver's case was different. She had not committed her thoughts to writing. The church trustees could only point to various oral statements which she had made. No offer could be inferred from these statements, nor had there been any definite acceptance: "There is in truth no contract at all averred here, but merely a promise to pay . . . "[4]

The guidance to be derived from these two cases has not proved particularly helpful to subsequent judges. Where possible they have avoided committing themselves to one analysis or the other. In *Bathgate* v. *Rosie*, a young boy broke a shop window while out playing one evening.[5] His mother told the shopkeeper's wife that she would pay for the cost of a replacement. However, when the window was installed, the mother refused to pay. The sheriff held that the mother was bound to pay the replacement cost because she had given an unqualified undertaking to do so, but he did not specify whether it was a promise or a contract. What is clear is that a promise cannot be converted into a contract. In the old case of *Miller* v. *Tremamondo* it was alleged that a man had married a lady on the strength of certain financial assurances made by her father.[6] When these assurances were not realised, the husband sued his (now) father-in-law to fulfil his promises. It was decided that the alleged assurances were promises and the mere fact that the husband-to-be had acted on the faith of the promises did not convert them into a contract.

A Presumption in Favour of Contract

There is no doubt that through time there has developed a general presumption in favour of an analysis in terms of contract rather than in terms of promise. Several cases can be cited in support of this proposition. In *Malcolm* v. *Campbell* a lady signed a document before witnesses which said "I have agreed to sell my house for £150 to Miss X" and delivered the document to Miss X.[7] The court decided that the lady was not bound by the document as it was only

[4] *per* Lord President Dunedin.
[5] 1976 S.L.T. (Sh.Ct.) 16.
[6] (1771) Mor. 12395.
[7] (1891) 19 R. 278.

one side of a bilateral arrangement. The circumstances of *Paterson* v. *Highland Railway Co.* arose out of the First World War. Various railway companies undertook to maintain freight rates for timber at a fixed rate while an arrangement they had with the government remained in force.[8] The companies sought to increase the rates before the arrangement had terminated. It was held that the undertaking did not amount to a contract and was therefore unenforceable. In *Muirhead* v. *Gribben* an assurance was given by one firm of solicitors to another.[9] They stated that the second firm's fees would be paid if they transferred to the first firm papers belonging to a particular client. This was held to be a contract rather than a promise.

Three factors have had a bearing on this preference for a contractual analysis. First, many situations which might possibly be regarded as a promise involve the satisfaction of a condition. The condition is that some act be performed. Let us take an example. Suppose a wealthy businessman makes the following statement: "I promise to pay £150 to the first person to climb Ben Nevis wearing roller skates." The businessman does not receive a return promise for his own obligation. No one is bound to fulfil the condition. But it is clear that if performance is made he must pay the sum stipulated. Now an offer can be viewed as a promise to perform, subject to a condition being satisfied, *viz.* that acceptance be given. It is not therefore difficult to view fulfilment of the condition by performance as implied acceptance. This is the line that the courts have tended to adopt.

Secondly, there is a strong presumption against donation in the law. The law is reluctant to hold that a person intended to benefit another without receiving anything in return, unless clear evidence of that intention is present. All promises appear on their fact to be gratuitous and, therefore, to be treated with caution. In a contract, even a gratuitous contract like the one in *Morton*, both parties know of and assent to the creation of the obligation. Clear evidence of both parties' intention is therefore present and it is expected that the person benefited will rely on the obligation. The third factor which has led to a presumption in favour of contract rather than promise is the influence of English law. A short excursus into English law is therefore required.

---

[8] 1927 S.C. (H.L.) 32.
[9] 1983 S.L.T. (Sh.Ct.) 102.

The English Requirement of Consideration

In England obligations are enforceable only when supported by "consideration." In essence, consideration means that there must be some reciprocity, or element of bargain, in the transaction. English law will not enforce a bare promise where the promisor receives nothing in return. Consideration is therefore an additional technical requirement beyond offer and acceptance which must be satisfied before obligations are upheld. A classic example of consideration in English law occurs in *Stilk* v. *Myrick*[10]:

> Nine seamen had been engaged to sail a ship on a return trip from London to the Baltic. Two of the crew deserted at Kronstadt. The captain promised the remainder of the crew extra wages if they would work the ship home shorthanded. However, when the ship arrived back in Britain, the owner refused to pay the extra amount and an action was brought by one of the seamen for the increased wage. He was unsuccessful. It was held that there was no consideration for the captain's promise—the crew were under an existing contractual duty to bring the ship home. The captain's promise to pay them extra was unsupported by consideration. He received nothing in return for his promise which he was not already due.

In theory, therefore, there is a wide gulf between the position of English law and that of Scots law. North of the border, the concept of simple promise is recognised. South of the border it is not. However, the true picture is less clear cut. In England, even where consideration is absent, a person can make a binding unilateral obligation in a deed under seal. This is not a difficult requirement to satisfy. All that is required is that a simple adhesive wafer be attached to the deed. This is the manner by which a parent in England might covenant to pay sums to a child at university in order to secure tax advantages. In addition, the concept of consideration has over the years become somewhat elastic. The English courts have been prepared—rather artificially—to "find" consideration in many instances. A promise in return for a promise is good consideration. So is an act in return for a promise. In determining whether or not there is consideration, no inquiry is made into the value of the other party's performance. It is enough that something is given in return, no matter how low in value. That is why the term "peppercorn rent" can be literally as well as

---

[10] (1809) 2 Camp. 317; 6 Esp. 129.

figuratively true. If a landlord stipulates that the rent for premises shall be 3 peppercorns, this will be binding. A recent example of this approach is provided by *Williams* v. *Roffey & Nicholls (Contractors)*[11]:

> Building contractors contracted to refurbish a block of 27 flats. Their contract provided that they would have to pay penalty damages in the event that there was a delay in completion. They subcontracted the joiner-work to a carpenter at a price of £20,000. The carpenter ran into financial difficulties. The contractors agreed to pay him an extra £10,300 to complete the work on time. He went on to complete several flats but only received one further payment of £1,500 from the contractors. He sued for the extra sum. The contractors maintained that there was no consideration. The Court of Appeal held that the advantage to be secured by the contractors in not having to pay under the penalty clause, nor having to find another sub-contractor, amounted to consideration.

It follows that in practice, the difference between the two legal systems is often not very great. But the underlying theory of consideration has resulted in English lawyers preferring to analyse all types of unilateral undertaking in terms of contract. By an unfortunate process of osmosis, this approach has become accepted in Scotland, a result which can lead to strained and artificial reasoning in analysing common situations where such undertakings occur.

THE PRACTICAL APPLICATION OF THE CONCEPT OF PROMISE

Firm offers

The first situation where the concept of promise is useful is in connection with promises to keep an offer open. In *Littlejohn* v. *Hadwen* the estate of Renniston was being sold.[12] In a postscript to a letter containing details of the estate, the seller's solicitor wrote "it is understood that Mr Littlejohn has the offer of the estate of Renniston for ten days from this date." Lord Fraser regarded this as "an obligation, no doubt unilateral, but still binding upon the offeror during the appointed period." Unless something was given

---

[11] [1991] 1 Q.B. 1; [1990] 2 W.L.R. 1153; [1990] 1 All E.R. 512.
[12] (1882) 20 S.L.R. 5.

in return for such a promise in England, it would not be binding upon the promiser. There is no consideration. Yet if the offerer truly intended to keep his offer open for a certain period it seems appropriate that the law should uphold this undertaking, as in Scotland.

Third party rights

The concept of promise has allowed Scots law to develop the principle that third persons may acquire rights under a contract to which they were not parties. Two contracting parties can bind themselves in favour of a third. This is known as *jus quaesitum tertio* and will be discussed in Chapter 9.

The Reward Cases

Those cases where a promise to pay a reward in the event of a condition being fulfilled are referred to generally as "the reward cases". Before the late nineteenth century, the precise analysis of such cases in Scotland was unclear. This can be seen by examining the case of *Petrie* v. *Earl of Airlie*[13]:

> The Earl of Airlie did not vote in support of the great Reform Bill which extended the franchise for the House of Commons. Subsequently, a poster appeared accusing the Earl of Airlie and others of conduct amounting to treason by not supporting the measure in Parliament. The Earl stated that he would pay 100 guineas reward for information leading to the detection of the author and printer of the placard. The reward was to be payable on conviction. Petrie informed the Earl that his brother and another person were the printers. When the Earl passed this information to the authorities, however, they declined to prosecute and he himself did not initiate a private prosecution (which was more common then). Accordingly, there was no conviction and the Earl refused to pay the reward. Petrie was successful in recovering the reward money when he sued the Earl. The opinion of the Lord Ordinary (Corehouse) was affirmed by the Inner House without their giving reasons.

Professor Smith regarded the case as being one of conditional promise.[14] Professor Walker states that it could have been dealt with on this basis, but in fact it was treated as a case of contract.[15] It

---

[13] (1834) 13 S. 68.

[14] Smith, *A Short Commentary on the Law of Scotland* (Edinburgh, 1962), p. 748.

[15] Walker, *Contracts* (2nd ed., 1985), 2.34.

is not clear from the opinion of Lord Corehouse which view is correct. He did not distinctly analyse the basis upon which the obligation was founded.

In the early twentieth century there were several Scottish cases dealing with rewards.[16] All proceeded on the basis of contract rather than promise, probably because of the influence of *Carlill*. The divergence between the two approaches has practical consequences. This is clearly demonstrated by considering an Australian case, *R.* v. *Clarke*[17]:

> A reward for information leading to the arrest of certain members was issued by the Government of Western Australia. If the information was provided by an accomplice it was further promised that he would receive a free pardon. Clarke, who was himself under suspicion of the crime provided the information. Later he found out about the reward and claimed payment.

The High Court of Australia held that Clarke was not entitled to the reward. In issuing the reward, the State Government was making an offer. Clarke gave the information without reference to that offer. There was therefore no acceptance and no contract. The Australian Chief Justice (Isaacs) instanced the case of an offer of £100 to anyone who would swim 100 yards in the harbour on the first day of the year. In his view, someone who had been thrown overboard and was simply swimming to save his life was not entitled to the sum. This argument reflects a hostility to persons acquiring money on a "something for nothing" basis. As the person would have given the information or swum the distance stipulated anyway, irrespective of the reward, the other person should not be bound to pay him anything. Perhaps it ultimately depends on one's moral perspective. On one view the condition is satisfied so the undertaking should be fulfilled. A person who issues a reward but wishes to withhold it from certain persons can do so by express stipulation. If he fails to make such a qualification, then he should be bound.

Another problem of analysing the reward in cases in terms of offers concerns the right to withdraw. When precisely does the offerer lose his right to cancel the reward? We have seen that offers can always be withdrawn before acceptance. How does that prin-

---

[16] see, *e.g., Hunter* v. *General Accident Corpn.*, 1909 S.C. (H.L.) 30; [1909] A.C. 404; 1909 2 S.L.T. 99.
[17] (1927) 40 C.L.R. 227.

ciple apply here? Suppose a man puts a notice in his local news-paper that he will pay £50 to anyone who will return his lost kitten "Shuggie" to him. A promise analysis means that the man must pay the money to anyone who satisfies the condition by returning the kitten to him. But if it is an offer, is the right of revocation lost when someone spies Shuggie, or picks him up, or starts going towards the man's home? English law has been over-elaborate in its attempt to explain why the offerer should be prevented from withdrawing his offer before acceptance is made. The approach of Scots law does seem both clearer and more appropriate.

Options

A typical option occurs where there is a provision in a contract which allows one party to acquire certain specific rights in the future by issuing a notice to the other party.

> *Example*: A agrees to lease B's estate for 15 years. Clause 3 of the lease allows A to purchase the estate after 8 years have elapsed. In order to exercise the option, A must issue a notice by means of recorded delivery letter served on B. The price for the estate will be its market value as at the date the option is triggered, which will be assessed by independent surveyors.

Some contracts are exclusively about options. A contract relating to the right to film a novel would fall into this category. A studio might agree to pay an author £20,000 in return for an option to film her novel within the next two years. Lord Ross has suggested that the better view is to regard options as a type of promise, rather than as an offer.[18] In effect, the granting of an option means "I oblige myself to do such and such provided you exercise the option." In our example, B promises to enter into missives to sell the estate to A provided that the option is exercised in terms of Clause 3. This overcomes the problem that arises with offer/acceptance, where an explanation must be given as to why the option is irrevocable even before any acceptance has been made.

The Potential for Development

The discussion above highlights a number of areas where the concept of promise might be useful. There are other areas where promise might potentially be employed.[19] A bank cheque-card, for example, can be viewed as a promise by the issuing bank to honour

[18] see *Stone* v. *MacDonald*, 1979 S.L.T. 288.
[19] MacQueen, 1987 S.L.T. (News) 1.

cheques drawn on a particular account up to a certain amount. A similar approach might be adopted in relation to "letters of intent."[20] These are documents where one person indicates to another that he intends to enter a contract with him if certain events occur. They are commonly used in the building trade, where a main contractor may request a subcontractor to provide a tender for certain specialist work such as plumbing. In return, the main contractor will provide a letter of intent, which indicates that he proposes to take the sub-contractor on if he is awarded the main contract. Such a letter of intent might, in appropriate circumstances, be regarded as a promise. Requirements contracts, where contractors undertake to take all their supplies from a particular supplier or retailer, might also yield to a promise analysis. These are areas where the concept of promise may provide a template for future legal development in Scots law.

CONCLUSION

1. Scots law recognises the unilateral voluntary obligation of promise. It is not bedevilled by the notion of consideration.
2. A promise is irrevocable from the moment it is made and does not require acceptance.
3. There is a presumption in favour of analysing situations in terms of offer and acceptance.
4. Promise is largely an undeveloped concept in Scots law despite the fact that it can provide an accurate analysis of several common situations.

[20] see *Uniroyal* v. *Miller*, 1985 S.L.T. 101.

CHAPTER 4

CAPACITY AND FORMALITIES

CAPACITY

EVERYONE aged over 18 years and in full command of their faculties can make contracts. Such persons are said to have full capacity. Special provisions apply to young people and to those who are not in full possession of their mental faculties.

Young Persons

So far as age is concerned, the law has recently been reformed by the Age of Legal Capacity (Scotland) Act 1991.[1] The Act distinguishes a person's capacity to act into three periods. Under the age of 16, a person is deemed to have no capacity to enter into transactions.[2] Any important legal step will generally be taken by that person's guardian.[3] A person's parents will usually act as their guardians. However, this general principle has an important qualification. Children are entitled to enter into a transaction provided two conditions are satisfied. First, the transaction is of a kind commonly entered into by persons of that age and circumstances. Secondly, the terms of the transaction are reasonable.[4] Accordingly, when a schoolgirl buys a bus ticket or a comic, this will be binding. If the two conditions are not met, however, the transaction is void.

Example: Archie is 15 years of age. He makes a contract, in terms of which he agrees to buy one computer game per month for a ten month period. The price of each game is £75, which is well above the retail price. There is no provision in the contract which allows Archie to cancel. Proceedings can be taken to declare the contract invalid on the basis that it is not

---

[1] c.50. The 1991 Act implemented the Bill annexed to the Scottish Law Commission's report "*Legal Capacity and Responsibility of Minors and Pupils*" (Scot. Law Com. No. 110) published in December 1987.

[2] s.1 (1) (a).

[3] s.5; and see Law Reform (Parent and Child) (Scotland) Act 1986.

[4] s.2 (1).

common for 15 year old children to enter contracts of this type
and that the terms are unreasonable.

When a person reaches the age of 16 years, the position changes.
Upon attaining that age, the general principle is that a person
acquires full legal capacity.[5] However, if between the ages of 16 and
18, someone enters into a "prejudicial transaction" then he or she
is entitled to apply to the court to have the transaction set aside. A
prejudicial transaction is defined by the Act as one which:
  (a) an adult, exercising reasonable prudence, would not have
       entered into in the circumstances of the applicant at the time
       of entering into the transaction, and
  (b) has caused or is likely to cause substantial prejudice to the
       applicant.
The application must be made before the person reaches 21 years of
age. A party may be reluctant to enter into a transaction with a
person under the age of 16 years, because of the possibility that the
agreement might subsequently be set aside on the ground that it is
prejudicial. In such a situation, a joint application can be made to
have the transaction ratified by the court.[6] The court is required to
scrutinise the bargain before ratifying it. Where a transaction has
been ratified, it cannot be challenged on the basis that it was
prejudicial.[7] Over the age of 18 years, a person has full capacity.

Summary Under 16 years   –   Limited capacity
          16–18 years   –   Qualified full capacity
          Over 18 years   –   Full capacity

Mental Capacity

The main category of person whom the law deems incapable of
giving consent comprises those who are insane. Insane people have
no capacity to make contracts. The law intervenes to protect such
people by making their contracts void. A curator must be
appointed to make contracts on behalf of an insane person.
Accordingly if an elderly person becomes demented and requires to
go into hospital or into a nursing home, a *curator bonis* may be
appointed to supervise that person's affairs. This can be an expensive and time-consuming process. It is often difficult for relatives to

[5] s.1 (1) (b).
[6] s.4 (1).
[7] s.3 (3) (j).

deal with an insane person's affairs expeditiously because of the need for a curator to be appointed.

A less important category of persons deemed to have no capacity are intoxicated persons. Persons who are drunk or under the influence of drugs can make contracts so long as they are not totally incapacitated. Erskine summed up the position as follows: "Persons while in a state of absolute drunkenness and consequently deprived of the exercise of reason, cannot oblige themselves, but a lesser degree of drunkenness which only darkens reason, has not the effect of annulling the contract."[8]

FORMALITIES

Introduction

The general principle is that no special formalities are required to make a valid contract. Scots law, said Stair, has adopted the canon law approach by which "every paction produceth action."[9] If, accordingly, the twin elements of agreement and intention to be bound are present, the contract is complete. This means that in Scotland most contracts have legal effect no matter what their form—whether written, oral or arising by implication from the way the parties act. Accordingly a verbal bargain to sell a Rolls Royce motor car, or a block of shares valued at £5 million, is binding on the parties. In this chapter we shall examine the exceptions to this general principle.

"Formalities" means that the law lays down further requirements beyond those of formation. These requirements must be satisfied before a contract is held valid and enforceable. The most common formality is to require some form of writing. How does this work in practice? In contracts where no formalities are required, a person wishing to prove that a binding agreement exists can rely on all relevant evidence. Witnesses can be heard and documents examined. But should a contract fall into a class where a particular formality is required, the validity of the contract will be determined by whether or not that formality has been complied with. Other evidence, however relevant, is excluded.

[8] *Institute* 1. III.16.
[9] *Institutions* I.x.7.

Reasons for Requiring Writing

It would be possible for a legal system to require no formalities for contractual obligations. Every contract could be made in any fashion and proved by any means. No system, however, entirely dispenses with formalities and there are several interlinked reasons for this:

1. To show the transaction is authentic

A formality may be important to demonstrate that a person truly intended to conclude a particular transaction. In the early law seals were used. Because seals could be easily lost or forged, signed writing came to be required as a better means of authenticating a person's intention. Today we regard signed documents as a mark that the signatory clearly intended to enter the transaction. A signed promise or I.O.U. is more cogent evidence of concluded intention.

2. To emphasise the importance of transaction

The law may insist on formalities to impress upon the contracting parties the importance of their acts. In some societies in the past, the requirements have been startling: "Herodotus tells us that the Scythians, when they desired to make a contract entirely binding, drew blood of one another into a bowl, dipt their arrows in it, and afterwards drank it off."[10] By putting their contract into writing, signing it and having the signatures witnessed, the parties are made aware of the serious nature of the transaction they are undertaking. The formality should deter them from entering contracts on a whim. It allows parties to pause and reflect before entering serious undertakings. The contracting party "is awaked from his reverie by the entrance of two or more people called in to witness what is going on" and "he will be more upon his guard and deliberate more coolly upon what he is doing."[11]

3. To produce certainty

When negotiations have been going on for a period, there may be certain issues which each contracting party thinks are settled. If, however, the agreement is oral and a dispute arises, each party may find that his recollection of the terms differs from that of the other. A written contract provides a fixed record of the agreement. This

---

[10] Smith, *Lectures on Jurisprudence*, ed. Meek, Raphael & Stein (Oxford, 1978), ii. 70.
[11] *Crichton and Dow* v. *Syme* (1772) Mor. 17047 (said in relation to probative writing, see *infra*).

allows disputes to be resolved more easily than by recourse to the parties' (or other peoples') impression of the terms of the agreement.

4. *To protect one of the parties*

There are some instances where it is helpful for one of the parties to have a written record of the terms of the transaction. A tenant or an employee may find himself in a situation where it is important to have in writing a statement of the terms of the contract. This can be particularly true where there is the possibility of exploitation by the stronger party. Some statutes require that one party's rights are to be specifically declared in the contract. Where goods are bought with finance provided by a credit company, for example, it is incumbent upon the company to provide a written statement of the contract to the consumer. This statement must include information telling the consumer about his rights.[12] A recent example is the Timeshare Act 1992; which relates to businesses which offer time-shares in holiday apartments. Such businesses must give written notice to the offeree that he has a right to cancel the agreement within 14 days.

Historical Development

The development of the present Scots law of formalities can be traced back to several statutes passed from 1540 onwards, which are known as the Authentication Statutes.[13] Those Acts laid down a variety of rules regarding the requirements to be satisfied to make a document legally binding. Subsequent cases amplified when and how these rules were to apply. The later statutes which have been passed in relation to this topic possess a common element, namely the relaxation of the more strict requirements of the earlier legislation.[14] Broadly speaking we can identify three categories in Scots law today where writing of some type is required: obligations provable by writ or oath, obligations which require formal writing (*obligationes literis*) and obligations which by statute require writing.

---

[12] Consumer Credit Act 1974, ss. 58, 60, 61.

[13] The most important of these are the Acts 1540 (cap. 117), 1579 (cap. 80), 1584 (cap. 4), 1593 (cap. 179), 1681 (cap. 5) (Lord Stair's Act).

[14] see Conveyancing (Scotland) Act 1874, Conveyancing and Feudal Reform (Scotland) Act 1970.

OBLIGATIONS PROVABLE BY WRIT OR OATH

The first category of obligations which require special formalities are those provable by writ or oath. These obligations can only be proved in two ways. There must either be a document signed by the person alleged to be bound, or he must declare the existence of obligation on oath in court. The evidence of witnesses or of other types of documentation which tend to prove the obligation is irrelevant. An example may help to illustrate this.

> *Example*: Sandy and Bryan are having a discussion over a drink in their golf club one day. Bryan agrees to lend Sandy some money to tide him over a difficult period and on the spot hands him £100. Several other members of the club witness this transaction. A month later Bryan asks Sandy to repay the money but Sandy refuses, alleging that the money was a gift not a loan. Because a loan is an obligation provable only by writ or oath, Bryan cannot enforce the obligation against Sandy by relying on the evidence of the other club members. He must produce a writing signed by Sandy, showing that he borrowed the money. A simple I.O.U. will suffice. Alternatively Sandy can be required to go into the witness box and be asked on oath whether it was truly a loan rather than a gift.

It may seem rather hard that Bryan may be prevented from recovering the £100. However, it must be remembered that a great deal of unnecessary litigation is prevented by having a rule of this nature. When money or goods are transferred from one person to another, the policy of the law is to try prevent one person subsequently alleging that the transaction was truly a loan if it was not. Signed writing performs this function. Bryan could have obtained an I.O.U. quite easily. Apart from loan, other obligations which are only provable by writ or oath are (a) gratuitous obligations, (b) obligations of relief and (c) innominate and unusual contracts.

(a) A gratuitous obligation is one which, in substance, places all the obligations on one of the parties, for instance an agreement to confer a benefit on another party.

(b) Obligations of relief arise where one person pays a debt or liability in full and then seeks to recover from others the share which they owe. For example in a partnership, if one partner pays a debt due by the firm, he has a right of relief against the other partners to recover the share of the debt for which they are liable.

(c) Put simply, an innominate and unusual contract is one where the terms of the contract are out of the ordinary. A recent example concerned an allegation by a husband that his wife had made an oral agreement to transfer a taxicab operator's licence to him on request.[15] Lord Hunter thought this was not only innominate and unusual but also anomalous. It followed that it could only be proved by writ or oath.

Proof by Writ

The writing (or writ) required to prove the obligation must be something signed by the party alleged to be bound. It can be informal and does not need to be witnessed. This was decided by a majority of the whole court in the case of *Paterson* v. *Paterson*.[16]

> A mother lent her son two sums of money. The son died and the mother sought to recover both sums. In respect of one sum, the only document she held was an acknowledgment signed by her son regarding payment of interest on the loan. Despite the informality of the document the mother was held entitled to recover the sum. The acknowledgment did amount to a "writ" sufficient to prove the obligation.

In some instances a document may be the party's writ even though unsigned. A handwritten entry in a business book may satisfy the requirement.

Proof by Oath

This archaic Scottish institution allows one party to peril his whole case on what his opponent states in court under oath.

> *Example*: A alleges that B has promised to gift him £10,000; B denies that he made any such promise. No writing exists. Under the procedure of reference to oath, A can require B to go into the witness box and answer under oath the question: "Did you promise to pay A £10,000 on Saturday 1st July?" No cross examination of B is permissible. If B's answer is "yes" the obligation is enforceable. But if the answer is "no" then the obligation is unforceable.

The person making the reference is bound by the answer, even if it is "palpably and disgracefully false."[17]

---

[15] *McCourt* v. *McCourt*, 1985 S.L.T. 335.
[16] (1897) 25 R. 144; 5 S.L.T. 209.
[17] *Hunter* v. *Geddes* (1835) 13 S. 369 *per* Lord Jeffrey at p. 377.

Reference to oath has never been a widely used procedure. In recent years it has almost disappeared. The reason for this stems mainly from the Scottish system of procedure. In civil cases the parties must draw up written pleadings before the case is heard in court. The purpose of these pleadings is to focus the issues about which the parties are in dispute. It prevents unnecessary evidence being led regarding matters upon which there is no dispute. Only the issues in dispute need be proved. If, accordingly, a person does not deny the existence of the obligation in the pleadings, it is not necessary for the other person to prove it. By contrast, if a person denies the existence of an obligation, both before the litigation begins, and in the written pleadings, he is unlikely to go into the witness box and admit that he lied.

An illustration of the rules relating to proof by writ or oath is provided by the case of *Smith* v. *Oliver* which was discussed in Chapter 3.[18] It will be recalled that Mrs Oliver allegedly made oral statements that she would leave a sum of money in her will to pay for structural alterations to her church. It was held that the obligation to benefit the church, being gratuitous, could only be proved by writ or oath. There was no reason to doubt the evidence given by the church trustees, but as the lady was dead and no writ dealing with the obligation existed, it could not be proved. Accordingly the trustees could not obtain the money from her estate.

CONTRACTS REQUIRING FORMAL WRITING (OBLIGATIONS LITERIS)

The second class of obligations is known as *obligationes literis*. In principle this class requires even more stringent formalities than those which apply to obligations proved by writ or oath. Such obligations must be constituted in formal writing. There are four main types of *obligationes literis*:

(a) Contracts relating to heritage (land and buildings).
(b) Contracts of employment for more than one year and contracts of apprenticeship.
(c) Submissions to arbitration and decrees arbitral.
(d) Contracts which the parties agree are to be constituted, and not merely recorded, in writing.

At the time of the institution of these categories, the first three classes were thought to relate to matters of "great moment." In particular, land was seen as the main source of wealth in the

---

[18] 1911 S.C. 103; 1910 2 S.L.T. 304.

community. The fourth class allowed parties to stipulate that a particular transaction should require full formalities before it was valid. Times have changed. Contracts of employment are largely drawn up to comply with the provisions of the Employment Protection (Consolidation) Act 1978. That Act requires that certain terms regarding pay and conditions must be notified to the employee. The common law requirements are rarely adhered to. So far as obligations relating to arbitration are concerned, these are not of widespread importance. With regard to the fourth class, parties rarely agree to constitute their agreements in formal writing unless the law itself requires it. It would, for example, be possible to stipulate that a contract for the sale of a car would only be binding if constituted in formal writing. Few people, if any, would wish to do this. Accordingly, by far the most important category of *obligationes literis* is that relating to heritage. Where a house or flat is sold, the missives relating to the transaction must be in formal writing to be valid. Similarly a lease for more than a year must be constituted in formal writing.

If a contract falls into the class of *obligationes literis* and the requisite formalities are not complied with, neither party is bound and each has the right to withdraw (*locus poenitentiae*). However, there is an important exception to this rule where performance has followed upon the agreement. This is discussed in greater detail below. The existence of the exception explains why an employer who has engaged an employee without using formal writing is not entitled to renege on his agreement.

The Writing Required

The formal writing required for *obligationes literis* can be one of two types:
1. *Probative*. A writing is said to be probative ("to prove itself") if it complies with the Authentication Statutes. Essentially this means it must be signed by the grantor and the signature witnessed by two persons.[19]
2. *Holograph* (in own hand). A holograph writing is one entirely in the handwriting of the granter and signed by him. A printed or typewritten sheet is treated as holograph if the granter writes the words "adopted as holograph" above his signature. This is the manner in which solicitors make offers and accept-

---

[19] see the definition in the Prescription and Limitation (Scotland) Act 1973, Sched. 1, para. 4 (*b*).

ances on behalf of their clients in house purchase transactions. Unlike probative writings, a holograph writing need not be witnessed.

For many purposes, probative and holograph writing are treated as similar. If, however, the deed is challenged then a difference emerges. A probative deed carries a presumption of authenticity on its face. In other words, it is assumed to be genuine and can only be set aside by a direct challenge. The onus is on the person challenging the deed. He must prove that it is not authentic. In general he can only do so in an action of reduction, which is within the exclusive jurisdiction of the Court of Session.[20] A further feature of a probative deed is that it proves its own date. With holograph writings the onus is on the person relying upon the deed. He must lead evidence to show that the deed was granted by the person who signed it and when it was signed. A third difference is that the obligations contained in a probative deed are not extinguished for 20 years, whereas those in a holograph deed are extinguished after five years.[21]

Terminology

Some problems have arisen over terminology in this area. "Attested" and "authenticated" are usually used as synonyms for probative writing. "Subscription" is another word for signature. "Resile" means withdraw. To confuse matters further, holograph writings are sometimes described as probative.

Both Parties' Writing must be Formal

If the obligation falls into the category of *obligationes literis* there must be formal writings of both parties. This is illustrated by the case of *Goldston* v. *Young*[22]:

> Young owned a shop which Goldston wished to purchase. They agreed a price of £790. Young wrote out an offer to purchase which Goldston signed. Young then wrote out an acceptance to this offer which he himself signed. Subsequently Young refused to go through with the transaction. Goldston raised an action to have the contract declared binding, claiming that Young must implement the sale. Alternatively he sought damages. The First Division held that there was no

---

[20] There are limited circumstances when the validity of a document can be challenged in the Sheriff Court. See Macphail, *Sheriff Court Practice*, paras. 12–71f.

[21] see Chap. 11.

[22] (1868) 7 M. 188.

contract. There was a valid acceptance but no valid offer. The purported offer had been signed by Goldston but not written by him so it was not holograph. Nor could it be probative as it had not been witnessed. Accordingly the contract was not properly constituted and both parties had the right to withdraw (*locus poenitentiae*) whenever they wished. As Lord Kinloch succinctly put it, "This being a contract about heritage, the want of a probative deed implies a want of completed agreement."

The rule that there be formal writing of both parties has not escaped criticism. No less an authority than Lord President Cooper said that it is a "fossil relic of feudalism" which is "completely out of touch with realities [in] the field of mutual contract."[23]

The Doctrine of Personal Bar

It is easy to see how the requirement of formality in *obligationes literis* might lead to unfairness. A party might act on the strength of an agreement even although the necessary formalities had not been completed. As we have seen, neither party is bound at this informal stage and each has the right to withdraw. Someone might incur a great deal of expense in reliance on the informal agreement and then find that the other party was claiming his right to withdraw from the contract. Suppose A is interested in buying B's house. They reach a verbal agreement on all the matters pertaining to the sale. Before the missives are completed between their respective solicitors A, with B's full knowledge and permission, sells his own house, orders a swimming pool for B's house and has B's roof repaired. To allow B to withdraw with impunity at this stage would be most unjust. Accordingly, the law has developed the doctrine of personal bar to cover this type of situation.

Personal bar is an equitable doctrine which prevents a party from withdrawing from an informal agreement if certain criteria are satisfied. In legal phraseology, *locus poenitentiae* is lost by operation of the doctrine of personal bar. What then is personal bar? One description often referred to was given by Lord Birkenhead:

"Where A has by his words or conduct justified B in believing that a certain state of facts exists, and B has acted upon such

---

[23] *McGinn* v. *Shearer*, 1947 S.C. 334.

belief to his prejudice, A is not permitted to affirm against B that a different state of facts existed at the same time."[24]

Its effect is "to rivet the obligations involved."[25] For the doctrine to be brought into play, a number of conditions must be satisfied. Firstly, it must be shown that there was an agreement. Secondly, either

(a) one party has changed his position in reliance upon the deed and his actions are permitted by the party now denying the validity of the obligation—*rei interventus* (subsequent actings), or

(b) the party now challenging the obligation has acted in such a manner as to show that he regarded the agreement as binding upon him—homologation (affirmation).

We shall consider each of these requirements in more detail below. It is worth stressing that while the doctrine of personal bar provides a large exception to the general principle which requires formal writing for certain contracts, not all cases of informality are cured by its operation. In *Goldston* v. *Young* the purchaser of the shop had not changed his position in reliance upon the informal agreement, nor had the seller done anything to indicate that he regarded himself as bound by the agreement. Accordingly neither *rei interventus* nor homologation was present, so the defect had not been cured.

The Informal Agreement

"There must, in my opinion, be *consensus in idem* as to the essentials of a contract before either of these doctrines can come into play."[26] The bedrock on which the application of the doctrine of personal bar rests is that there is an agreement, albeit informal. So where a holograph offer to sell a shop was met by an informal acceptance which contained the words "subject to contract," it was held that no binding obligation existed.[27] The words "subject to contract" qualified the acceptance. There was, accordingly, no agreement on which *rei interventus* or homologation could follow.

---

[24] *Gatty* v. *MacLaine*, 1921 S.C. (H.L.) 1 at p. 7; [1921] 1 A.C. 376.

[25] Gloag, *Contract* (2nd ed., Edinburgh, 1929), p. 174.

[26] *Mitchell* v. *The Stornoway Trs.*, 1936 S.C. (H.L.) 56 at p.66 *per* Lord Macmillan.

[27] *Stobo Ltd.* v. *Morrisons (Gowns) Ltd.*, 1948 S.C. 184.

Rei Interventus

Where a person claims that he has changed his position in reliance upon an informal agreement and that his actions were known to the other party, the plea is one of *rei interventus*. Bell made the classic statement on this branch of the law[28]:

> "*Locus Poenitentiae* (a corollary to the rule of final engagement) is a power of resiling from an incomplete engagement . . . *Rei Interventus* raises a personal exception, which excludes the plea of *locus poenitentiae*. It is inferred from any proceedings not unimportant on the part of the obligee, known to and permitted by the obligor to take place on the faith of the contract as if it were perfect; provided they are unequivocally referable to the agreement and productive of alteration of circumstances, loss, or inconvenience though not irretrievable."

In this statement, Bell identified a number of criteria which had to be satisfied before *rei interventus* could operate. Let us consider each in turn.

1. *Not unimportant*—The actings in question must not be trivial. A person who purchases a new door-mat on the strength of an informal agreement to buy a house is in a different position from someone who has sold his own house in reliance on the agreement. Nevertheless it is a "not very exacting standard,"[29] and easily satisfied.

2. *Known to and permitted by the obligor*—Secret acts cannot cure the informality because the essence of the doctrine of personal bar is that of "fair play". It is only where a person actually allows the actings in question that it is equitable to deprive him of his right to withdraw. So a farmer will not lose his right to withdraw if a prospective purchaser of one of his outlying fields, with whom he has an informal agreement, travels to the field and, without the farmer's knowledge, sows new crops and repairs the fences. But the farmer will be bound if he knows about these actions and does not do anything to prevent them.

3. *Unequivocally referable to*—The actings must take place in reliance upon the agreement. Otherwise there is no reason to suggest that the actor has suffered in consequence of relying on the informal agreement. Suppose the owner of a hotel enters into an informal agreement to sell the hotel building for development. He cannot claim *rei interventus* simply by selling all the

[28] Bell, *Prin.*, ss. 25, 26.
[29] *per* Lord Macmillan in *Mitchell* (*supra*).

hotel's bedlinen. That might be something he was proposing to do in any event. He must therefore establish that he sold the bedlinen in reliance upon the informal agreement.

4. *Alteration of circumstances, loss or inconvenience*—This ties in with the requirement that the actings be "not unimportant." If the actings have not prejudiced the actor's position and he has suffered no loss or inconvenience then there is no equitable reason to invoke the doctrine. What is looked for is some form of detriment. Arranging for the preparation of a draft disposition together with ancillary documents did not satisfy this test in a case involving a shop said to be worth £215,000.[30]

Homologation

As with *rei interventus*, the effect of the plea of homologation is to prevent a person from taking unfair advantage of the rules relating to *obligationes literis*. Homologation prevents a party who acts in a way which shows he regards an agreement as binding from changing his mind and denying its validity.

> *Example*: Crispin sends a short note to Bartholomew offering to lease Bartholomew's salmon fishing for a five year period. Bartholomew replies agreeing to the proposal. Neither letter is in formal writing. Subsequently Crispin sends Bartholomew a cheque for the first term's rent of the fishings which Bartholomew pays into his bank account. By accepting the rent Bartholomew has homologated the agreement and lost his right to resile.

"The law of homologation proceeds upon the principle of presumed consent by the party who does the act to pass from grounds of challenge known to him and *sciens et prudens* [in full knowledge] to adopt the challengeable deeds as his own."[31] At the heart of homologation is the view that a person cannot affirm or deny an agreement as it suits him. He cannot have his cake and eat it. Either the engagement is binding or it is not binding. Homologation focuses on the acts of the party now denying the existence of the obligation. His words and deeds are examined to see whether he has formerly recognised the validity of the informal agreement. By contrast, *rei interventus* is concerned primarily with the acts of the party seeking to uphold the bargain. The plea of homologation is only available if the person in question knew of his right to

---

[30] *Rutterford* v. *Allied Breweries Ltd.*, 1990 S.L.T. 249, 252.
[31] *Gardner* v. *Gardner* (1830) 9 S. 138 *per* Lord Moncrieff at p. 140.

withdraw. If he did not know of his right to withdraw, his actions could not be deemed to affirm the informal agreement.

The pleas of *rei interventus* and homologation can both arise in the same case. In *Mitchell* v. *Stornoway Trs.*[32]:

> Mitchell wished to buy certain land for the purpose of building a garage. Although no formal agreement was concluded, he submitted a site plan to the owners showing the building he proposed to erect. The owners signed and approved this plan. As their signature was not witnessed it was not probative. Mitchell applied for planning permission to build the garage. The owners' factor gave assistance in the proceedings by explaining the details of the building plans to the court. Before these proceedings had been completed, however, the owners decided not to sell the land to Mitchell.

It was held that the trustees had homologated the informal agreement and were therefore barred from resiling. By assisting in the application for planning permission the trustees had acted in a manner "inconsistent with the reservation . . . of any *locus poenitentiae*." Three of the judges also thought that Mitchell's application to the Dean of Guild court amounted to *rei interventus*. He acted to his loss in the full knowledge and with the full permission of the trustees.

Extending the Doctrine of Personal Bar

We have seen that for personal bar to operate, two elements must be present. First there must be an informal agreement. Secondly there must be subsequent actings. The actings which are relied upon to establish personal bar can be proved by any means. However, the informal agreement itself can only be proved by writ or oath. So there must usually be a written acknowledgment of the obligation by the person now denying its validity. If the only evidence is that of witnesses, the agreement cannot be proved in court. In *Walker* v. *Flint* there was an alleged agreement to let a plot of land for three years for the purpose of feeding pigs.[33] It was held that the agreement could only be established if there was a writ (or the defender was prepared to state under oath that an agreement truly existed). As the alleged agreement was oral, it is unlikely that the pursuer was able to succeed at the proof.

---

[32] 1936 S.C. (H.L.) 56.
[33] (1863) 1 M. 417.

In at least two cases, the distinction between actings required to prove the underlying agreement and those required to support a plea of *rei interventus* appears to have collapsed. Both cases involved situations where it was impossible to prove the existence of the informal agreement without relying on the subsequent actings. The first of these cases is *Colquhoun* v. *Wilson's Trs.*[34]:

> Wilson offered to buy certain premises from Sir James Colquhoun. Colquhoun accepted this offer subject to certain conditions. Both offer and acceptance were in informal writing. No further written communications passed between the parties on the matter. But Wilson made extensive alterations to the premises. After Wilson's death, Colquhoun sued Wilson's representatives to have the transaction declared a binding contract. It was held that a valid contract had arisen.

A considerable difficulty faced the court. As the offer had been met by a qualified acceptance, the writings did not disclose a completed contract. Nor was it possible to prove by parole evidence that the parties were truly in agreement, for proof was restricted to writ or oath. It was, however, competent to prove parole the actings which constituted *rei interventus*. As these actings were only explicable on the footing that agreement had been reached between the parties, it was held that Wilson's alterations and other acts not only cured the informality but also purified the conditional agreement. As Lord President Inglis put it: "the contract, which was originally conditional and incomplete became unconditional and complete."

In a later case, Lord Macmillan doubted the soundness of the decision in *Colquhoun*.[35] However, despite his reservations, the case was followed in *Errol* v. *Walker*[36]:

> Walker made a probative offer for the purchase of part of Errol's property. Although he never received a formal acceptance, Walker was put in possession of the property, paid instalments on the price and made extensive improvements, all of which Errol knew. It was held that the actings both proved acceptance and cured the informality of the agreement.

The effect of these two decisions is to dilute substantially the requirements of *obligationes literis*. Personal bar was originally

---

[34] (1860) 22 D. 1035.
[35] *Mitchell (supra)*.
[36] 1966 S.C. 93.

introduced to cure the informality of an agreement in circumstances where it appeared fair to hold it binding. Indeed in the early nineteenth century it was viewed with such disfavour that a judge referred to *rei interventus* as an "unwarrantable evasion of a statute."[37]

The effect of *Errol* following on *Colquhoun* is to allow subsequent actings both to set up an agreement and to make it binding where otherwise formal writing would be required. This suggests that as long as the party seeking to set up the contract can point to some actings, it is open to the court to infer the existence of the obligation. If this were true, the category of *obligationes literis* would be a quaint anachronism. In effect, the exception would swallow up the rule. Instead of holding fast to the requirement of formal writing, a wide interpretation of personal bar means that parties do not need to bother whether or not such formal writing is obtained. Their actings will cure the formal defects. In addition, the interpretation of the rule in this way is almost worse than no rule at all. Consider a tenant farmer who offers to purchase the farm from his landlord. No acceptance is given but nevertheless the tenant subsequently makes alterations. One or other of the parties may later claim that there is a binding contract for the sale of the farm. As a result of the decisions in *Colquhoun* and *Errol*, the court could hold that there was a contract even although one of the parties, with good reason, did not think that any contract had been concluded.

The question of whether homologation can be extended in the same way has been canvassed but not finally determined. Lord Maxwell has suggested that the actings in question would have to impinge upon the other party before agreement could be held to have occurred.[38] Merely obtaining the keys to a hotel on the strength of an uncompleted agreement did not mean that the purchaser had homologated.

At a theoretical level there is a difference between *obligationes literis* and obligations provable only by writ or oath. The former is concerned with the constitution (or creation) of the contract, the latter solely with the mode of proof. But the practical consequences can often be the same: without the requisite document the obligation cannot be enforced. It has accordingly been said of the distinction that "to the layman the whole is a legal chimera."[39] A particular paradox is that as the doctrine of personal bar only

---

[37] *Johnston* v. *Grant* (1844) 6 D. 875 *per* Lord Justice-Clerk Hope at p. 888.
[38] *Law* v. *Thomson*, 1978 S.C. 343.
[39] Gow, 1961 J.R. 3.

applies to *obligationes literis*, such obligations may be easier to prove than an obligation provable by writ or oath.

Writings in Re Mercatoria

In order not to hamper commerce by unnecessary formalities, mercantile documents are supposedly relieved from the requirements of *obligationes literis*. The privilege of writings *in re mercatoria* is said to cover "all the varieties of engagements, of mandates, of acknowledgments which the infinite occasions of trade may require."[40] But as the dispensation does not apply to contracts relating to heritage or service, it does not have much importance. The writ *in re mercatoria* thus remains "one of the mysteries of Scots law."[41] Its main importance lies in the law of evidence, where a writ *in re mercatoria* operates as a liquid document of debt. The creditor in such a situation does not need to lead any other evidence to prove the matter.

Statutory Provisions Requiring Writing

There are many pieces of legislation stipulating that particular transactions are to be in writing. For example, the Consumer Credit Act 1974 requires all hire purchase agreements to be legible, to embody all the terms of the agreement, including those prescribed by the Act, and to be signed by both hirer and creditor. Other contracts which require to be in writing include marine insurance contracts and agreements between employers and employees for making certain deductions from wages. One provision which has caused particular difficulty is s.6 of the Mercantile Law Amendment (Scotland) Act 1856. It states that all guarantees and other cautionary obligations should be in writing and signed by the person undertaking the obligation. It has never been authoritatively decided whether such documents need to be probative or holograph. In one case it was accepted by the defender that formal writing was required and the court therefore did not pronounce upon the point.[42] Despite the concession the better view would seem to be that informal writing is all that is required.

---

[40] Bell, *Comm.*, 1. 342.
[41] Scottish Law Commission, Memorandum No. 66 at p. 20.
[42] *B.O.C.M. Silcock* v. *Hunter*, 1976 S.L.T. 217.

PROPOSALS FOR REFORM

The present state of the Scots law of formalities has received much criticism. First, the charge of injustice may be levelled against it. Let us take one example. In *Thiem's Trs.* v. *Collie* an I.O.U. was found amongst a deceased person's papers.[43] It was several years old. The person who had granted the I.O.U. stated that he paid it off by instalments and that the deceased had promised to destroy it. Nevertheless he was held bound to pay the debt, even though the judge who heard the evidence believed that the debt had been paid. Because of the rule that proof was restricted to writ or oath, there could be no finding in favour of the debtor. Secondly it has been stated that:

> "the law which requires writing for the constitution or proof of certain obligations is so uncertain and unsatisfactory that it is almost impossible to state a principle which is of general application."[44]

In other words it is so haphazard that it does not appear clear or rational. The Scottish Law Commission has recently made a detailed study of this area of law. They began by canvassing a number of possibilities, including a requirement that all transactions above a certain value should be in writing. They then consulted widely before coming to a final view on the matter. The Commission has now proposed a comprehensive scheme of reform, which is contained in the draft Bill entitled *Requirements of Writing (Scotland) Bill*, which is annexed to their final report.[45] The main features of the draft Bill are as follows:

1. Proof by writ or oath and the rules relating to *obligationes literis* are abolished. Holograph writings will cease to have any special status.
2. The contractual obligations which require writing are (a) those relating to an interest in land, and (b) gratuitous obligations. (Writing is also required for conveyances, wills and trust obligations.)
3. Otherwise contractual obligations can be constituted and proved in any fashion.
4. Where writing is required but that requirement has not been complied with, the obligation will still be binding if reliance has

---

[43] (1899) 1 F. 764; 7 S.L.T. 4.

[44] Walkers, *Evidence* (Edinburgh, 1964), p. 84.

[45] Scottish Law Commission, *Report on Requirements of Writing* (1988 Scot. Law Com. No. 112).

taken place (i) with the knowledge and acquiescence of the
other party, and (ii) prejudice would otherwise result.
5. For validity, all that is required is simple signature. With regard
to companies, the document can be signed by a director of the
company or by the company secretary.
6. If a document is witnessed by one witness, then depending on
the terms of the document, certain presumptions will arise in
relation to the signature and the date and place of signature.

At present the Scottish Law Commission's proposals await
Parliamentary time being made available for their implementation.
A simplification of the present law, along the lines the Commission
suggest, would be a most welcome improvement to our law.

CHAPTER 5

GROUNDS OF INVALIDITY

EVEN where a contract complies with the rules relating to formation and to formalities, one party may still seek to have it declared invalid. In order to challenge the contract successfully, that party must show that there is some fundamental infirmity or defect in its constitution. There are several grounds on which such a challenge can be made. A person may allege that he was coerced or deceived into making the contract, or that the other party took unfair advantage of him, or that he was mistaken as to some central feature of the contract. All the grounds of challenge have one thing in common—an allegation that one party did not truly consent to the contract. If the challenge is successful, the contract is invalid and neither party is bound.

THE GROUNDS OF CHALLENGE

Force and Fear

The clearest case of invalidity is where some form of coercion or unfair pressure is applied to secure consent to the contract. A person who is threatened with a gun to make him sign a contract cannot be regarded as acting freely. Were the law to hold such bargains binding, this would legitimise terrorism and extortion. In Scotland this ground of challenge is known as force and fear (*vis ac metus*). It is the subversion of consent by fear, rather than the force, which is important:

> "Although . . . we couple together force and fear as one ground of reduction, the act of force is truly . . . only one means of inducing fear, the true ground of reduction being extortion, through the influence of fear, induced in the various ways . . ."[1]

---

[1] *Priestnell* v. *Hutcheson* (1857) 19 D. 495 *per* Lord Deas at p. 499.

An early and colourful example of force and fear is provided by the case of *Earl of Orkney* v. *Vinfra*.[2]

> The Earl sued Vinfra for payment of 1,000 merks which he said were owed to him under a deed which Vinfra had signed. Vinfra claimed that he had initially refused to sign but then "the said Earl was so offended that with terrible countenance and words and laying his hand upon his whinger [short sword], he threatened with execrable oaths to bereave this Vinfra of his life and stick him presently through the head with his whinger, if he subscribed not."
>
> The Earl maintained that he had only used boisterous words. The court preferred Vinfra's account of events and held the contract invalid.

Sometimes lawyers speak in this connexion of the "overborne will." But we should be clear that the person threatened has a choice—he chooses the lesser of two evils. He consents to sign the document to avoid the threat being carried out. Indeed, the greater the threat, the more likely it is that the person will do the act in question. It is not therefore strictly correct to say that one person's will is actually overborne. That is simply a convenient way of expressing what happens. More accurately, the person threatened is influenced or pressurised in such a way as to choose one course of action instead of the course he would have adopted had he not been subject to such pressure. So it is the illegitimacy of the threats which is the crucial factor. Some forms of pressure will not ground an action for force and fear. It is legitimate, for example, for one party to tell the other that he will resort to litigation in order to induce consent. A creditor can tell his debtor that he will raise an action for payment unless the debtor agrees to pay off the debt. This is a proper course of action for "If the only threat is a threat to do a lawful act then the plea of force and fear must fail."[3] In *Hunter* v. *Bradford Property Trust Ltd*[4]:

> Two sisters were in financial difficulties. They signed an agreement with a property company. The terms of the agreement were that the sisters would be paid certain sums of money when properties belonging to them were sold by the company.

---

[2] (1606) Mor. 16481.
[3] *Hunter* v. *Bradford Property Trust*, 1977 S.L.T. (Notes) 33 *per* Lord Migdale at p. 34.
[4] 1977 S.L.T. (Notes) 33.

On the night before the sale was due to take place, one of the company's directors found that the written contract did not accurately record the agreement that he thought had been reached. He told the sisters that unless they signed a second contract, he would cancel the sale. After discussion long into the night, the sisters signed. They sought to reduce this second contract on the ground that it had been signed through force and fear. They claimed that they were anxious about their financial position should the sale not go ahead the following day. It was decided that the sisters had not made out a case of force and fear. The threat to cancel the sale could not be regarded as illegitimate.

The threats employed to induce the contract must not have resulted in "vain or foolish fear."[5] Rather, they must have been such as would have overcome the fortitude of a person of reasonable constancy. In the case of a woman or child, however, the degree of pressure or force required to maintain a successful plea may be less. Where a weapon is used, or actual violence is threatened, then the issue is clear-cut. Usually, however, some more insidious pressure is brought to bear. Then it is a question of evidence as to whether or not the plea of force and fear is made out.

The plea of force and fear is relatively rare in modern times. If one considers the various types of extortion that a person might wish to deploy to secure a contract, this is perhaps not surprising. At one end of the extortion scale is robbery, at the other blackmail. Robbers are unlikely to tarry to ask for apparent consent from their victims, while persons who are blackmailed are often unwilling to reveal what has happened in case confidential material comes to light. Most of the reported cases involve some form of pressure midway between these two extremes and the real question is—was consent subverted or not? A good illustration is provided by *Hislop v. Dickson Motors (Forres) Ltd.*[6]

The cashier of a garage in Forres was confronted by her employer. He shouted at her and accused her of embezzling sums from the garage accounts. She admitted the allegation and agreed to try and repay the sums. The next morning the employer arrived at her home with another director of the company. She handed over her car registration documents and keys together with a blank deposit-account withdrawal form

---

[5] Stair, *Institutions*, I.x.14.
[6] 1978 S.L.T. (Notes) 73.

which she signed. The directors drove her car away and withdrew all the money from her deposit account (£385). At the bank they found out that the cashier also had a current account. They returned to her house and after further argument obtained a signed blank cheque from her which they used to withdraw the total credit balance (£195) from her current account. Subsequently the cashier was prosecuted in respect of the sums which had disappeared from the garage accounts. A not proven verdict was returned. She raised an action for reduction of the two transactions with her employer on the ground of force and fear. It was held that the transaction involving the car and deposit account was valid, but that the transaction involving the current account was invalid through force and fear.

It is not easy to draw a clear distinction between the two transactions. On both occasions the pursuer was prepared to trade off her assets against the threat of a criminal prosecution. Although her optimism on that point proved unfounded, that was not a relevant factor in the decision reached. The line drawn by Lord Maxwell was to say that in giving over the documents relating to the car and the deposit account the cashier was acting voluntarily: she was handing them over in return for not being prosecuted. On the second occasion, however, she was not acting voluntarily. Instead, she was coerced by her two employers into handing over the blank cheque in respect of an account about which she thought they knew nothing. By disclosing certain of her assets she was indicating the extent to which she was prepared to go to avoid prosecution. But when she was confronted by the two men returning with information which she had not volunteered, no true consent on her part was discernible. Accordingly the second arrangement was struck down. This is probably the correct analysis of a fact situation where, superficially at least, it is difficult to measure the consent given and the degree to which it was undermined.

Some English cases have given colour to the notion that there can be economic duress, as opposed to physical duress or pressure to the person. Thus, where a creditor accepted a lesser sum from the debtor than that due, solely because he himself was in difficult financial circumstances and the debtor took advantage of his position, the bargain was declared invalid.[7] The threat by the debtor not to pay at all unless the lesser sum was accepted amounted to

---

[7] *D. & C. Builders Ltd.* v. *Rees* [1966] 2 Q.B. 617.

unfair pressure. It followed that the balance of the debt was recoverable. Similarly, where shipowners only agreed to a contract when faced by the threat of industrial action, the contract was reducible on the ground of economic duress.[8] As yet there has been no discussion of such types of pressure in Scots law but there would not appear, in principle, to be any objection to such a development here. The essence of force and fear is that agreement is extorted from one party by the other's use of illegitimate pressure. Today that pressure can be as effective economically as physical violence was of old.

Facility and Circumvention

A contract is reducible for facility and circumvention when, for example, a weak-minded [facile] party has been imposed upon unfairly and misleadingly [circumvented]. Facility and circumvention involves one party taking unfair advantage of another who, for some reason, is in a vulnerable state.

> *Example*: Motorist X is in a state of shock after a car accident: Y takes advantage of X's condition to purchase X's car from him at 25% of its market value.

Three elements must be present before such a challenge will be successful. The person attempting to set aside the contract must prove
(a) weakness and facility (if the person is insane rather than merely weak-minded then he is incapable of giving consent),
(b) circumvention, and
(c) loss (lesion).
The greater the facility and loss, the less circumvention required. In each case it is a question of degree. The court will examine whether the person seeking to be released from the obligation was easily influenced or preyed upon because of his or her vulnerable mental state at the time. A person who is ill and in hospital is not on that account alone "of facile disposition"[9] but a recently bereaved widow may be in such a condition.[10]

---

[8] *Universe Tankships of Monrovia* v. *International Transport Workers' Federation* [1983] 1 A.C. 366; see also *Dimskal Shipping Co. S.A.* v. *International Transport Workers' Federation* [1992] 2 A.C. 152.

[9] *Mackay* v. *Campbell*, 1967 S.C. (H.L.) 53; S.L.T. 337.

[10] *MacGilvary* v. *Gilmartin*, 1986 S.L.T. 89.

Undue Influence

A contract obtained in consequence of the exercise of undue influence by a person in a position of authority or trust is reducible. The law recognizes that where parties are not at arm's length, any transactions between the parties must be closely scrutinised to make sure that one party does not abuse his position. As Lord President Inglis put it in the leading case of *Gray* v. *Binny*[11]:

> "If . . . the relation of the parties is such as to beget mutual trust and confidence, each owes to the other a duty which has no place between strangers . . . the party trusted and confided in is bound, by the most obvious principles of fair dealing and honesty, not to abuse the power thus put in his hands."

There, a 24 year old man, on the advice of his mother and the family solicitor, sold his inheritance rights for an inadequate amount. It was decided that if he could show that he had only entered the contract because of the advice he had received, it could be set aside.

At one time it was thought that the classes of relationship which could ground an action of undue influence were closed. It is now accepted that it is always a question of fact whether such a relationship is present and it can exist as much between client and art-dealer as between doctor and patient, or parent and child.[12] The issue is whether one person actually did repose trust and confidence in another; and whether that confidence was abused.

Extortion and Inequality of Bargaining Power

So far we have been considering grounds of challenge where it is alleged that something improper has occurred in the course of the bargaining process, such that one party's consent has not truly been given. However, it may be that without being able to point to anything specific at the time of negotiating, one party claims that the contract should not be enforced because its terms are grossly unfair. In common parlance, someone has made a "bad bargain" and seeks relief. This can occur where there is a gross disproportion between the relative bargaining strengths of the parties. Take, for example, a contract between a small business and a large multi-national company. Because of the company's superior bargaining

---

[11] (1879) 7 R. 332 at p. 343.
[12] *Honeyman's Exrs.* v. *Sharp*, 1978 S.C. 223.

strength, it can ensue that the terms of the completed contract are entirely in its favour.

There is some early authority in Scots law to the effect that such bargains may be reducible. "All bargains which from their very appearance discover oppression, as an intention in any of the contractors to catch some undue advantage from his neighbour's necessities, lie open to reduction on the head of dole or extortion, without the necessity of proving any special circumstances of fraud or circumvention on the part of that contractor."[13] But the general principle is that such contracts must stand. It is not for the court to determine whether or not a person has made a good or bad bargain. A flood of claims would occur, it is argued, if the courts had power to set aside a bargain on the ground of "fairness" alone. In certain areas provisions have, however, been enacted. For example, there are regulations relating to licences and levels of interest to cover those involved in money-lending and consumer credit agreements.[14] An extortionate credit bargain can be re-opened by the court.[15] There is a "cooling-off" period for those entering consumer credit agreements, time-share agreements and life assurance transactions off trade premises.[16] This gives individuals an opportunity to pause and reflect before committing themselves to such major financial relationships. Otherwise, reduction can probably only be granted where a contract is so inequitable in its terms as to raise an overwhelming presumption that it has been involuntarily granted.

Other countries have been less reluctant to enact a general principle into their law. In the United States, for example, both the Uniform Commercial Code and the Restatement of Contracts (Second) have provisions relating to unconscionability.[17] A contract deemed to be unconscionable can be set aside. No such general ground of challenge exists in Scotland and the courts have been unwilling to intervene directly to decide whether a bargain is or is not unfair. To do so, it is argued, would be to usurp the function of the parties in making their own contract.

A move toward a general principle of inequality of bargaining power was at one stage discernible in English law. Two cases, heard

---

[13] Erskine *Institutes*, IV.i.27.

[14] Consumer Credit Act 1974, Pts III & IX.

[15] Consumer Credit Act 1974, ss. 137–140.

[16] Consumer Credit Act 1974 ss. 67–73; Timeshare Act 1992; Insurance Companies Act 1982, s. 76.

[17] Uniform Commercial Code S.2–302; Restatement of the Law, Second, Contracts 2d, S.208.

within days of each other in July 1974, suggested the development of such a principle. In *A. Schroeder Music Publishing Co. Ltd.* v. *Macaulay*[18]:

> A contract was entered into between a young songwriter and a music publishing company. In terms of the contract, the company were to have the exclusive right to publish the songwriter's compositions for a five-year period. There was an automatic right of renewal for a further five years if his royalties reached a certain amount. The company also had the right to terminate the contract at any time. Conversely, there was no duty upon them to publish any songs which might be submitted by the songwriter and he had no right to terminate the contract. When the songwriter became successful he sought to be released from the contract.

His claim was upheld by the House of Lords on the ground that it was a contract in restraint of trade because it sterilised his earning capacity for an excessive period. Remarks, however, were made *obiter* in several of the speeches, notably that of Lord Diplock, who thought that one-sided contracts of this nature should be closely scrutinised by the courts.

The second case, *Lloyds Bank* v. *Bundy*, concerned a guarantee given by an elderly farmer in respect of his son's overdraft.[19] When the son failed to repay the loans, the bank sought to realise their security. The Lloyds Bank representative who obtained the farmer's signature was alleged not to have fully explained the consequences of the contract to him. In particular, it was claimed that he had not stressed to the farmer that he stood to lose the roof over his head if the guarantee and second mortgage over his home was called up. All three judges in the Court of Appeal held that the contract could be avoided on the ground of undue influence. Because Lloyds were his bankers, as well as his son's, he was entitled to expect them to give him independent advice, which they had failed to do. Lord Denning M.R. was prepared to go further. He proposed that several of the grounds of challenge should be regrouped under a new heading: inequality of bargaining power. His formula for the test was compendious. It applied to a person

> "who, without independent advice, enters into a contract upon terms which are very unfair . . . when his bargaining power is

---

[18] [1974] 1 W.L.R. 1308.
[19] [1975] Q.B. 326.

grievously impaired by reason of his own needs or desires, or by his own ignorance and infirmity, coupled with undue influences or pressures brought to bear on him by or for the benefit of the other.''

That should be the new test, he suggested, by which the validity of contracts should be judged. Lord Denning's view has been followed in at least one other jurisdiction, Australia.[20] But as such a diffuse concept would potentially allow the courts to intervene in a great many contracts, it is unlikely to be developed. This is particularly true given, as we have seen, that in certain instances legislation provides a degree of protection to potential victims of sharp practices. Lord Scarman has spoken out against adopting a general ground of challenge along the lines suggested by Lord Denning.[21] His view was that any such principle would further restrict freedom of contract and that it was for Parliament, not the courts, to legislate in this area if that were thought desirable.

ERROR

Introduction

If one or both parties to a contract enter into it under some misapprehension, can the contract be declared invalid? Suppose, for example, that a person buys a car by post and only discovers when it arrives that it is left-hand drive. Or imagine a person booking for a performance of *Carmen* only to discover after paying the price that it is a filmed rather than a live performance. In both cases the purchaser has made a mistake. Can the contract be set aside on the basis that it would never have been made if the true situation had been known? This is the key question to be discussed under the heading of error, which is one of the most controversial topics in contract law. The nub of the problem is the conflict between two different theoretical approaches to contract law. A subjective approach suggests that where error is present there can be no true consent and therefore no contract. In our examples this would mean the contracts would be set aside. The purchasers never intended to make the bargains with which they are now landed. The objective approach, on the other hand, takes the view that parties are bound by what they say, not what they think. So the purchaser in our examples would be bound by the respective contracts they

---

[20] see *Commercial Bank of Australia* v. *Amadio*, (1983) 57 A.L.J.R. 358.
[21] *National Westminster Bank plc* v. *Morgan* [1985] 1 All E.R. 821 at p. 830.

had entered into. This conflict can be seen as far back as Stair. In an early passage in the *Institutions* he seems to take a broad subjective approach: "These who err in the substantials of what is done, contract not."[22] But later on he narrows the compass of this passage considerably: "But the exception upon error is seldom relevant, because it depends upon the knowledge of the person erring, which he can hardly prove."[23]

Stair's view seems to have been that while difficult to prove, error in the substantials would render a contract void. It remained to lay down with precision what constituted error in the substantials (or essential error). Bell's formulation has been expressly adopted by Lord Watson and is generally regarded as the *locus classicus*[24]:

> "I concur . . . as to the accuracy of the general doctrine laid down by Professor Bell [*Prin.*, s.11] to the effect that error in substantials such as will invalidate consent given to a contract or obligation must be in relation to either (1) its subject-matter; (2) the persons undertaking or to whom it is undertaken; (3) the price or consideration; (4) the quality of the thing engaged for; if expressly or tacitly essential; or (5) the nature of the contract or engagement supposed to be entered into. I believe that these five categories will be found to embrace all the forms of essential error which, either *per se* or when induced by the other party to the contract, give the person labouring under such error a right to rescind it."

Classifying Error

We can illustrate the five categories of essential error as follows:

1. Subject-matter	–	A thinks he is buying wheat from B, B thinks he is selling barley to A
2. Identity	–	A thinks he is contracting with B, whereas he is contracting with C
3. Price	–	A thinks the price is £1,000, B thinks it is $1,000
4. Quality	–	A thinks he is buying a stallion, when in fact the beast is a gelding
5. Nature of the Contract	–	A thinks he is signing a lease, whereas in fact the document is a guarantee

[22] I.x.13.
[23] IV.xxxx.24.
[24] *Stewart* v. *Kennedy* (1890) 17 R. (H.L.) 25 at p. 28.

If the error is not essential, the contract stands. For example, A's belief that he will make a profit from his contract affords no ground of relief should he prove mistaken. His error is one of motive not intention, so it does not affect the contract.

While Bell explained the factors that are required to make an error "essential" and therefore legally relevant, he did not distinguish between the situation where only one party is in error and the situation where both parties are in error. A further classification is therefore required.

(a) *Unilateral error* As its name indicates, in unilateral error only one party is mistaken as to some feature of the contract.
> *Example*: X believes the painting he is buying is an original by Ernst. The seller Y knows it is a copy.

(b) *Common error* Here, both parties make the same mistake. They share an assumption about the state of affairs upon which the contract is based, which turns out to be erroneous.
> *Example*: In a contract for the sale of a painting, both parties think the painting is in existence, whereas it was destroyed the day before the contract was made.

(c) *Mutual error* Where the error is mutual, the parties misapprehend each other's intention. This results in the parties being at cross purposes.
> *Example*: X believes that he is selling the 1628 "Madonna and Child", Y that he is buying the 1630 version, which X also owns.

Mutual error results in the parties not achieving *consensus* (or agreement), but rather *dissensus* (misunderstanding). Normally the cases concern situations where there is potential ambiguity. The most famous case concerned the sale of a cargo of grain which was to be transported on a ship called the *"Peerless"* from Bombay to England.[25] Unknown to the parties at the time they made the contract, there were two ships of that name, one sailing in October, the other in December. The buyer thought that he was contracting in respect of the October *"Peerless"*. The seller meant the December *"Peerless"*. It was held that there was no contract. At no stage were the parties at one regarding the contract both had thought they had entered into. An equivalent Scottish case is *Stuart*

---

[25] *Raffles* v. *Wichelhaus* (1864) 2 H. & C. 906.

& *Co.* v. *Kennedy.*[26] There, a quantity of stone-coping was sold at
so much per foot. One party thought that the measure was the
lineal foot, the other that it was the superficial foot. It was held that
there was no contract. Nevertheless, the purchaser was bound to
pay the market price for the quantity of stone-coping which had
actually been delivered. The payment was held to be due on the
basis of the principle of unjust enrichment, rather than being due
under the purported contract between the parties.

Unilateral Error

A unilateral error is usually treated as irrelevant. In one case,
parties were negotiating an out of court settlement. A number of
communications took place between the parties' solicitors. One
issue which required to be resolved was the date from which
interest was to run on the sum due to be paid. For most of the
negotiations, this date remained constant. Finally, one party's
solicitor accepted an offer to settle the action, omitting to notice
that the date on which interest was to run had been altered.[27] The
solicitor was not able to plead his own mistake to avoid the
transaction. He ought to have read the offer more carefully, as it
clearly stated the new date from which interest was to run. Similarly, a commercial party erroneously believes that a property
being sold by it is subject to a lease of 990 years, rather than 99
years, he will not be relieved of that mistake if it is not engendered
by the other party.[28] Even a lay person is expected to understand
that a document signed by him gives rise to obligations. In *The
Royal Bank of Scotland* v. *Purvis*[29]:

> A wife signed a guarantee to the bank in respect of a loan to a
> company of which she and her husband were directors. Sub-
> sequently, the bank sued both the husband and wife under the
> guarantee for payment of a sum of £21,635.17. The wife
> defended on the basis that she was in essential error at the time
> that she signed the document. She pointed to the following
> factors: (a) she signed at the request of her husband, (b) she
> had not read the document nor had it explained to her, (c) she
> was not formally educated and was unfamiliar with commer-
> cial documents, and (d) she did not realise that the document
> was a guarantee and would not have signed it if she had.

---

[26] (1885) 13 R. 221.
[27] *Steel* v. *Bradley Homes (Scotland) Ltd.*, 1974 S.L.T. 133.
[28] *Spook Erection (Northern) Ltd.* v. *Kaye*, 1990 S.L.T. 676.
[29] 1990 S.L.T. 262.

Lord McCluskey repelled this defence and stated:

> "The whole point of committing such obligations to writing is
> to avoid any inquiry into antecedent states of mind unless the
> whole picture is one of a signature induced by misrepresenta-
> tion. I find it virtually impossible to envisage a situation in real
> life in which a person could repudiate a document signed by
> him when he was innocently, unilaterally and not negligently
> in ignorance of the character of the document which he was
> signing at the time. I think one would need to wait and see
> what circumstances were averred that could give rise to such a
> special exception to a rule upon which so much commerce
> depends.[30]

Unilateral error may, however, be relevant where the other party
knew of the error and took unfair advantage of the situation. A
person is not allowed unfairly to "snatch at a bargain". This is the
ratio of *Steuart's Trs.* v. *Hart*, where a seller sold some land
believing it to be burdened with a feu-duty (annual land charge) of
£9 15s.[31] The purchaser knew that the feu-duty was only three
shillings and also knew of the seller's mistake. The seller was held
entitled to reduce the contract since the mistake was essential and
his error had been taken advantage of by the purchaser. This
decision has attracted considerable controversy. Those comment-
ators in favour of the decision point to its equity in the circumstances which had occurred. It emphasises the good faith of the
bargaining process. Those against the decision note the untoward
consequences that a wide application of this principle would bring.
A person who picked up a book or an antique "for a song" might
find that the seller would seek to have the sale set aside on the basis
of his own error.[32]

The ratio in *Steuart's Trs.* v. *Hart* has been considered in the
recent Outer House case of *Angus* v. *Bryden*.[33]

> Annbank Angling Club were the tenants of certain river
> fishings in the River Ayr. The river fishings were owned by
> Angus, who also owned sea fishings at the mouth of the river.
> In 1986, the club offered Angus £30,000 to purchase the

---

[30] *Ibid.* at p.266; see also *McCallum* v. *Soudan*, 1989 S.L.T. 522 *per* Lord Morison
at p. 523.
[31] (1875) 3 R. 192.
[32] see Gloag, p. 438.
[33] 1992 S.L.T. 884.

fishings. This was accepted and subsequently a disposition was granted transferring the whole fishings. Angus claimed that on a true construction, all that was agreed to be transferred was the river fishings and the disposition had proceeded upon a mistake. As an alternative argument, he contended that if the sea fishings had been disponed, this was an error on his part known to and taken advantage of by the club. Lord Cameron of Lochbroom disposed of the action by upholding Angus' position on the principal argument. However, he went on to consider the alternative argument and stated " . . . I consider that *Steuart's Trs.* v. *Hart* is still good law and is therefore binding upon me."[34]

While unilateral error has little relevance to onerous contracts, it may be sufficient to reduce a gratuitous transaction. It is not difficult to see the logic of this distinction. As the obligee in a gratuitous transaction is receiving something for nothing, it is thought equitable to allow the obligor to be relieved of his obligations if he has made a mistake. Suppose that B makes a written promise to give £500 to X, believing X to be his long lost cousin. If B subsequently discovers that X is not related to him, he should be discharged from his obligation. In the case of *Hunter* v. *Bradford Trust Ltd.*, which was discussed above with regard to force and fear, the sisters successfully set aside the contract in a second action where they pled that it had been entered gratuitously under essential error.[35]

Mutual Error

In the case of mutual error, a finding that the parties have not truly reached agreement will result in the contract being set aside. There are relatively few cases of this type and two factors account for this. First the court will normally prefer one party's version of the contract to that of the other. For example, they will declare that it is a contract of credit sale rather than hire-purchase.[36] Secondly, where it does find that there is no *consensus*, a court is more likely to classify the situation as falling under the heading of offer and acceptance than of mutual error. An example is provided by *Mathieson Gee* v. *Quigley*, where the parties' mistaken view that they had achieved agreement was held to have arisen because the

---

[34] *Ibid.* p. 887.
[35] 1970 S.L.T. 173.
[36] *Muirhead & Turnbull* v. *Dickson* (1905) 7F. 686; (1905) 13 S.L.T. 151.

offer did not meet the acceptance.[37] Accordingly, the only situation where mutual error is likely to operate occurs when there is a latent ambiguity in the contract. The two cases cited above regarding *The Peerless* and the lineal/superficial foot are examples.

Common Error

So far as common error is concerned, a similar phenomenon exists. In principle, common error as to some essential feature renders a contract invalid, but in practice few such cases arise. This is mainly because rules exist as to the allocation of risk. Where a house is sold, risk passes on completion of the missives. This means that if both parties believe that the house is in existence at the time the contract is made, whereas in reality it has been destroyed by fire, the risk is with the seller. But once the missives are completed, any damage to the house which occurs subsequently is the risk of the buyer.

Alternative Analysis

It can be argued that there has been no case of error proper in the twentieth century. No case, that is, where an onerous contract has been set aside on the basis of uninduced error in intention. Instead, the law uses various other principles in resolving error-type situations. As well as the two already mentioned—of offer and acceptance and passing of risk—there are two other important techniques: implied terms and personal bar. The use of implied terms converts a problem of error into a breach of contract question:

> *Example*: A person buys a pair of shoes which fall apart after two weeks' light wear. Clearly it would be possible to say that the person seeks redress because he bought the shoes under mistake—he thought they would be hard-wearing. However, such cases are invariably treated as a question of breach of the implied term of merchantable quality under the Sale of Goods Act 1979.

The second technique is personal bar. Where performance follows on from an agreement alleged to be defective, the subsequent actions of the parties may prove decisive in determining whether the parties are bound or not. In *Morrison-Low* v. *Paterson*, both parties believed that the defenders had inherited the tenancy of an

---

[37] 1952 S.C. (H.L.) 38.

agricultural lease.[38] This belief arose because the solicitor, who had acted for both parties, told them that this was the position. The House of Lords accepted that the tenancy had not been validly transferred under the relevant statutory provisions. Both parties were therefore mistaken as to their legal position. Nevertheless the subsequent actions of the parties, which involved *inter alia* the defenders remaining in occupation and paying rent for six years, were only explicable on the footing that a new agreement had been entered into. Accordingly, the House of Lords held that despite the error there was a contract of lease and the landlord's action of removing must fail. He was personally barred from founding on the error.

Historically, however, the most significant change in this area of law, the one which has substantially eclipsed the role of error, has been the development of the law relating to misrepresentation. Misrepresentation means induced error. In Scots law, the shift from uninduced to induced error can be traced to two House of Lords' decisions in the late nineteenth century. In *Stewart* v. *Kennedy*,[39]

> A contract for the sale of an entailed estate was made "subject to the ratification of the court." The seller, Sir Archibald Stewart, mistakenly thought that the phrase meant that the court would determine if the price was fair and reasonable. In fact, it was a simple statutory requirement which had to be followed in the case of entailed estates. He sought to reduce the missives of sale, claiming amongst other things that he had entered the contract under essential error. In the Court of Session it was held that there was no essential error, as the person, the price and the subject-matter of the contract were clearly established. The House of Lords took an entirely different line. First, it decided that the error was an essential error. Secondly, the House of Lords decided that although there had been essential error, that of itself was not enough to set aside the contract. But, it decided, the essential error would be relevant if it were induced.

This marked the beginning of a sea-change in the law. The House of Lords decided that essential error was present but then said it was not operative in the circumstances. Error, they said, would only be effective if shown to have been induced. Accordingly, the focal point was the cause of the error rather than the error itself. To

---

[38] 1985 S.L.T. 255.
[39] (1890) 17 R. (H.L.) 25.

demonstrate this, let us return to our two initial examples. Whether the person who bought the left-hand drive car, or the tickets to the film version of *Carmen*, can set aside the contract will depend on the circumstances in which his belief was formed. If his mistake was attributable to the other party then there is misrepresentation and the contract can be challenged. But if the mistake arose simply through his own uninduced error he would be unlikely to be able to set aside the contract.

The confirmation of this view is to be found in the second of the two House of Lords' cases, *Menzies* v. *Menzies*.[40] Lord Watson stated that:

> "Error becomes essential whenever it is shown that but for it one of the parties would have declined to contract. He cannot rescind unless his error was induced by the representations of the other contracting party, or of his agent, made in the course of negotiation, and with reference to the subject matter of the contract. If his error is proved to have been so induced, the fact that the misleading representations were made in good faith affords no defence . . . "[41]

Two propositions can be drawn from this statement: (a) misrepresentation, rather than error, is the true ground of challenge; and (b) the standard required is no longer that of Bell's five categories, rather the issue is whether or not the party would have declined to contract.

Conclusion on Error

Although, as we have seen, the law on uninduced error is fairly well developed, it is of little practical importance today. The courts are reluctant to relieve people of their obligations simply because they allege that they made a mistake on entering into them. Perhaps only in the case of gratuitous obligations is it still important.

MISREPRESENTATION

A person who is induced to enter a contract as a result of a misleading statement has the right to be relieved of his obligations under the contract.

---

[40] (1893) 20 R. (H.L.) 108.
[41] *Ibid.* at pp.142–143.

Examples:
1. X buys Y's car on the faith of an assurance that the car possesses an M.O.T. certificate, Y's statement in this regard turns out to be false. X is entitled to return the car and receive back the purchase price.
2. B arranges for A to instal central heating in his house. B chose A because A told him that he was a registered plumber and that he could arrange finance for B. Both statements are false. B can withdraw from the contract.

To be relevant, a misrepresentation must be material and made in the course of negotiations. A trivial statement, for example, cannot be relied upon. Moreover, the misrepresentation must be an inaccurate statement of fact and not simply an expression of opinion. In one case, the seller stated that a farm would carry so many head of sheep.[42] It was known by both parties that the farm had never been used for sheep before. The statement was held not to amount to a misrepresentation. It was merely a statement of the seller's opinion which a reasonable buyer would not have relied upon. But a deliberately false statement of opinion is a representation of fact. "Trade puffs" (*verba jactantia*) are allowed a degree of latitude. Reasonable people are not expected to place too much reliance on the material to be found in advertisements. No one should really expect a new brand of shampoo to improve their social life. Accordingly, material which might fairly be termed "misleading" does not allow a consumer to set aside the contract, although the Trade Descriptions Act 1968 provides certain criminal sanctions in the event of serious misdescriptions.

Normally there is no duty of disclosure in contract, so silence cannot constitute a misrepresentation. But silence may amount to misrepresentation in a number of situations, of which the most important class is contracts *uberrimae fidei* (of utmost good faith). The most important example of such a contract is that of insurance. Here, there is a duty to disclose all material facts. In *The Spathari*:[43]

A vessel was registered and insured in the name of a British subject. It sank in calm waters and a claim was made under the insurance policy. The insurance company then discovered that the true owner was a Greek subject. The company refused to

---

[42] *Bisset* v. *Wilkinson* [1927] A.C. 177.
[43] 1925 S.C. (H.L.) 6.

pay out on the policy. It was held that the company were entitled to do so. At the time, Greek ships were virtually uninsurable because they had bad risk records. Accordingly, the nationality of the owner was material in this instance. As it had not been disclosed, there had been a misrepresentation which rendered the contract voidable.

Other situations where silence may amount to misrepresentation occur where the parties are in a fiduciary relationship, for example parent and child, trustee and beneficiary, solicitor and client; where there is a half-truth that has not been completed; and where a statement, true when made, is falsified by circumstances. Further, in contracts of sale, if it is impossible for the purchaser to examine a specific object, the seller is bound to reveal all known defects.

The Degree of Misapprehension Produced

At one time it was suggested that for misrepresentation to be relevant, there must be essential error in the sense of Bell's five categories. Although this proposition has never been expressly overruled it probably is no longer the law. It is directly counter to Lord Watson's statement in *Menzies* quoted above. The most accurate statement of the present law is that given by Lord Carmont:

> "It appears clear that Scots law recognises, as indicated by Bell, that when misrepresentation by a party is alleged inducing error in the other in regard to some matter, that matter need not be an essential of the contract, *but it must be material and of such a nature that not only the contracting party but any reasonable man might be moved to enter into the contract*; or put the other way, if the misrepresentation had not been made, would have refrained from entering into the contract."[44]

In other words, the court is directed to look at the reasons why the person was induced to enter the contract. If they are material and pass the "reasonable man" test then the contract can be set aside, even though they do not relate to Bell's five categories.

The remedies open to a person depend upon whether the misrepresentation is fraudulent, negligent or innocent. If the misrepresentation is innocent, the only remedy is to set aside the contract.

---

[44] *Ritchie* v. *Glass*, 1936 S.L.T. 591 at pp. 593–594 (emphasis added).

But if negligence or fraud is present, damages may also be recovered.

Fraudulent misrepresentation

Fraud is a "machination or contrivance to deceive."[45] Since the end of the nineteenth century, a statement has been regarded as fraudulent if (a) the maker of the statement was aware that his representations were untrue, or (b) he made them recklessly, without knowing or caring whether they were true or not. That proposition was established in the case of *Derry* v. *Peek*.[46]

> The directors of the Plymouth Devonport and District Tramways company issued a prospectus which stated that the company had the right to use steam power in its trams. The plaintiff bought shares in the company on the strength of this statement. In fact the company was only entitled to use steam power if it was issued with a certificate by the Board of Trade. The certificate was refused. It was held that the plaintiff could not succeed in his action of damages for fraud. The directors had made the statement in the honest belief that it was true.

This decision changed the law. Until that point, almost any statement which turned out to be untrue and induced a person to enter a contract grounded an action for fraud. In effect the decision in *Derry* raised the standard for civil fraud to that of criminal fraud. Damages became much more difficult to recover. It has been suggested that the judges were swayed in arriving at their decision by the argument that to call a man "fraudulent" was tantamount to expelling him from polite society. As the judges looked at the directors, Victorian gentleman all, it was a telling point.

The actual effect of the decision in relation to directors' liability was overturned by statute. But its general importance as a test of fraud remains undiminished. In the Scottish case of *Boyd & Forrest* v. *Glasgow & S.W. Railway Co.*,[47] which occurred shortly after *Derry*, it was held that contractors who had built a railway line could not recover damages against the railway company in respect of wrong information which the latter had given. This was because the employee who had furnished the information had altered it honestly but mistakenly, so he could not be guilty of fraud.

[45] Erskine, *Institute*, III.i.16.
[46] (1889) 44 App.Cas. 337.
[47] 1912 S.C. (H.L.) 93.

Negligent misrepresentation

A representation is negligent if the person failed to take reasonable care in making the representation and was in the circumstances under a duty to do so. This category has only been developed in the post-war period and originated in a dissenting judgment of Lord Denning M.R.[48] His view was adopted by the House of Lords in *Hedley Byrne* v. *Heller & Partners*, where a bank gave information regarding the credit-worthiness of one of its customers.[49] When it was found that the information was incorrect and the bank had not exercised sufficient care in assessing the situation, it was held they could be liable to the person who had requested the information.

These cases were concerned with non-contractual situations. Originally it was thought that negligent misrepresentation did not apply to contracts, because the parties did not owe one another a "duty of care". Because they are at arm's length, each was thought bound to rely on his own means of information. If he was deceived by misrepresentation, then he could set aside the contract and, if the misrepresentation was fraudulent, he could also claim damages. However, the concept of negligent misrepresentation was extended to pre-contractual negotiations in England in *Esso Petroleum Co.* v. *Mardon*.[50]

An oil company was held liable in respect of statements made to a prospective tenant of a petrol filling station. An employee of the company with many years' experience had misled the tenant regarding the throughput of petrol the station could expect. Normally when parties are negotiating, each must rely on his own means of information. Because they are at arm's length neither owes a duty of care to the other. Although a false statement allows one party to withdraw from the contract it does not ground an action for damages unless there is fraud.

The effect of the decision in Esso was to extend the right to recover damages to a situation where one party had special skill or knowledge and the other party was reasonably entitled to rely on that knowledge, which turned out to be false. The Scottish position regarding negligent misrepresentation was unclear. Some courts felt bound by a nineteenth century decision which decided that unless fraud was established, damages were not recoverable for

---

[48] *Candler* v. *Crane Christmas & Co.* [1951] 2 K.B. 164.
[49] [1964] A.C. 465.
[50] [1976] Q.B. 801.

statements made at the stage of negotiation between the parties. However, statute now provides that damages for negligent misrepresentation are recoverable under Scots law.[51] So if a designer builds a ship which does not have the carrying capacity that he represented, he will be liable in damages. Likewise a seller who informs a buyer that the factory he is selling has been passed by the factory inspectorate and is asbestos-free.[52]

Innocent misrepresentation

Here the representation, although inaccurate, is made with the honest belief that it is true. The only remedy is to reduce the contract. There is no additional right to damages as in the previous two categories.

THE EFFECT OF A SUCCESSFUL CHALLENGE

The traditional view is that a successful challenge renders a contract either void or voidable. A contract which is *void* is a complete nullity. It is treated as if it had never existed at all. There are two important consequences which flow from a contract being declared void. First, there is in theory no need to have a court decree that it is void. It is enough to notify the other party that the contract is no longer regarded as binding. If, however, he disputes that the contract is void the issue will have to be determined by a court. Secondly, no one can acquire rights under a void contract. Accordingly, a third party who has property which has been transferred under a void contract is obliged to restore it to its original owner. The court may however impose an equitable solution on the parties. For example, if goods are delivered under a void contract, the courts may stipulate that the buyer must pay the appropriate market price for the goods.

A contract which is *voidable* is valid and effective until it is set aside. Unlike void contracts, a contract which is voidable can confer rights. Accordingly, third parties who acquire rights before the contract has been set aside are protected. There are certain requirements which must be satisfied before a voidable contract can be set aside:

(a) Restoration to the original position (*restitutio in integrum*) must be possible. In *Boyd & Forrest* this condition could not

---

[51] Law Reform (Miscellaneous Provisions) (Scotland) Act 1985, s.10.
[52] These examples are based upon *Kenway* v. *Orcantic Ltd.*, 1980 S.L.T. 46 and *Foster* v. *Craigmillar Laundry*, 1980 S.L.T. (Sh.Ct.) 100, both of which were decided before the 1985 statutory provision was in place.

be satisfied as the contractors had gone ahead and construed the railway line.[53] It was impossible to restore the parties to their original position.

(b) The contract must not have been affirmed by homologation.

(c) There must have been no unnecessary delay in bringing the action.

(d) The rights of third parties must not be affected.

The crucial difference between void and voidable contracts concern the rights of third parties. The difference is demonstrated by contrasting two well-known cases: *Morrisson* v. *Robertson*[54] and *Macleod* v. *Kerr*.[55]

In *Morrisson*, a man claiming to be the son of Wilson of Bonnyrigg approached Morrisson and offered to buy two cows from him. Although Morrisson did not know the man, he knew of Wilson, who was a neighbouring farmer of good financial standing. Accordingly, he let the man have the two cows on credit. In fact, the man was not the son of Wilson but a rogue called Telford. Telford sold the two cows to Robertson. When Morrisson found this out he sought to recover the cows from Robertson. The action was successful. It was held that there had been no contract between Morrisson and Telford. The purported transaction was a complete nullity. Accordingly, Telford had no rights which he could pass on to Robertson, so Morrisson was entitled to recover his cows.

Macleod v. *Kerr* provides a modern setting for the same problem.

A rogue paid for a Vauxhall Cresta car with a stolen cheque. As soon as the seller discovered that the cheque had been dishonoured, he notified the police. Shortly afterwards, the car was sold by the rogue to an innocent third party. It was held that the contract between the seller and the rogue was voidable rather than void. As it had not been reduced before the rogue had sold the car, title to the car had passed. It followed that third parties could acquire good title.

The distinction between the two cases is a narrow one. In *Morrisson* it was held that the seller had never intended to contract

---

[53] 1915 S.C. (H.L.) 20.

[54] 1908 S.C. 332.

[55] 1965 S.L.T. 358.

with the person before him, Telford, but rather with Wilson. As Wilson knew nothing of the transaction there could be no contract. The seller in *Macleod*, on the other hand, was prepared to contract with the person in front of him because he did not know the identity of the person with whom he was dealing. What is important to notice is the varying results between a finding of void or voidable. In the first case, the owner was protected, in the second, the third party purchaser. It can be argued that it boils down to a question of policy. Should the law protect the seller or the innocent party? As the seller is normally in a better position to prevent the fraud, it is better if he takes the risk. He could have taken precautions—in the first case by contacting Wilson himself; in the second by accepting only a certified cheque. This is the reason that there has been a move toward holding contracts voidable rather than void.

Reform

It may be argued that the distinction between the two types of nullity has now become so obscure that legislative action is required to dispel confusion. The Scottish Law Commission has recommended that where a vitiating factor is present the contract should come to an end either: (a) by agreement between the parties, or (b) by judicial decree (or decree arbitral).[56] In the case of (b), the Commission recommend an accelerated annulment procedure. There ought, says the Commission, to be a swift court procedure to determine the parties' respective rights. This would be a significant improvement on the present position.

DEFECTIVE EXPRESSION

The parties may reach agreement but the terms of their agreement are incorrectly recorded. This is sometimes referred to as an "error in expression". But error is not the appropriate term to use since the error is not as to the parties' intention. Rather, it is a defect in its expression. There is a discrepancy between what A and B have agreed and the terms of the document expressing the agreement. At common law in Scotland there was an equitable power to deal with such situations. So where a clerk improperly recorded an agreement that a hotel manageress should receive one fifth instead of one twentieth of the annual profits of the hotel this could be rectified.[57] Likewise where there was a discrepancy between the

---

[56] Scot. Law Com. Memorandum No. 42.
[57] *Krupp* v. *Menzies*, 1907 S.C. 903.

missives of sale and the disposition as to the ambit of the subjects to be sold.[58]

The courts have now been granted a wide power under statute to rectify documents which are defectively expressed.[59] Under these provisions, the court can rectify a document to give effect to the true intention of the parties "in any manner that it may specify in order to give to that intention." However, the court will not order rectification if it would adversely affect the interests of a party who has (a) not known (or ought to have been aware) of the defective expression; and (b) has placed reliance upon the deed; with the result that his position has been affected to a material extent; and (c) does not consent to the proposed rectification.

It has been suggested that six conditions must be present before rectification can take place under the statutory provision:[60]

1. that there is a document to be rectified;
2. that that document was intended to express or give effect to an already existing agreement arrived at by two (or more) parties;
3. that there was, when the document was executed, such a pre-existing document—whether or not enforceable;
4. that that agreement itself embodied and was an expression of one or more intentions common to (that is to say, shared by) the parties;
5. that the intentions were actual (not deemed) intentions;
6. that the agreement itself must have been reached at a definite point in time.

---

[58] *Anderson* v. *Lambie*, 1954 S.C. (H.L.) 43.

[59] Law Reform (Miscellaneous Provisions) (Scotland) Act 1985, ss. 8, 9.

[60] *Shaw* v. *William Grant (Minerals) Ltd.*, 1989 S.L.T. 121, *per* Lord McCluskey at p. 121H; see also *Bank of Scotland* v. *Graham*, 1992 S.C.L.R. 306; *cf. Angus* v. *Bryden*, 1992 S.L.T. 884.

CHAPTER 6

THE TERMS OF THE CONTRACT

IN A PERFECT legal world, all contracts would stipulate unambiguously the terms which had been agreed. They would also provide for every contingency which might occur. It is rare for parties to have the time or the prescience to achieve such goals. The opportunity to negotiate is often limited. What happens after the contract is made is just the occurrence which the parties failed to foresee. When a dispute arises, the parties frequently differ over the scope of the obligations they have undertaken. The duty of the court is to determine with precision (a) what the terms of the contract are; and (b) what effect is to be given to those terms.

The general principle is that the scope of the contract depends upon the intention of the parties. Of course, this can only be gleaned from their words and acts. If the contract was made orally, the crucial question is: what did the parties say? In one case the evidence was criticised by the court hearing the appeal because at the proof the parties were asked what obligations they thought they had undertaken. They should have been asked what words they had actually used.[1] If the contract is written, the court's attention is directed to the terms contained in the writing.

A variety of factors will determine the detail into which the parties go in making the contract. Commercial leases are frequently the result of detailed negotiations which result in documents of great length. Sometimes the parties will use a detailed contract which has been prepared in advance on standard terms with some minor modifications to cover their particular transaction. Contracts relating to building and engineering works are usually based on one or other of the forms which have been developed to deal with these operations. Examples of such conditions of contract are those produced by the Institute of Civil Engineers (the I.C.E. conditions of contract) and the Joint Contracts Tribunal (the J.C.T.). These forms attempt to cover most situations which arise in the course of a contract in which construction work is undertaken. Usually they

---

[1] *Muirhead & Turnbull* v. *Dickson* (1905) 7F. 686, *per* L.P. Dunedin at p. 693.

have clauses dealing with the application of Scots law. They may even have distinctive Scottish editions.

In many contracts virtually none of the potential contractual risks are expressly set out. Life would become immeasurably more complicated if we had to discuss all the legal implications arising from the purchase of a theatre ticket or a car-wash token. Accordingly, in the most common contracts, the obligations entered into by the parties are not determined by terms expressly agreed by them. Instead their legal relationship is governed by terms implied by law. This is particularly true where the pecuniary exchange is of low value. But even in some transactions of high value, such as the purchase of a new Rolls Royce car, much will be left to implication.

COMMON EXPRESS TERMS

Apart from terms detailing the main aspects of the contract, such as price and subject matter, there are a number of other express terms which are commonly found in contracts.

Arbitration Clauses

The parties may wish that any dispute which arises under the contract should be resolved by an arbiter rather than by the courts. The advantages of arbitration are said to be that it is cheaper and faster than normal litigation. In addition the person appointed as arbiter will often be a "man of skill" with knowledge of the type of contract involved. Such clauses are frequently found in building contracts, where an architect or engineer may be appointed as the arbiter. A reference to arbitration effectively excludes the jurisdiction of the courts. The courts only have a limited right to review arbiters' decisions on questions of law and to ensure that the principles of natural justice—regarding the right to be heard, and so on—are upheld.

Exemption Clauses

One party may seek to restrict, or even entirely exclude, his liability to the other party. A common example of such a clause is "the management accept no liability for any loss or damage caused to customers on these premises". Such clauses are referred to generally as exemption clauses. They are of great importance and will be discussed in detail in the next chapter.

Indemnity Clauses

A clause may provide that liability is to be borne by another party. A person who purchases a manufacturing process may for example require the seller to indemnify him, if he is found liable in respect of any breach of a patent owned by a third party. An indemnity clause is similar to an exemption clause except instead of stating "I am not liable" it states that "X shall be liable to indemnify me in respect of any liability I incur." Such clauses are increasingly common in large scale industrial works, such as off-shore oil rigs, or the construction of submarines.[2] Two contractors may provide one another with cross-indemnity clauses. The effect of such clauses is that each contractor becomes solely responsible for compensating its own employees in respect of any personal injury claims which may arise.

Liquidate Damage Clauses
The parties may wish to provide in advance how much compensation is to be payable in the event of a breach of contract. For example, a construction contract might stipulate that the builder will pay £100 per week in respect of each week beyond the date on which an extension to a factory is due to be completed. Such clauses are referred to as "liquidate damage" or "penalty" clauses and will be considered in Chapter 8.

Retention of Title Clauses
In a contract for the sale of goods, ownership normally passes when the goods are transferred or delivered. A seller may, however, stipulate that title (ownership) shall not pass until the goods have been paid for. Such a clause attempts to place the seller in a favourable position with regard to other creditors should the purchaser become insolvent. These retention of title clauses are also known as "Romalpa" clauses after the name of the case in which they were first discussed.[3] After some dispute about their legal validity under Scots law, it has been authoritatively determined that they are effective.[4]

TERMS INCORPORATED BY REFERENCE

In some cases a contractual document may refer to terms contained in another document. A contract of employment may state that superannuation conditions, which are contained in a separate booklet, are to be part of the contract. The most common example is to be found in the use of tickets, which often bear on their face phrases such as "issued subject to the terms and conditions printed in the company's timetable". Questions about whether such terms are incorporated or not normally arise in relation to exemption

---

[2] *Scott Lithgow* v. *Secretary of State for Defence*, 1989 S.L.T. 236.
[3] *Aluminium Industrie Vaaseen B.V.* v. *Romalpa Aluminium* [1976] 2 All E.R. 552.
[4] *Armour* v. *Thyssen Edelstahlwerke A.G.*, 1990 S.L.T. 891.

clauses, so we shall discuss them in more detail in the next chapter.
But it is worth stressing here that such terms will only be incorporated if the reference is clear and unambiguous.

IMPLIED TERMS

The parties can never provide for every contingency that may arise
under the contract. Accordingly, they will leave some terms to be
implied. If it is a typical contract which occurs in a familiar context,
few difficulties will arise. Over the years the incidents of these
contracts have been fully worked out. Originally the courts were
most willing to imply terms in contracts of everyday occurrence,
such as sale, hire and lease. Implication would usually be based
upon the custom which had grown up regarding such transactions.
Many of these individual instances of implication of terms eventu-
ally found their way into statute. The contract of sale of goods
provides the classic example of this process. By the end of the
nineteenth century the implied terms of this contract had been so
well worked out by judicial decisions that it was possible to codify
the law. This was done by the Sale of Goods Act 1893. Over the
years various amendments were made to the 1893 Act and the law
was consolidated in the Sale of Goods Act 1979.

> *Example*: Fred paid £600 for a chair which was described in the
> catalogue as "a reclining chair". Shortly after taking delivery
> Fred discovers that the chair can only remain in a fixed position
> and cannot recline. In a sale by description there is an implied
> term that the goods correspond with that description. Fred is
> entitled to return the chair to the seller and to recover his
> money.

In contracts of less common occurrence, the courts were in the
beginning reluctant to imply terms unless they were satisfied that
the term represented the parties' true intention. Two general
principles may be stated regarding implication by the courts in such
contracts. First, no term will be implied which is directly contradict-
ory to an express term (*expressum facit cessare tacitum*). Secondly,
a term will more easily be implied in a verbal than in a written and
formal contract.[5] Beyond those two principles it becomes more

---

[5] Gloag on *Contract* (2nd ed.) pp. 288–289; approved in *Crawford* v. *Bruce*, 1992
S.L.T. 524, *per* L.P. Hope at 531G.

difficult to state the law with precision. The classic statement on this branch of contract law was made by Lord McLaren:

> "The conception of an implied condition is one with which we are familiar in relation to contracts of every description, and if we seek to trace any such implied conditions to their source it will be found in almost every instance that they are founded either on universal custom or in the nature of the contract itself. If the condition is such that every reasonable man on the one part would desire for his own protection to stipulate for the condition, and that no reasonable man on the other would refuse to accede to it, then it is not unnatural that the condition should be taken for granted in all contracts of this class without the necessity of giving it formal expression."[6]

It is worth noting that in this passage, Lord McLaren flirts with two different bases for the implication of terms. The first basis is that of "universal custom or the nature of the contract itself." We have already seen that this applies perfectly to everyday contracts. It is assumed in such cases that the parties simply did not trouble to express the term. But the passage goes on to discuss terms being implied by reference to the test of the "reasonable man." True, it is not a full blown "reasonable man" test. The court must have regard to the interests of both the contracting parties. Such an approach might allow a court to imply a term when it thought that it was reasonable to do so.

Lord McLaren's approach has recently been approved and adopted in the Inner House.[7] In *G.M. Shepherd* v. *North West Securities Ltd.*[8]:

> Retail chemists hired a compact processor to develop films on their premises at Cults. As is so frequently the case today, the equipment was supplied by one company, Photosystems (U.K.) Ltd., but the actual contract of hire was with the defenders, a finance company. Clause six of the hire agreement stated that the hirers had inspected and approved the equipment and that the defenders would not be subject to any implied terms. The processor failed to work satisfactorily and the chemists purported to reject it and rescind the contract.

---

[6] *Morton & Co.* v. *Muir Bros.*, 1907 S.C. 1211 at p. 1224.

[7] *G.M. Shepherd* v. *North West Securities Ltd.*, 1991 S.L.T. 499; *Crawford* v. *Bruce*, 1992 S.L.T. 524.

[8] 1991 S.L.T. 499.

They claimed that they were entitled to do so because the contract included an implied term that the equipment was hireworthy. At issue was whether or not such a term fell to be implied into the contract. It was held that no such term fell to be implied. The Second Division recognised that typical contracts of hire were subject to the item being hireworthy. However, they found that this contract was atypical in that "the owner never had possession of the compact printer processor, and he only purchased it from the supplier at the special request of the hirer who acknowledged that he, the hirer, had inspected and approved the equipment."[9]

In *Crawford* v. *Bruce*, shop premises were leased for an initial period of ten years.[10] It was provided that the rent should be reviewed every three years, but no mechanism was provided to determine how that rent should be assessed. The landlord contended that a term fell to be implied into the lease that the rent should be market rent at each three year review. The First Division rejected this contention. Delivering the opinion of the court, Lord President Hope stated that

> "The hypothesis on which we are asked to say the rent should be fixed is that the rent should be a market rent, and that the duration on the expiry of each three year period is to be the same as the initial duration of the lease. But both points could be said to be likely to operate to the disadvantage of the tenant, and it is far from clear that the hypothesis is one which satisfies the test which Lord McLaren described in *Morton & Co.* v. *Muir Bros.*, namely that the implied condition is such that no reasonable man in the tenant's position would have refused to accede to it."[11]

By considering the matter from the position of the tenant, the court was able to reject the idea that a term fell to be implied.

ENGLISH LAW

In arriving at their views on implied terms, the Scottish courts have carefully considered the English cases on this subject. In order to

[9] *Ibid. per* L.J.C. Ross at p. 507A; see also Lord Murray at p. 511C and Lord McCluskey at p. 513G–514B.
[10] 1992 S.L.T. 524.
[11] *Ibid.* at p. 532I.

have a full understanding of this topic, it is necessary to consider these cases in some detail. Various tests have been adopted by the English judiciary to determine whether or not a term should be implied into a particular contract. The first is known as the "*Moorcock* test". In the *Moorcock*[12]:

> A vessel had arranged to discharge its cargo at a pier on the River Thames. At low tide the keel of the vessel was damaged when it grounded on the bed of the river. There was held to be an implied term in the contract between the owner of the vessel and the wharfingers that the latter had taken reasonable steps to ensure that it was safe anchorage. In awarding damages against the wharfingers, Bowen L.J. framed the test for implying terms as follows: "I believe if one were to take all the cases, and they are many, it will be found that in all of them the law is raising an implication from the presumed intention of the parties with the object of giving to the transaction such efficacy as both parties must have intended that in all events it should have."[13]

The court approached the question from the angle of "efficacy". Was the term required to give the contract "efficacy"? Later jurists have used the term "business efficacy" to refer to the test which is said to derive from the *Moorcock*.

A different approach was formulated in the case of *Shirlaw* v. *Southern Foundries*. There the test adopted was that of the "officious bystander".[14] If such a fictitious person were to be standing close to the contracting parties and were to propose a further term in the contract, would they "testily suppress him with a common 'Oh of course' "? In other words, was the term sought to be implied so obvious in the minds of both contracting parties that they did not trouble themselves to express it? Such a test is clearly based on fact whereas the *Moorcock* test seemed to allow that a term might be implied in law. In other words the *Moorcock* test suggested circumstances might arise where the court itself might imply a term independent of the parties' intentions if it thought it were required to give the contract "efficacy".

More recently, the House of Lords has stated that the courts should not imply terms simply because it is reasonable for them to

[12] (1889) 14 P.D. 64.
[13] at p. 68.
[14] [1939] 2 K.B. 206.

do so.[15] That is a usurpation of the function of the parties. Instead
Lord Wilberforce has propounded the test of "necessity". A court
will only imply a term when it is necessary to do so: " . . . such
obligation should be read into the contract as the nature of the
contract itself implicitly requires, no more, no less . . . ". The
distinction between what is "reasonable" and what is "necessary"
is a fine one. In a subsequent case it was asserted that a petrol
supplier was subject to an implied term that it would not discrimin-
ate amongst its retail garages during a petrol price war.[16] The term
was thought capable of being implied on the ground of "necessity"
by one Lord Justice of Appeal but not by his two colleagues. They
held that although it was "reasonable" it was not "necessary" for
the term to be part of the contract.

IMPLYING TERMS IN PRACTICE

It can be difficult to decide whether a term falls to be implied in a
particular case. In *Lothian* v. *Jenolite* a company sought to terminate its contract with an agent which sold industrial chemicals on its
behalf.[17] The company claimed that the agent had sold a competitor's products. They argued that this breached an implied term of
the agreement that the agent would work exclusively for it. It was
held that there was no implied term to that effect. The company
had not stipulated that the agency was to be an exclusive one in the
written contract. Such a term could not be implied, either on the
grounds of efficacy or on the basis of Lord McLaren's test.

By contrast in *North American Continental Sales Inc.* v. *Bepi
Electronics Ltd.*, an American company gave a Scottish company
sole rights to distribute its software in the United Kingdom.[18]
Under the contract, the Scottish company was to pay the American
company a proportion of the value of the sales it achieved. The
Scottish company failed to market the software, alleging that it did
not work. In consequence the American company raised an action
claiming that there was an implied term in the contract that the
Scottish company would use its best endeavours to sell the process.
It was held that business efficacy did require such a term to be
implied into the contract.

In one Australian case, an attempt was made by the Privy

---

[15] *Liverpool City Council* v. *Irwin* [1977] A.C. 239 (H.L.); [1975] 3 All E.R. 658
(C.A.).
[16] *Shell* v. *Lostock Garages Ltd.* [1977] 1 All E.R. 48.
[17] 1969 S.C. 111.
[18] 1982 S.L.T. 47.

Council to rationalise the law of implication.[19] It was said that the following conditions (which may overlap) must be satisfied before a term can be implied:

1. it must be reasonable and equitable.
2. it must be necessary to give business efficacy to the contract so that no term will be implied if the contract is effective without it.
3. it must be so obvious that "it goes without saying".
4. it must be capable of clear expression.
5. it must not contradict any express term in the contract.

These criteria provide useful signposts in considering whether a term falls to be implied in a particular case.

CONSTRUCTION OF THE CONTRACT

Most contracts consist of a mixture of express terms, implied terms and terms imported by reference. The mixture will be different in each case. One contract may be entirely housed in a written document which sets out the terms in detail. It is their private "legislative act". Another contract may be dependent almost entirely on implied terms. Once ascertained, these terms demarcate the ambit of the parties' respective contractual obligations. The next stage is for the courts to determine the exact import of the terms. In other words they must construe the contract. The aim of the courts is to give effect to the intention of the parties. This may appear paradoxical, for, if a case is before the court, the parties are in dispute and it is likely that their respective interpretations of the contract differ. Accordingly they have no such common intention. But the courts take an objective approach and consider what a reasonable observer would take to be the "intention", looked at from a neutral point of view. There are certain established guidelines which courts follow in ascertaining that person's intention.

Priority of Express Terms

Express terms take priority over implied terms. When parties state their terms, whether orally or in writing, these express terms provide the best key to the parties' intention. Accordingly terms will only be implied where needed to "fill in the gaps". An example is provided by the contract of partnership. The partnership document drawn up and signed by the partners will regulate the manner in which the partnership is to be conducted. But where the docu-

---

[19] *B.P. Refinery (Westernport) Pty. Ltd.* v. *Hastings Shire Council* [1978] 52 A.L.J.R. 20.

ment is silent, the relationship will be governed by implied terms. The partners may choose to modify or override terms which would otherwise apply. A partnership deed may, for example, stipulate that profits are to be distributed unequally between the partners. This would vary the term which would otherwise be implied by the Partnership Act 1890. Certain implied terms cannot be displaced by express terms. This is unusual but occurs, for example, in relation to the Sale of Goods Act 1979 where businesses are prevented from contracting out of their obligation to provide a consumer with goods of merchantable quality.[20]

Parole Evidence Rule

When the parties have reduced the contract to writing, the written document is presumed to be not only the best but also the complete expression of their will on the matter. Oral evidence of the parties' intentions on the matter is in principle inadmissible. This is known as the parole evidence rule. It allows the courts to restrict their inquiry when disputes arise. Instead of having oral evidence on the parties' respective understanding of their contract, the court can concentrate on the written deed. The parties' meaning is to be found within the "four corners of the deed". For instance a clause in a contract for the supply of steel for the erection of the four main spans of the Forth Railway Bridge stated: "The estimated quantity of the steel we understand to be 30,000 tons, more or less."[21] This was held to mean precisely what it said. Evidence to the effect that according to trade custom, the term meant 30,000 tons exactly, or with a margin of variation not exceeding 5 per cent, was not allowed. The supplier was entitled to provide all the steel that was necessary for the work under the contract.

However, it should be stressed that the parole evidence rule is not applied rigorously in every case. Scottish courts are in general entitled to hear evidence where it is appropriate to do justice between the parties. Usually the evidence in question will have a bearing on the parties' intention.

> *Example*: Gertrude accepts a written tender from Shunt Ltd., to knock down two walls in her flat and install a shower. During the course of the work, Gertrude asks the workmen to repair a skylight and tile the shower area. In the event of a

[20] Unfair Contract Terms Act 1977, s. 20.
[21] *Tancred, Arrol & Co.* v. *The Steel Company of Scotland* (1890) 17 R. (H.L.) 31; (1887) 15 R. 215; (1889) 16 R. 440.

dispute Shunt Ltd., would be allowed to lead parole evidence to show how the original written contract had been varied.

In England it appears that the parole evidence rule is largely obsolete. One Scottish writer lists eight exceptions to the rule.[22] The leading textbook on Evidence states " . . . the exceptions to this part of the Scottish rule are so numerous and extensive that little harm would probably result if the English method of statement were to be adopted."[23]

Prior Communings

Where there is a formal contract, all prior negotiations between the parties, oral or written are irrelevant in determining the parties' respective obligations. This is similar to the parole evidence rule. However, as it excludes written communings, it goes somewhat further. "The principle is well established, that, when communings are followed by a written contract, it is not competent to allow any part of the communing . . . to be held as part of the written contract, or to apply to them so as to enlarge or control the terms of the contract."[24] By entering a formal contract the parties have crystallised their obligation. The whole purpose would be lost if the deed was not seen as the final statement of the terms.

This principle is particularly important in sales of heritage, where the written disposition normally supersedes the parties' missives. When an obligation which is stated in the missives is not repeated in the disposition this can lead to hardship. In *Winston* v. *Patrick* an obligation was placed on the seller by the missives of sale to the effect that he warranted that the building had been erected in accordance with the relevant statutory and local authority requirements.[25] It was held that the buyer could not found on the missives once the disposition had been granted: the parties' respective rights and duties were thereafter governed by the disposition (which was silent on the matter), not the missives. The validity of the principle has been challenged. But it remains true that, in general, the prior communings may only be looked at where it is alleged either that the disposition improperly records the parties' intention, or where there is some invalidity such as force and fear in its constitution.

---

[22] Gow, *Mercantile Law* (1963), pp. 13, 14.

[23] Walkers, *Evidence*, pp. 254–5.

[24] *Walker* v. *Caledonian Ry Co.* (1858) 20 D. 1102 *per* Lord Justice-Clerk Hope at p. 1105.

[25] 1981 S.L.T. 41; there have been several subsequent cases on this point.

The *Contra Proferentem* Principle

Where a clause is ambiguous, it is construed against the interest of the party who seeks to rely upon it. "The rule is related to the simple proposition that he who seeks a privilege or protection by way of exemption from a liability which the law otherwise imposes in a contract must justify it: that and no more." In one case an insurance company stipulated in a contract of life insurance that the contract would be void should any of the statements made by the proposer turn out to be untrue.[26] A lady made statements on the proposal form indicating that she was not suffering from any malady. Unknown to her, at the time of filling out the form, she was already suffering from the disease which was to cause her death some months later. The company initially refused to pay out on the policy. The court held that the company was bound to do so. Construing the clause *contra proferentem* it meant that the proposer required to disclose any illness known to her; it did not apply where she did not know of her true medical condition.

Certainty

Sometimes, the court determines that construction of the contract yields such uncertainty that it is unable to give effect to either part or all of the parties' bargain. For example, there may be insufficient precision about some central feature of the pact. The essential features of a particular contract will depend upon the nature of the contract in question. Often the essential elements are threefold: (1) the identity of the parties, (2) the subject-matter of the contract, and (3) the price. If the parties do not agree these elements, there is insufficient certainty to hold that a contract has been concluded.

It should be possible to crystallise the duties of the parties with enough precision for a court to frame an order against one of them, should a dispute arise. In *McArthur* v. *Lawson*[27] an employee received a written contract of employment in which the employer stated that "at the expiry of the second year I engage to give you a substantial interest by way of partnership in my business, so that your annual income may be considerably increased." This was held to be too vague and indefinite to be enforceable. In *Crawford* v. *Bruce*, the court considered the clause regarding the rent review too uncertain to receive effect:

---

[26] *Life Association of Scotland* v. *Foster* (1873) 11 M. 351.
[27] (1877) 4 R. 1134.

"As it is, the clause must be regarded as void for uncertainty because it lacks the elements which would be necessary for the court to arrive at a figure which could be taken to be the result of what the parties had always intended to agree as the basis on which the rent was to be calculated."[28]

If possible, however, the court will try to give effect to the contract. So where the price has not been agreed upon, the court will still enforce the contract if the parties have agreed a mechanism for arriving at the price. Sometimes it may even fix a reasonable price itself. The general approach is well summed up by Lord Guthrie:

"The object of our law of contract is to facilitate the transactions of commercial men, and not to create obstacles in the way of solving practical problems arising out of the circumstances confronting them, or to expose them to unnecessary pitfalls."[29]

Terms and Misrepresentation

A statement which is made during the course of negotiations leading up to the contract may: (1) have no legal effect; (2) amount to a misrepresentation; or (3) be a term of the contract. Whether a pre-contractual statement has legal force or not is largely a question of intention and reliance. Was it sought to induce the other party to enter the contract by means of the statement? Was it intended and understood that it became a term of the contract?

Statements in advertisements usually have no legal effect because reasonable persons know they are exaggerated to "puff up" the product. By contrast, in many contracts for the sale of goods, statute decrees that there is a term in the contract that the goods are of merchantable quality. Difficulties arise in cases which fall between these positions. Usually the pursuer will wish to argue that the statement on which he founds his claim is a term of the contract. This is because it is easier to prove breach of contract than misrepresentation. Moreover in a breach of contract case, damages can be recovered even though fraud or negligence are not proved. On the other hand, where the contract has been reduced to writing, the parole evidence rule may exclude evidence to explain or qualify

---

[28] *Ibid.* at p. 532G.
[29] *R. & J. Dempster* v. *Motherwell Bridge & Engineering Co.*, 1964 S.C. 308; 1964 S.L.T. 353; approved in *Neilson* v. *Stewart*, 1991 S.L.T. 523, 526.

the terms of the contract. In this situation a claim for misrepresentation may be the only remedy available. In *Fortune* v. *Fraser*[30]:

> In May 1991, Mr Fortune purchased a sandwich bar in Edinburgh from Mr Fraser. One clause of the offer stated that Fraser warranted that the business account provided "a true and fair view of the business". Subsequently, Fortune claimed that the results of trading were lower than those stated in the account. He sued Fraser for damages of £150,000. A subsidiary argument was that there had been a misrepresentation by Fraser. It was held that a term of the contract could not also amount to a misrepresentation.

CLASSIFICATION OF CONTRACTUAL TERMS

Frequently the terms of the contract are referred to as conditions: the "conditions of sale" or "the conditions of hire". What does this mean? The explanation requires a short excursus into English law. In England the word "condition" is used in a technical sense. It is a term which is deemed to be an important provision of the contract. By contrast a "warranty" is a term of lesser importance. A breach of a "condition" allows the other party to treat the contract as at an end. Breach of a "warranty" only gives rise to a claim for damages. Through the course of time certain terms were always regarded as conditions, others as warranties. So the consequences depended entirely on the nature of the term broken, irrespective of the seriousness of the breach which had occurred.

In Scotland the corresponding terminology is between "material" and "non-material" terms. This is a more flexible approach which enables a court to decide what remedy the degree of breach justifies. "Warranty" is used in its more common meaning of "guarantee". Certain provisions of the Sale of Goods Act 1893 (now consolidated in the 1979 Act) caused confusion by introducing English terminology. More recent U.K. legislation has provided that in relation to Scotland the words "condition" and "warranty" mean "stipulation".[31] As indicated in Chapter 1, the more proper usage of "condition" in Scotland refers to "conditional" obligations. A contract may not come into question until a

---

[30] 1993 S.C.L.R. 470 (at the time of writing, this case is under appeal).
[31] Consumer Credit Act 1974, Sched. 4, paras. 35, 36; Supply of Goods (Implied Terms) Act 1973, s. 16.

particular event occurs. Such an obligation is subject to a condition. But we cannot ignore the fact that the phrase, "conditions of contract" is often used in which "conditions" is simply another word for "terms".

CHAPTER 7

EXEMPTION CLAUSES

A PERSON may insert a term into a contract restricting his legal liability to the other party. Such clauses are known as exemption clauses. They may seek to either totally or partially exclude liability on the part of one party. Here are some familiar examples: "The management accepts no liability for any article lost on the premises"; "In the event of any damage occurring to this item when in the control of the company, the company shall not be liable for any loss in excess of £100"; and "Persons enter these premises at their own risk."

Exemption clauses are found on tickets, in cloakrooms, at car parks and in many other locations and guises in modern life. They may attempt to exclude or restrict liability not only for contractual liability but for delictual liability as well. In the case of *McKay* v. *Scottish Airways* the pursuers sought damages against an airline in respect of the death of one of their relatives, who had been killed in a crash caused by the airline's negligence.[1] The claim was unsuccessful because of an exemption clause in the contract of carriage. This was held to cover the airline's liability for breach of contract —not carrying the passenger safely from A to B—as well as exempting the company from its delictual liability—the duty to pay damages for harm occasioned by negligent actings.

Exemption clauses can have much to commend them. By allocating the risk of a particular event, the liability of the parties is determined in advance. This avoids unnecessary litigation, indicates who is to bear the cost of insurance and enables the value of goods and services to be accurately priced.

> *Example*: Blunt Ltd., supplies widgets to Klim Ltd. In their contract it is stipulated that Blunt shall not be liable if a widget is defective and causes loss to Klim. Should, accordingly, a widget prove defective, the parties know their legal position. Klim can insure against loss if it wishes while Blunt can keep the price of the widgets down, because it does not have to pass on the cost of insurance premiums to its customers.

---

[1] 1948 S.C. 254.

Regrettably, however, there is another side to the coin. Often these terms appear on standard printed forms in situations where the person who drafted the form simply seeks to evade his duties. The absence of negotiation means that he seeks to impose terms which are advantageous to himself without any belief or expectation that the other party will make provision for the contingency. To rent a car or purchase a package holiday the consumer is asked to sign a form prepared in advance by the company. It sets the terms which are to apply and cannot be varied. The consumer must "take it or leave it." His sole decision is whether to make the contract or not. There is no opportunity to bargain about the terms. In particular he cannot vary or delete a clause which exempts the company from the legal liability they would otherwise owe to him. Although such standard forms apply particularly to consumers, they can also affect businesses. Goods or services are often supplied subject to a standard printed form. The other party, albeit a business itself, will have no opportunity to negotiate the terms. Sometimes, as we have seen, this can be advantageous in terms of an efficient economic allocation of risk. But at other times one business may seek to exploit a superior bargaining position by inserting an unfair exemption clause into the contract.

The idea of one party exempting itself from legal liability for its own negligence is not one which the courts view with favour. Various legal controls have been developed to regulate the use of such clauses. The story of this development begins with the controls the courts themselves fashioned and culminates in statutory regulation under the Unfair Contract Terms Act 1977. Today when considering the legal effect of an exemption clause we must consider in turn the common law and statutory controls to establish whether it is valid or invalid.

REGULATION AT COMMON LAW

At common law only those exemption clauses which (1) are incorporated into the contract, and (2) unequivocally apply to the breach in question, are effective.

1. Incorporation

A clause is clearly incorporated when the party against whom it is designed to operate has signed the contractual document. By signing a document a person is deemed to have assented to its terms and consequently to be bound by it:

" . . . where an action is brought on a written agreement which is signed by the defendant, the agreement is proved by proving his signature and, in the absence of fraud, it is wholly immaterial that he has not read the agreement and does not know its contents."[2]

This principle holds even where the clause in question is in "legible, but regrettably small print"[3] but not where the writing is illegible, or where the effect of the clause has been misrepresented. Dissatisfaction with this rule has frequently been expressed:

> "If it were possible for your Lordships to escape from the world of make-believe which the law has created into the real world in which transactions of this sort are actually done, the answer would be short and simple. It [signature] should make no difference whatsoever. This document is not meant to be read, still less to be understood. Its signature is in truth about as significant as a handshake that marks the formal conclusion of a bargain."[4]

There is force in this contention. Even contract lawyers are unlikely to pore over the fine print of every holiday booking form, car hire document and receipt which they sign. Like Homer, their heads may nod. Nevertheless signature is the outward and visible sign of assent to the terms of an agreement. It remains an important factor in determining whether or not an exemption clause has been incorporated.

Where no document is actually signed, one party may, at the time of contracting, point out an exemption clause and say "I am contracting on the basis of this term being part of our contract, do you agree?" Following the signature principle, the term will be held to be part of the contract if the other party does expressly agree. Unfortunately such a procedure is rarely followed. Instead the party seeking to incorporate the exemption clause will rely upon a notice. The notice may itself contain the clause, such as those one sees on dry-cleaners' counters. Alternatively it may refer to another document which actually contains the clause. Bus tickets often refer to clauses contained in the terms and conditions of carriage which are printed in the company's timetable. Over the years the courts have had to consider the question of incorporation in relation to such notices many times.

---

[2] *Parker* v. *S. E. Railway Co.* (1877) 2 C.P.D. 416, *per* Mellish L.J., at p. 421.
[3] *L'Estrange* v. *Graucob* [1934] 2 K.B. 394.
[4] *McCutcheon* v. *MacBrayne*, 1964 S.C. (H.L.) 28, 39–40 *per* Lord Devlin.

The issue was first authoritatively considered in the English case
of *Parker* v. *S.E. Railway Company*[5]:

> Mr Parker deposited a bag worth £24 10s, in a railway cloak-
> room. He was charged 2d. and received in return for his money
> a ticket which bore on its face the opening hours of the
> cloakroom and the words "see back." On the reverse it stated
> that the company would not be responsible for any bag worth
> more than £10. A notice to the same effect hung in the
> cloakroom. Although Parker admitted that he knew there was
> writing on the ticket he denied that he had read either it or the
> notice. He said that he imagined that the ticket was a receipt
> for the bag.

By a majority, the court held that if the plaintiff knew that there
was writing and also knew that it was the other party's intention
that these constituted terms of the contract he would be bound. But
if he had not read the term, nor knew that the intention was to
constitute contractual terms, then the correct question to ask was
"whether the railway company did what was reasonably sufficient
to give the plaintiff notice of the condition."[6] The test was therefore
one of reasonable notice. *Parker* has been accepted as good authority in Scotland.

A steamship company was held to have satisfied the test by
handing passengers an envelope which stated conspicuously on the
outside "please read contents of enclosed contract."[7] The envelope
contained a ticket with an exemption clause. The company had
successfully incorporated the clause into the contract.

But the "reasonable notice" approach received a significant setback in the English case of *Thompson* v. *London Midland &
Scottish Railway Company*.[8]

> Mrs Thompson sustained injuries when alighting from a train
> due to the railway company's negligence. Her claim for
> damages was held to be subject to an exemption clause despite
> the following: Mrs Thompson could not read; the ticket had
> been bought for her by her niece; and the relevant exemption
> clause referred to in the ticket was contained on page 552 of a
> separate timetable which itself cost 6d. At first instance the

[5] (1877) 2 C.P.D. 416.
[6] *Ibid. per* Mellish L.J. at p. 424.
[7] *Hood* v. *Anchor Line*, 1918 S.C. (H.L.) 143.
[8] [1930] 1 K.B. 41.

jury had held on these facts that the railway company had not given reasonable notice of the exemption clause. It awarded Mrs Thompson £167 10s. On appeal, Lord Hamworth M.R. distinguished *Parker* on the ground that it concerned a contract of deposit where no written document was required. The plaintiff was therefore entitled to treat the ticket as a mere voucher. But in a contract of carriage, the ticket was required to get onto the platform and thence the train. The issue of a railway ticket accordingly ought to indicate to a reasonable person that there were conditions to be found upon it.

Subsequent courts have been reluctant to follow *Thompson*. In a neat piece of judicial conjuring, a distinction has been drawn between the different types of function a ticket may perform. This is demonstrated by the case of *Taylor* v. *Glasgow Corporation*[9]:

Mrs Taylor went weekly for a hot bath to her local public baths in Glasgow. On one such occasion she fell down a stair and suffered serious injury. The corporation sought to rely on an exemption clause. This clause appeared on the ticket with which all bathers were issued when they entered the building and paid the price for the facility they sought. On the front of the ticket it said "For conditions see other side" and on the reverse were words to the effect that the corporation accepted no liability for an injury which was caused to anyone using the establishment. Mrs Taylor said that she knew there was writing on the ticket but not that it referred to contractual terms.

It was held that the corporation had not brought the clause to Mrs Taylor's notice and therefore it had not exempted itself from liability in respect of her injury. Lord Justice-Clerk Thomson said that the ticket performed the following functions: (a) it was a domestic check on the running of the establishment; (b) it was a receipt for the price; and (c) it was a voucher, indicating what facility had been paid for. He regarded the voucher aspect as the significant one. A person would not regard a voucher as containing contractual conditions, unlike a railway or cloakroom ticket where it was accepted that the ticket was a contractual document. Today this reasoning appears specious but we can applaud the result which prevented the corporation from escaping their liability to compensate Mrs Taylor.

More recent cases have tended to examine all the circumstances

[9] 1952 S.C. 440.

before deciding whether reasonable notice has been given. A factor which has been closely scrutinised is the degree of exemption sought. In *Thornton* v. *Shoe Lane Parking Ltd.*, the owners of a car-park attempted to exclude liability not only for damage to property but also for personal injury to those parking their cars on the premises.[10] The clause appeared on a ticket issued by an automatic machine at the entrance to the car-park and on a notice inside the car-park. The Court of Appeal held that no reasonable notice of the clause had been given. To see the clause, a customer had either to take a ticket from the machine, or to leave his car at the entrance and enter the car-park to see the notice. As no one was likely to follow this second course of action it was held that the term came too late. In seeking to exempt liability for personal injury as well as damage to property, very clear notice would have to be given. Lord Denning M.R. suggested it would have to be "in red ink with a red hand pointing to it."[11] So far as the "reasonable notice" test could be applied to automatic machines he thought that "None of those [older] cases has any application to a ticket which is issued by an automatic machine. The customer pays his money and gets a ticket. He cannot refuse it. He cannot get his money back."[12] Lord Denning believed that in the case of ticket machines, incorporation ought not to be presumed, even in the case of contracts of carriage and deposit.

Incorporation by Course of Dealing

Even though no notice is given, a person may nevertheless be bound by an exemption clause because he knows of it as a result of a course of dealing. In each case the question to be asked is whether or not the circumstances yield the inference that both parties proceeded on the basis that the exemption clause was a term of the contract.[13] The most famous case on this topic is *McCutcheon* v. *MacBrayne*[14]:

> The pursuer sought damages in respect of his car which had been lost when the defenders' ferry sank on a trip from Islay to Tarbert. His brother-in-law had arranged the shipment of the car and both men had transferred items on the ferry in the past.

---

[10] [1971] 2 Q.B. 163.
[11] *Ibid.* at p. 170.
[12] *Ibid.* at p. 169.
[13] *Continental Tyre & Rubber Co. Ltd.* v. *Trunk Trailer Co. Ltd.*, 1987 S.L.T. 58; *Wm. Teacher & Sons Ltd.* v. *Bell Lines Ltd.*, 1991 S.L.T. 876.
[14] 1964 S.C. (H.L.) 28.

In principle the defenders required shippers to sign a risk note exempting them from liability, but the pursuer and his brother-in-law had sometimes, but not always, signed such a note. Inadvertently no such note had been signed on this occasion. Notices containing the exemption clause were also displayed in the defenders' office and on the pier but the pursuer had never read them.

The House of Lords first distinguished *Parker* on the ground that there was no contractual document such as a ticket or receipt seeking to import conditions. Further as the notices had not been read they could not bind the pursuer. On the question of the prior dealings of the parties, the House held that while a consistent course of dealing could in principle bind the parties, there had been no consistent course here. The risk note had sometimes been signed, sometimes not. Accordingly the defenders had also failed to establish that the clause had been inserted on the basis of notice by means of course of dealing. Mr McCutcheon was accordingly entitled to full compensation in respect of his car.

Surprisingly few examples of a course of dealing leading to incorporation can be given. One case where a parallel principle was successfully invoked occurred when a crane was hired under an oral contract made by telephone.[15] Both the companies concerned were engaged in the business of hiring cranes and both used the standard industry conditions of contract when hiring out cranes. The standard conditions contained an exemption clause. Although there was not strictly a course of dealing between the parties, both ought to have reasonably assumed that the term in question would be part of the contract. Long usage of the term by both parties indicated that it was to be incorporated. A contrasting case is *Grayston Plant Ltd. v. Plean Precast Ltd.*[15a] Over a period of four years there were 12 instances in which the pursuers followed up an oral contract by sending an "acknowledgement of order form" which referred to the general conditions upon which they traded. It was held that the general conditions were not incorporated into the contract.

2. Construction of the Clause

Once it is established that an exemption clause is incorporated, the next question to be asked is "Can it be relied upon in the circumstances which have arisen?" This is essentially a question of con-

---

[15] *British Crane Hire Corpn. Ltd.* v. *Ipswich Plant Hire Ltd.* [1975] Q.B. 303; [1976] 1 All E.R. 1059.
[15a] 1976 S.C. 206.

struction. Is the clause drawn in such a way that it is clear that the parties intended it to cover the situation which has occurred? The strong presumption of the law is that one party will not agree to release the other from liability for his own negligence. Such a course is regarded as "inherently improbable."[16] So in a series of cases it has been established that unless the draftsman is particularly precise, actually uses the term "negligence" itself or some synonym and exempts from all other forms of liability, the defender might still be liable. One example will illustrate the rigour with which the courts follow this approach[17]:

> A clause in a contract for the carriage of household goods from Aberdeen to Glasgow stated: "The contractors shall not be responsible for loss and damage to furniture and effects caused by or incidental to fire or aircraft but will endeavour to effect insurance on behalf of the customer on receipt of instructions." The goods were destroyed by fire and the owners sought compensation from the transport company. It was held that the clause did not exempt the carriers from liability.

This apparently surprising result was reached because the clause could be construed to refer both to the carrier's liability under contract and also to its liability under statute. Construing the clause strictly, the court decided that it only exempted the carriers from their statutory liability. What the decision shows is the willingness of the courts to prevent a contracting party from relying on an exemption clause by adopting a strict construction of the contract.

Fundamental Breach

Because a skilled draftsman could, with careful drafting, always exclude liability in the 1950s and 1960s the courts in England, particularly the Court of Appeal, developed a new doctrine, that of fundamental breach. Let us begin with an example:

> Dealer A agrees to sell a new Rolls Royce to B. Under the contract there are several duties upon A. He must deliver the particular car agreed upon to B in return for the price. If A delivers a car which is scratched, or a different colour to that specified, or with a different engine, he is in breach of contract.

---

[16] *Gillespie Bros. & Co. Ltd.* v. *Roy Bowles Transport Ltd.* [1973] Q.B. 400, *per* Buckley L.J. at p. 419.

[17] *Graham* v. *The Shore Porter's Society*, 1979 S.L.T. 119; see also *Golden Sea Produce Ltd.* v. *Scottish Nuclear plc*, 1992 S.L.T. 942.

Of course if the car is second-hand or A does not deliver a car at all, then the breach is even more serious. Suppose that in the contract of sale there is a blanket exemption clause which states that B cannot sue A notwithstanding any of the breaches set out above occurring. This reduces the contract to something of a sham. A's apparent promise to assume certain responsibilities is refuted by the exemption clause. Its effect is to exempt A from legal liability even if he does not fulfil any of his promises. The agreement thus becomes a statement of intent rather than a contract with obligations on both sides.

When a serious breach had occurred the courts were reluctant to hold that this was the legal result which the parties had achieved. A number of terms were used to describe such a breach: one that "went to the root of the contract", one that removed the purpose of the contract or, more simply, a fundamental breach. Although the seeds of the doctrine were sown in 1922,[18] the term "fundamental breach" itself was first used in this context by Devlin J. in 1953.[19] But it was Denning L.J., who gave a new gloss to the use of this term by suggesting that once a fundamental breach had occurred the whole contract was swept aside, including any exemption clause it contained.[20] So it was impossible for a draftsman to exclude liability for such a breach. The first time this idea was considered by the House of Lords it received a severe setback.[21] The Lords affirmed that whether or not the exemption clause covered the breach in question is always a question of construction. Accordingly it was possible for one party to exclude liability even where the breach was "fundamental", or "went to the root of the contract."

The principle of fundamental breach has received little judicial attention in Scotland. Lord Kincraig probably gave the correct opinion when he stated that "fundamental breach was not a term of art in Scots law". He suggested that it should be equiparated with the term "material breach."[22] So in Scots law it has always been possible for a clause to exempt liability, even for a fundamental breach. Three recent decisions by the House of Lords have restated the law in this area. In one of these cases Lord Bridge summed up

---

[18] *Pollock* v. *MacRae*, 1922 S.C. (H.L.) 192.

[19] see, *e.g. Smeaton Hanscomb & Co. Ltd.* v. *Sasoon L. Setty & Co. Ltd.* [1953] 1 W.L.R. 1478.

[20] see *Karsales (Harrow) Ltd.* v. *Wallis* [1956] 1 W.L.R. 936.

[21] *Suisse Atlantique Société D'Armement Maritime* v. *N.V. Rotterdamsche Kolen Centrale* [1967] 1 A.C. 361; [1966] 2 W.L.R. 944; [1966] 2 All E.R. 61.

[22] *Alexander Stephen (Forth)* v. *J. J. Riley (U.K.) Ltd.*, 1976 S.L.T. 269.

the position when he said that the House of Lords had "forcibly evicted" fundamental breach from the law.[23] Because those decisions were taken against a backdrop of new statutory provisions which came into force in the 1970s, we shall defer examination of the present state of the common law until consideration of the statutory controls.

REGULATION UNDER STATUTE

Until 1973 statutory intervention on the topic of exemption clauses was haphazard. Usually a statutory provision was enacted to deal with a specific matter which was regarded as giving rise to concern. To take one example, it was provided that the user of a road vehicle could not exclude liability for negligence which resulted in personal injury or death to a passenger in the vehicle.[24] This put an end to the practice of drivers sticking notices on dashboards which sought to exempt the driver from liability for damage caused to any passenger in the vehicle.

THE SUPPLY OF GOODS (IMPLIED TERMS) ACT 1973

The Supply of Goods (Implied Terms) Act 1973, which implemented the proposals of the Law Commissions' first joint report on Exemption Clauses,[25] covered contracts for the supply of goods, in particular sale of goods and hire-purchase. It had become common for sellers in contracts for the sale of goods to exempt themselves from the standard terms implied into such contracts by the Sale of Goods legislation. New controls were thought necessary to prevent this and it was also thought desirable that the law relating to hire-purchase was brought into line with that of sale of goods. Accordingly terms attempting to exempt a seller's obligations in respect of title were made void. Terms which sought to exempt a seller's obligations in respect of correspondence with description or sample, and quality or fitness for purpose were made void in the case of consumer sales, and made subject to a reasonableness test in other instances.

Example: Font Ltd. supply bathroom suites to both private

---

[23] *George Mitchell (Chesterhall) Ltd.* v. *Finney Lock Seeds Ltd.* [1983] 2 A.C. 803; [1983] 2 All E.R. 737.

[24] Road Traffic Act 1972, s. 148(3).

[25] (1969) Law Com. No. 24; Scot. Law Com. No. 12.

and trade customers. Font sells a bath to Alf and six bidets to Alf's brother-in-law Sid, who is a builder currently involved in converting a large house into flats. The bidets do not belong to Font and the bath delivered to Alf has a large crack in it. Any attempt by Font Ltd. to exempt its liability to Alf and Sid is void. If the bath had been supplied to Sid the question would be whether it was fair and reasonable for the term to be inserted.

So far as sale of goods is concerned these provisions now appear in the Sale of Goods Act 1979 which consolidated the earlier statutory provisions.

THE UNFAIR CONTRACT TERMS ACT 1977

Whilst the first report of the Law Commissions had tackled a particular problem in contracts for the supply of goods, it did not deal with the more widespread problem of exemption clauses. Such clauses were to be found in almost every species of contract. This was the subject of their Second Report on Exemption Clauses.[26] The two Commissions were in broad agreement as to the nature of law reform in this area but there were some differences between them and this is reflected in the 1977 Act. Part I applies to England and Wales, Part II to Scotland and Part III to all of the U.K.

It should be emphasised at the outset that the title of the Act is a misnomer. It does not cover all unfair contract terms, only exemption clauses. Originally it was to be called the "Avoidance of Liability Act", which would have come closer to the mark. Its main purpose was described in Parliament to be "to strengthen the protection for consumers against the mischievous use of small print." In brief, the 1977 Act regulates the use of exemption clauses by business parties. Some exemption clauses are declared void; others are subject to a "fair and reasonable" test.

The Scope of the Act

The provisions of the 1977 Act apply to a variety of contracts: contracts for the sale and supply of goods, contracts to enter upon land, employment contracts and contracts for services.[27] These contracts are the most common ones in which exemption clauses appear. To take some examples which are subject to the Act, it

---

[26] (1975) Law Com. No. 69; Scot. Law Com. No. 39.
[27] Unfair Contract Terms Act 1977 (hereinafter "1977 Act"), s. 15.

covers contracts to (i) park a car; (ii) attend a sporting venue; (iii) have an item repaired; and (iv) deposit luggage. But the 1977 Act does not apply to contracts of insurance, nor to contracts relating to the formation or dissolution of a company or partnership.

The 1977 Act not only covers clauses which actually appear in a written document, but also to notices.[28] Before the Act was amended in 1990, it was only contractual notices which were covered by its controls. Such notices are to be found in restaurants, hotels and dry-cleaners. Non-contractual notices have now also been brought within the ambit of the 1977 Act.[29] Such notices often accompany information or professional advice proferred by a person in a non-contractual setting. For example, a surveyor providing a house report to a building society has no contract with the prospective purchaser. However, the purchaser will usually learn of the contents of the report and rely upon it in determining whether or not to buy the house. An attempt by the surveyor to exclude liability is now capable of being struck down under the 1977 Act.[30] An example is provided by *Melrose* v. *Davidson & Robertson*[31]:

> Mr and Mrs Melrose wished to purchase a house in Rumbling Bridge. They sought a loan from the Alliance Building Society. They completed an application form which contained a statement that the Society would obtain a valuation of the property. It also disclaimed liability for the contents of the report on the part of the society and the valuers. A report was obtained and the house purchased. Subsequently, Mr and Mrs Melrose claimed damages for alleged negligence. The surveyors contended that the disclaimer exempted them from liability. It was held by the First Division that there was a contract for the provision of a report, that the 1977 Act applied and that the surveyors were not entitled to the benefit of the disclaimer.

Types of Clause

The commonest clauses are those which expressly seek to exclude or restrict liability. We have already given some examples of such

---

[28] 1977 Act, s. 25 (3) (*d*), (4).

[29] Law Reform (Miscellaneous Provisions) (Scotland) Act 1990, s. 68.

[30] *Smith* v. *Eric S. Bush* [1990] 1 A.C. 831; [1989] 2 W.L.R. 790; *cf. Robbie* v. *Graham & Sibbald*, 1989 S.L.T. 870; 1989 S.C.L.R. 578 (decided prior to the amendment to the Act).

[31] 1993 S.L.T. 611.

clauses at the beginning of this chapter. To ensure that other devices are not used to circumvent the 1977 Act, its scope is widened to include other attempts to hinder or prevent one party's right to pursue his normal legal remedies:[32]

— "Refunds must be accompanied by a receipt."
— "The purchaser's claim shall be restricted to damages and he shall not be entitled to sue for delivery."
— "Any claim relating to this contract must be made within fourteen days of the date hereof."

Business

The 1977 Act only applies to the attempted exclusion of liability by businesses. For the purpose of the Act, "business" covers most forms of enterprise: companies, firms, professionals, sole traders as well as government and local authority departments.[33] The only clear exception is individuals acting in a personal capacity.

Clauses invalid not prohibited

When exemption clauses are declared void it means they are deprived of legal effect. The 1977 Act does not prohibit such clauses being inserted into contracts. It simply provides that they cannot be relied upon in the event of a claim for damages arising.

Liability for "Negligence"

The 1977 Act talks about "breach of duty". That term is designed to refer to one party's liability for breach of a contractual term and for delictual liability. It is, however, rather unwieldy and in most instances simply means "negligence". We shall use "negligence" in preference to "breach of duty" in our discussion of the Act's provisions.

The Primary Controls

Death or Personal Injury

Parliament took the view that there was no justification for allowing businesses to avoid liability where their negligence had occasioned death or personal injury.[34] In the past, as we have seen, an exemption clause in a ticket or other contractual document could exculpate a party from all liability, even where the negligent act had resulted in death. After 1977 such terms are void and of no effect.

---

[32] 1977 Act, s. 25 (3) (a), (b) and (c).
[33] 1977 Act, s. 25 (1).
[34] 1977 Act, s. 16.

Economic loss

Negligence on the part of one party will often give rise to financial loss rather than to death or personal injury. This is particularly true of contracts for services. If dry-cleaners negligently clean your garment it is more likely that you will suffer financial loss because your garment is ruined, rather than that you will be injured by getting a skin inflammation. Similarly, if a solicitor or architect does not take reasonable care, the loss sustained by a client will normally be a pecuniary one. Under the 1977 Act clauses which attempt to evade liability for financial loss are not automatically void. Rather they are subject to a "fair and reasonable" test. If the court thinks they are justified in the circumstances, such clauses will be upheld. Otherwise they will not be given effect. It has, for example, been held that it is not reasonable for a photographic developing company to exclude liability in respect of films deposited with it for processing which are lost or damaged as a result of its negligence.[35]

Liability for Breach of Contract not Involving Negligence

Many breaches of contract are not concerned with "negligence". A builder does not complete a house extension on time, a coach tour goes to a different destination from that advertised, a wedding photographer fails to turn up at the church, a plumber uses different fittings from those specified in his tender. In each of these cases one party has failed to fulfil his contractual obligations, but the breach has not necessarily occurred as a result of negligence. There may be no duty of care between the parties. The controls in the 1977 Act here apply to exemption clauses in two types of contract: consumer contracts and standard form contracts.[36] In both cases the test of fairness and reasonableness is used.

Consumer contracts

The term "consumer contract" is defined in the 1977 Act.[37] It is a contract where (a) one party deals in the course of a business; and (b) the other does not; and (c) in contracts involving the transfer of ownership or possession of goods, the goods are of a type ordinarily supplied for private use or consumption.

> *Example*: Oswald is keen to begin windsurfing. He goes to his local shop and books a series of lessons from its instructor. In

---

[35] *Woodman* v. *Photo Trade Processing Ltd.*, noted in (1981) Scolag 281.
[36] 1977 Act, s. 17.
[37] 1977 Act, s. 25 (1).

addition he orders a beginner's windsurfing board. The shop switches the lessons from Saturdays to Sundays and delivers a seagoing surfboard for advanced users. Oswald asks for his money back, but the shop points him to a clause which appears in the two contracts he has made with it. The clause attempts to relieve the shop from liability in the event (i) that there is any change in the instruction arrangements and (ii) where the board supplied does not conform to the one ordered. The clause is subject to the "fair and reasonable" test.

Standard form contracts

Standard form contracts are not defined in the 1977 Act. It was thought that, however the definition was drawn, there would always be a danger of evasion. Clever draftsmen would draft around the definition. In the debate in Parliament it was suggested that judges recognised such contracts when they saw them. Common features of such contracts are that they are prearranged, not subject to negotiation and offered to everyone with whom the business deals.[38] Where a transaction is made using a standard form contract the provisions of the 1977 Act apply. This applies even where the recipient of the standard form is a business.

> *Example*: Easiclean Windows arrange to clean the windows of a large office building owned by Bright Ltd. Easiclean make the contract with Bright on its own standard form in which it seeks to exempt liability for any damage to the windows and the stonework of the building. If damage does occur and Easiclean seek to rely on the clause, Bright can challenge its validity under the 1977 Act. It will then be subject to the fair and reasonable test.

In the case of consumer and standard form contracts, the fair and reasonable test applies not only to exemption clauses but also to clauses which allow a party (a) to render no performance or (b) to render a performance substantially different from that which the other party reasonably expected from the contract.[39] So in the example above, an attempt by Easiclean to evade liability for breach if it fails to turn up to clean the office windows, or to use automatic sprinklers instead of trained window cleaners, would be caught under the 1977 Act.

---

[38] see *McCrone* v. *Boots Farm Sales*, 1981 S.L.T. 103.
[39] 1977 Act, s. 17 (1) (*b*).

The Fair and Reasonable Test

Clearly the "fair and reasonable test" is of key significance in applying the 1977 Act. A number of points can be made about it:
  (a) The onus is on the party seeking to rely upon the clause to show that it is fair and reasonable.[40]
  (b) Whether the clause was fair and reasonable is determined at the time the contract was made, not with regard to the subsequent events which have occurred.[41]
  (c) In the case of limitation clauses the court must have regard to
      (i) the resources open to the party seeking to rely on the term;
      (ii) how far he can cover himself by insurance.[42]
So far as exemptions from the implied terms in sale and supply of goods are concerned, the fair and reasonable test is elaborated even further.[43] In such cases the courts are directed to consider:
1. the parties' relative bargaining positions;
2. whether an inducement was offered to accept the exemption clause or other offending term;
3. whether the customer knew or ought to have known of the term;
4. in the case of conditional terms, the likelihood of the condition not being complied with; and
5. whether in the case of supply of goods the goods were specially made for the customer.
It is likely that the courts would have these factors in mind when considering other situations where the fair and reasonable test applied.

Three illustrations of the test can be provided. First, a power boat was supplied which was a total loss within 27 hours of delivery as a result of electrical defects.[44] A clause seeking to exempt the sellers was held not to be fair and reasonable. Secondly, a man who had deposited a suitcase worth over £300 was held entitled to recover full compensation from British Rail when the suitcase disappeared, despite a limitation clause which attempted to restrict their liability to £27.[45] This clause was held not to be reasonable since the suitcase had disappeared whilst in British Rail's control. The third illustration provides an example of a clause which was

---

[40] 1977 Act, s. 24 (4).
[41] 1977 Act, s. 24 (4) (10).
[42] 1977 Act, s. 24 (3).
[43] 1977 Act, s. 24 (2) and Sched. 2.
[44] *Rasbora* v. *UCL Marine* [1977] 1 Lloyd's Rep. 645.
[45] *Waldron-Kelly* v. *British Rail*, 1981 C.L.Y. 303.

held to be fair and reasonable.[46] It was a clause inserted into a contract for the repair of a ship designed to exempt the shipowners from various types of loss. It was decided that their attempt to exclude liability for loss was not unfair or unreasonable given that the two parties were of equal bargaining strength.

Further Controls

In order to prevent draftsmen using devices to avoid the implication of the 1977 Act controls, the Act itself specifies that it is not possible to evade its provisions by means of a secondary contract. Manufacturer's guarantees and indemnity clauses are also regulated.[47] Nor is it possible to attempt to avoid the negligence provisions of the 1977 Act by defining the obligations undertaken rather than exempting liability for breach of duty.[48] Suppose the owner of a sports stadium sought to exempt himself from liability to spectators using the premises. Instead of inserting an exemption clause in respect of negligent acts by himself and his employees, he might state that his sole obligation under the contract was to provide a spectator with a seat with a reasonable view of the event. Under the 1977 Act this would not exempt him from his liabilities. Finally, it is not possible to use a "choice of law" clause to evade the operation of the 1977 Act.[49] This prevents parties from inserting a clause such as "this contract shall be subject to the law of Burkina Faso as administered by the courts in Ouagadougou" to circumvent the Act.

Negligence—the Defence of Consent

It is a complete defence to a delictual action if it is proved that the injured person voluntarily assumed the risk of the harm that occurred. A person who deliberately interferes with an electrical socket which he knows to be faulty cannot claim compensation from the person responsible for the socket. This defence is called *volenti non fit injuria* (to he who consents no wrong is done). Because it denies the person harmed any compensation at all it is rarely a successful plea. Instead, the courts prefer to use the more flexible concept of contributory negligence, whereby blame can be apportioned between the parties and reflected in the amount of damages awarded. Recently, however, the House of Lords has

---

[46] *The Zinnia* [1984] 2 Lloyd's Rep. 211.
[47] 1977 Act, ss. 18, 19.
[48] 1977 Act, s. 25 (5).
[49] 1977 Act, s. 27.

affirmed that the defence of *volenti* will still be applied in appropriate circumstances.[50] An argument might be made that the negligence provisions of the 1977 Act would not apply where a person had his attention specifically drawn to the exemption clause at the time of contracting and consented to assume a particular risk. In order to guard against such an argument, the 1977 Act specifically provides that the fact that a person agreed to, or was aware of, the term would not of itself be sufficient evidence of voluntary assumption of risk.[51] Something more is required. As yet this provision has not been the subject of judicial scrutiny and it remains to be seen just how it will be construed.

> *Example*: A motor-racing circuit displays notices on its tickets and on conspicuous hoardings around the premises stating that neither the organisers nor the drivers accept any responsibility for any injury to spectators, howsoever occasioned. The 1977 Act means that such a clause will have no effect should a spectator be injured by, say, a car leaving the track and plunging into a grandstand in circumstances where it is shown that the owner or organisers have been negligent. But if the spectator himself leaps on to the track then any injury which results will probably not be the responsibility of the organisers or drivers.

The Common Law Position Since the 1977 Act

Three cases have restated the common law subsequent to the 1977 Act. In the first case, *Photo Production Ltd.* v. *Securicor Transport Ltd.*[52]:

> Securicor entered into an agreement to provide security inspection at a factory. One of their employees started a fire at the factory which resulted in loss totalling £615,000. He was subsequently convicted of arson. In an action by the factory owners to recover compensation for their loss, Securicor relied on a clause in their standard conditions under which their liability was totally excluded "unless such act or default could have been foreseen and avoided by the exercise of due diligence on the part of the Company."

[50] *Titchener* v. *British Railways Board* [1983] 3 All E.R. 770.
[51] 1977 Act, s. 16 (3).
[52] [1980] A.C. 827; [1980] 1 All E.R. 556.

When the case came before the Court of Appeal the doctrine of fundamental breach was applied and the plaintiffs were successful. Lord Denning M.R. put the position as follows:

"Securicor were not doing what they had contracted to do. They were doing the complete opposite. Whatever formula be taken from the various cases, it is plain that they cannot rely on the exemption or limitation clause . . . the breach was so fundamental that at that very moment (the throwing of the match on to the cardboard box) the contract was ended in respect of all further performance from that moment onwards and Securicor cannot rely on the exemption clause so as to escape the consequences of it."[53]

Shaw L.J. and Waller L.J. decided that on a true construction the exemption clause did not cover the situation which had occurred. In the House of Lords the decision of the Court of Appeal was reversed. To understand the decision, which, on the face of it, seems rather harsh, it must be remembered that the Unfair Contract Terms Act 1977 was already on the statute book, although it did not apply to the facts in this case. Delivering the leading speech, Lord Wilberforce reiterated the view that it was always a question of construction whether or not an exemption clause applied. If parties expressed themselves clearly and unambiguously, liability could be excluded even for a total breach of contract. He indicated that fundamental breach had been developed as a means of protecting the weaker party in circumstances where it was felt that he had made an unfair bargain. Now that the courts had been given statutory powers to control exemption clauses, the Lords seem to have felt that, as between business parties, a return to freedom of contract was justified. Here the cost of each visit by Securicor worked out at about 26 pence. To hold it liable would have meant it would have had to provide insurance (or be its own insurers) for all the myriad properties which it protected. This would have had the consequence of raising Securicor's charges to all its clients. As the factory owners were in a better position to know the exact value of their property they were the best and cheapest insurers. At one level the decision can therefore be regarded as being about the most efficient allocation of risk.

The second of the trio of cases was a Scottish case, *Ailsa Craig Fishing Co. Ltd.* v. *Malvern Fishing Co. Ltd. & Anr.*[54]:

---

[53] [1978] 3 All E.R. 146 at p. 152 (C.A.).
[54] 1982 S.L.T. 377; [1983] 1 All E.R. 101; [1983] 1 W.L.R. 964.

Two fishing boats were tied up together in Aberdeen Harbour
on New Year's Eve 1971. When the tide rose the bow of one of
the boats was caught under the deck of the quay and it sank,
fouling and sinking another boat in the process. Securicor had
been engaged to patrol the harbour to provide against the risk
of just such an event occurring. Unfortunately its employees
seem to have been celebrating the New Year themselves and
accordingly the accident to the vessels was not discovered until
too late. Securicor relied on a clause in the contract limiting its
liability to £1,000 in respect of any one claim and £10,000 in
respect of total claims arising out of any one incident.

Without a great deal of discussion this clause was accepted by the
House of Lords as effective. It was, however, noted that the courts
would approach limitation clauses slightly differently from clauses
which totally exempted liability:

> "Clauses of limitation are not regarded by the courts with the
> same hostility as clauses of exclusion; this is because they must
> be related to other contractual terms, in particular to the risk
> to which the defending party may be exposed, the remune-
> ration which he receives and possibly also the opportunity of
> the other party to insure."

The development of the common law was rounded off by the case
of *Mitchell* v. *Finney Lock Seeds* and one cannot do better than
quote from Lord Denning's own judgment to indicate the change
which had occurred:

> "Before the decisions of the House of Lords in the two
> *Securicor* cases, I would have been . . . 'hostile' to the clause
> . . . but in the light of the House of Lords cases, I think that
> that approach is not available . . . To my mind these two cases
> have revolutionised our approach to exemption clauses."[55]

These three cases show a return to a "hands-off" approach by the
courts. Business parties are given freedom to negotiate their own
terms with which the court will not interfere. Today fundamental
breach is effectively dead. Now that the statutory controls of the
Unfair Contract Terms Act 1977 are in place it is no longer
necessary for the judges to engage in artificial and difficult ques-

---

[55] [1983] 2 A.C. 803; [1983] 2 All E.R. 737 (H.L.); [1983] 1 All E.R. 108 at p. 113
(C.A.).

tions of interpretation as to whether a breach is or is not "fundamental".

SUMMARY

In determining whether or not an exemption clause is to be given effect the following route must be taken:

I. Common law controls

(a) Decide whether the exemption clause is incorporated into the contract. It will be incorporated if:
1. The contract has been signed by the party against whom it is designed to operate.
2. Attention is specifically drawn to the term (whether in a notice or otherwise) before the contract is concluded.
3. There is writing and it is known that the writing contains conditions. (This is presumed in contracts of carriage and deposit although the presumption is not a strong one.)
4. (Assuming none of the above apply.) If reasonable notice has been given. Whether such notice has been given or not will depend on the nature of the contract, the terms of the clause and the attempt made to bring it to the attention of the other party.
5. If there has been a consistent course of dealing between the parties.

(b) Decide whether the clause applies to the facts which have arisen.

II. The 1977 Act controls

Check
1. contract of a type covered by Act,
2. that the party seeking to exclude liability is a business,
3. the type of liability involved,
4. whether the fair and reasonableness test is satisfied.

THE LEGAL CONTROL OF EXEMPTION CLAUSES IN CONTRACTS

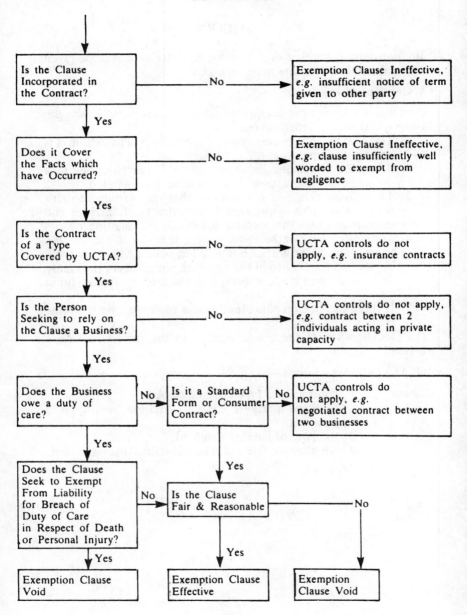

CHAPTER 8

BREACH OF CONTRACT

THE TERMS of the contract determine the obligations owed by the parties to one another. Breach of contract occurs when a party breaks one or more of those terms. Breach can occur in a number of ways:

> *Example*: Gas company A contracts to instal a central heating system in B's house.
>
> 1. A telephones B a week before the work is due to begin and informs B that it will not do the job because it has found more profitable work elsewhere. (*Anticipatory Breach*)
> 2. A fails to turn up on the due date. (*Failure to Perform*)
> 3. A instals the system in such a manner that it seriously damages the fabric of B's house. Moreover, the system itself does not work. (*Defective Performance*)
> 4. A takes an unreasonably long time to complete the job. (*Failure to Perform Timeously*)

In each instance, A fails to fulfil its obligations under the contract. For the sake of convenience, throughout this chapter we shall refer to the party faced by a breach of contract (in the example, B) as the innocent party.

When breach occurs, the innocent party is afforded a legal remedy. The nature of the remedies available to him depends upon the materiality of the breach. Materiality means the degree of importance or seriousness of the breach.

> "It is familiar law, and quite settled by decision, that in any contract which contains multifarious stipulations there are some which go so to the root of the contract that a breach of those stipulations entitles the party pleading the breach to declare that the contract is at an end. There are others which do not go to the root of the contract, but which are part of the contract, and which would give rise, if broken, to an action of damages."[1]

---

[1] *Wade* v. *Waldon*, 1909 S.C. 571 *per* L.P. Dunedin at p. 576.

The more serious the breach which has occurred, the greater the range of remedies open to the innocent party. It is one thing to deliver a Lada instead of a Rolls Royce, it is quite another to deliver a Rolls Royce with a slight scratch.

THE REMEDIES FOR BREACH

Rescission

A person faced by a breach of contract may wish to be released from the contract. If a supplier fails to deliver flowers to a hotel on time, the hotel may wish to rescind (that is, cancel) the agreement and obtain the flowers elsewhere. Rescission is the response to repudiation. Repudiation occurs where one party refuses to fulfil his contractual obligations. It is a form of material breach of contract. Courts are slow to hold that there has been repudiation:

" . . . it is a drastic conclusion which should only be held to arise in clear cases of a refusal, in a matter going to the root of the contract, to perform contractual obligations."[2]

It is important to note that repudiation of itself does not terminate the contract, because it is not open to one party unilaterally to declare the contract terminated. By rescinding the contract, the innocent party accepts that neither party requires to perform future obligations under the contract.[3] However, the contract may remain alive for some purposes. For example, certain debts may have accrued. Further, there may be an arbitration clause or a liquidate damage clause to regulate any dispute which has arisen. Accordingly, it is more correct to say that the effect of rescission is to terminate the innocent party's future obligations under the contract.

Two further points about terminology need to be made. First, in the case of sale of goods, a buyer's remedy faced by the seller's material breach is described in the Sale of Goods Act 1979 as to "reject the goods and treat the contract as repudiated."[4] Accordingly, should V receive a washing machine which fails to work, V is entitled to return the equipment to the shop (rejection) and to claim his money back (rescission). Secondly, "rescission" is some-

---

[2] *Woodar Investment Development Ltd.* v. *Wimpey Construction (U.K.) Ltd.* [1980] 1 All E.R. 571 *per* Lord Wilberforce at p. 576; [1980] 1 W.L.R. 277.
[3] *G.L. Group P.L.C.* v. *Ash Gupta Advertising Ltd.*, 1987 S.C.L.R. 149.
[4] S. 11 (5).

times used in a different sense. In the context of misrepresentation, a person induced to enter the contract through error may "rescind" the contract. In my view, it is preferable to avoid using the term "rescission" in this second sense. A person who decides not to go ahead with a contract because of the other party's misrepresentation should be said to have withdrawn (or resiled) from the contract. The term "reduction" is appropriate in the case of a contract judicially set aside on the ground of misrepresentation.

What amounts to Repudiation?

There is a narrow line between rescission and repudiation. In the case of *Wade* v. *Waldon*:[5]

> George Robey, a famous comedian of the time, contracted to appear a year later at two Glasgow theatres, the Palace and the Pavilion, for a one-week engagement. Shortly before his performances were due to take place, Robey looked in vain for advertisements for his show. He contacted the management. They informed him that the booking was cancelled. They referred to clause six of his contract which stated: "All artistes engaged . . . must give fourteen days' notice prior to such engagements, such notice to be accompanied by bill matter (publicity material)." He had omitted to provide such material. Robey offered to fulfil his engagement but the management refused. He pointed out that he had not given notice or "bill matter" for his last engagement, and sued them for £300. The defenders argued that breach of clause six was a serious one and they were entitled to rescind the contract. The court held that the failure to provide bill matter did not go to the root of the contract and found against the management. By refusing to allow Robey to appear, the management itself had repudiated the contract, thereby giving him a claim for damages.

Some writers have argued that this is a hard decision. Why should the management be forced to accept Robey without proper notice or advertising material? The answer may be that his fame was such that the theatre simply had to put up his name for an audience to appear. Further, the management had waived the requirement for bill matter in the past. It therefore seems that justice was done.

Two further cases underline the difficulties of determining who has repudiated the contract. In *Blyth* v. *Scottish Liberal Club* an employee refused to perform certain duties which he believed

[5] 1909 S.C. 571.

formed no part of the scope of his employment.[6] Although it was accepted that his belief was an honest one, it was held to be mistaken. Accordingly, his employers were entitled to terminate the employment as a result of his breach. His belief was unjustifiable in the circumstances. In *G.L. Group plc* v. *Ash Gupta Advertising*, an advertising company became concerned about the financial position of their clients.[7] They wrote seeking payment of all their work to date, together with a sum in respect of future work. The letter also stated that if payment was not received within twenty-four hours they "would have no alternative to resile from the contract." This was held to amount to repudiation.

Anticipatory Breach

In contracts where performance is due to take place at some future date, one party may indicate in advance that he is not going to fulfil his side of the bargain. He thus repudiates the contract before the time for performance arrives. This is known as anticipatory breach and leaves the innocent party with three options:
1. To rescind the contract and immediately sue for damages.
2. To wait until the time for performance has arrived (in case the other party changes his mind) then sue for damages.
3. To perform his side of the bargain and claim the contract price.

The third of these options has proved the most controversial. It is worth stressing that it is only a viable option in a limited number of cases. This is because firstly, contracts normally require the co-operation of both parties in order for performance to take place. If, for example, X repudiates a contract to have an extension built on to his house, the builder cannot enter on to the land and commence construction without X's permission. Secondly, few parties will wish to render a performance which is no longer desired. The builder will be unlikely to try to build the extension in the teeth of X's opposition. Exceptionally, however, the innocent party will not require the co-operation of the other party to fulfil his side of the bargain and will ignore the fact that performance is no longer required. The leading case on this topic is *White & Carter (Councils) Ltd.* v. *McGregor*[8]:

A representative from an advertising agency called at a garage to arrange a new advertising contract which was to last for

---

[6] 1983 S.L.T. 260; see now *Ghaznavi* v. *B.P. Oil (U.K.) Ltd.*, 1992 S.L.T. 924.
[7] 1987 S.C.L.R. 149.
[8] 1962 S.C. (H.L.) 1; [1961] 3 All E.R. 1178.

three years. Terms were agreed with the manager and the contract completed. Later the same day, the owner of the garage telephoned the agency to cancel the contract. The agency ignored the purported cancellation, continued with the contract and sued for the full contract price. By suing for a debt (the contract price) rather than for damages, the agency were thus able to avoid having to show that they had mitigated their loss. For the garage, it was argued that the proper course of action that the agency should have adopted was to sue for damages (if any) when the cancellation was notified.

An earlier Scottish case had held that the proper test in such situations was: what was the "reasonable and proper course" for the pursuer to take?[9] By a narrow 3:2 majority, the House of Lords overruled this view and held that the agency were entitled to succeed in this claim:

> "It might be, but it never has been, the law that a person is only entitled to enforce his contractual rights in a reasonable way and that a court will not support an attempt to enforce them in an unreasonable way. One reason why this is the law is no doubt because it was thought that it would create too much uncertainty to require the court to decide whether it is reasonable or equitable to allow a party to enforce his full rights under a contract."

Subsequent courts have been reluctant to follow the decision. Lord Denning said that he would only follow the decision in a case which was "on all fours with it."[10] Other judges have fastened upon Lord Reid's qualification that the innocent party can only perform where he has a "legitimate interest, financial or otherwise" to do so. It has been suggested that the question to be answered is whether the innocent party's conduct was merely "unreasonable" or "wholly unreasonable". Keeping a ship at anchor off Piraeus for seven months after an anticipatory breach was held to be wholly unreasonable.[11] A Scottish case has, however, reaffirmed the *White & Carter* approach[12]:

Tenants took a 34-year lease of premises on an industrial

---

[9] *Langford* v. *Dutch*, 1952 S.C. 15.
[10] *Attica* v. *Ferrostahl* [1976] Lloyd's Rep. 250.
[11] *The Alaskan Trader* [1984] 1 All E.R. 129.
[12] *Salaried Staff London Loan Co. Ltd.* v. *Swears & Wells*, 1985 S.L.T. 326.

estate. Five years into that lease, the tenants gave notice that they wished to renounce the lease. The landlord was held entitled to ignore this anticipatory breach. Only in exceptional circumstances, said the court, would it decline to enforce the legal rights of an innocent party. It was, however, noted that there might be cogent reasons for the landlord to accept the renunciation of the lease and sue for damages. In other words, he could not sit back and accept the rent from the tenants indefinitely without attempting to secure new tenants for the premises.

Retention and Lien

The breach may not be sufficiently material to justify rescission. In *Linn* v. *Shields*, a purchaser requested 12 stacks of corn to be delivered, payment on delivery.[13] He received 3 stacks but made no payment. In an action by him for the remaining 9 stacks, the seller was held entitled to withhold delivery, although it was observed that the breach was not sufficiently material to justify the seller rescinding. Alternatively it may be disadvantageous to the innocent party to rescind. Contracts of lease furnish a useful illustration. The tenant may wish to withhold payment of the rent until the landlord fulfils his obligation to keep the premises in good repair. He will often not wish to terminate the lease. Faced by breach, a person may withhold performance of his own obligations under the contract (retention) or retain possession of the other party's goods (lien). Retention and lien are ways of exerting pressure on the other party to perform his side of the bargain. A solicitor who has carried out work for a client may not wish to rescind when the client refuses to pay the fees. Instead he may refuse to carry out any further work he had agreed to do for the client. In addition, he may exercise a lien by holding on to documents such as title deeds or share certificates which belong to the client.

Lien is really a particular type of retention. It takes the form of holding on to property which should otherwise be delivered to the other party. A special lien arises when a person is employed to do work on specific goods belonging to another. For example, a garage may hold on to a car until the repairs that have been carried out have been paid for. Certain persons such as solicitors have a general lien over all documents in their hands against the balance of their account.

[13] (1863) 2 M. 88.

Action for Payment

The most common action which arises out of contract is a simple action for the payment of money. Where the contract price is not paid, the creditor will seek payment by way of an action to recover his debt. The creditor will be entitled to interest on the sum due. The date and rate from which interest will run will depend on the terms of the contract.

Specific Implement and Interdict

A person faced by breach may apply to the court to require the other party to fulfil his obligations under the contract. In the case of a positive obligation, the remedy is specific implement. Suppose D purchases an antique bureau at auction. Subsequently, the seller decides that she no longer wishes to sell the bureau and refuses to deliver it to D. D can raise an action concluding for specific implement of the contract of sale. In the case of a negative obligation the remedy is interdict. Take an example drawn from the law of options: E pays G £10,000 in return for an option to purchase G's factory on or before a date three years from the date of payment. Should G attempt to sell the factory to L before the time limit has expired, E may seek an interdict to prevent him from doing so. Failure to obey an interlocutor (*i.e.*, decree) pronouncing specific implement or interdict may amount to contempt of court and be visited by a fine or imprisonment.

Under Scots law, implement is in theory the primary remedy to which the innocent party is entitled.[14] In English law the primary remedy at common law was damages. The right to specific performance of a contract was an equitable remedy developed in the courts of Chancery. But Scottish courts retain an equitable power to refuse the remedy:

> "It appears to me that a superior court, having equitable jurisdiction, must also have a discretion, in certain exceptional cases, to withhold from parties applying for it that remedy to which, in ordinary circumstances, they would be entitled as a matter of course. In order to justify the exercise of such a discretionary power there must be some very cogent reason for depriving litigants of the ordinary means of enforcing their legal rights."[15]

---

[14] *Stewart* v. *Kennedy* (1890) 17 R. (H.L.) 1, 9–10 *per* Lord Watson.
[15] *Grahame* v. *Magistrates of Kirkcaldy* (1882) 9 R. (H.L.) 91.

Accordingly, although the two systems approach specific implement from opposite angles, in practice courts in Scotland and England will tend to grant or refuse the remedy in similar circumstances. Specific implement will be refused if there are "equitable grounds" or "good and sufficient grounds" for doing so. There are a number of situations where it is recognised that the innocent party has no right to implement:

    (a) A decree of specific implement cannot be obtained to enforce an obligation to pay money. Otherwise a debtor would be in contempt of court for defaulting in payment and liable to imprisonment.

    (b) The courts will not enforce contracts involving a personal relationship. It would be an undue restraint on personal liberty to compel persons to work together. The manager of the pop group "The Troggs" could not keep his post when the group members lost faith in him and sacked him.[16] Similarly, where the boxer Nigel Benn changed management and his original manager sought to prevent the new manager from inducing a breach of the original contract.[17]

    (c) The court will not grant decree if a decree could not be enforced, or if it is impossible for the party to fulfil performance under the contract.

    (d) Where the subject matter is of no special significance in itself and money compensation would be adequate specific implement will not be granted.

These exceptions mean that the remedy of specific implement is sought and granted less commonly than one might expect. It is frequently used to enforce restrictive convenants, which will be discussed in Chapter 10. However, its utility as a contractual remedy should not be ignored. It has been granted to enforce an agreement to oblige an electricity supply company to purchase coal from one supplier.[18] It is also used to enforce missives.

Damages

Every breach of contract gives rise to a claim for damages:

> "The contract and the breach of it are established. That leads of necessity to an award of damages. It is impossible to say that

---

[16] *Page One Records Ltd.* v. *Britton & Ors.* (t/a The Troggs) [1967] 3 All E.R. 822; cf. Employment Protection (Consolidation) Act 1978, s. 69.

[17] *Warren* v. *Mendy* [1989] 1 W.L.R. 853; [1989] 3 All E.R. 103.

[18] *British Coal Corporation* v. *South of Scotland Electricity Board (No. 2)*, 1993 S.L.T. 38.

a contract can be broken even in respect of time without the party being entitled to claim damages—at the lowest, nominal damages."[19]

Despite this general right to damages, in the case of minor breaches, parties will rarely wish to undergo the financial (and sometimes emotional) outlay involved in vindicating their rights in a court of law. Suppose a customer has a complaint which is not satisfactorily dealt with by personal representation at the shop. He may well seek help from a newspaper consumer column or a trade association, rather than raise an action in the sheriff court.[20]

Causation

Before an award of damages can be made it must be established not only that there has been a breach, but that there is a direct causal link between the breach and the loss which has occurred. In *A/B Karlhamns Oljefabriker* v. *Monarch Steamship Co.*[21]:

> A charterparty was entered into for the transport of soya beans from Manchuria to Sweden. The contract included two clauses which provided (a) that the ship should be seaworthy, and (b) that it would not be a breach if the ship deviated, if required to do so by government. This second clause was inserted because the parties recognised the risk of war and thought there was a real chance that the ship might be requisitioned during the course of its voyage. Unknown to the shipowners, the ship was unseaworthy when it left port and it was delayed in both Colombo and Port Said to effect repairs. When it reached Britain it was detained by the government, war having broken out. The characters sought to recover from the owners the extra cost of transhipment of the soya beans from Glasgow to Sweden. The owners defended the action on the basis that the real cause of the extra cost was the act of the British government in requisitioning the ship. As the contract stated the government action was not to be a breach, no claim for damages could succeed.

The House of Lords rejected this argument and found that the dominant cause of the loss was the initial unseaworthiness of the ship. Without that, the ship would in all likelihood have arrived on

---

[19] *Webster* v. *Cramond Iron Co.* (1875) 2 R. 752 *per* L.P. Inglis at p. 754.
[20] Although there are simplified forms of procedure to deal with small claims in the sheriff court.
[21] 1949 S.C. (H.L.) 1.

time and avoided requisition by the government. Accordingly, the pursuers had established the link between their loss and the defenders' breach of contract and were entitled to damages.

The Measure of Damages

Every day, courts assess damages. However, "the assessment of damages is not an exact science."[22] It is easier to state the general principles than to determine the exact level of award in a particular case.

> " . . . the broad general rule of the law of damages [is] that a party injured by the other party's breach of contract is entitled to such money compensation as will put him in the position in which he would have been but for the breach."[23]

Damages are measured according to the loss suffered by the innocent party, not by reference to the gain made in consequence of the breach by the contract-breaker. In *Teacher* v. *Calder*[24]:

> A agreed to lend £15,000 to B to use in his business as a timber-merchant under an agreement which was to last 5 years. B agreed to keep at least £15,000 of his own money in the business during that period. B broke the contract and withdrew sums which he invested in a distillery where they earned lucrative profits. Damages were assessed by reference to A's loss, not by reference to the profits made by B.

Contract and Delict

In theory, the measure of damages in delict and contract are different. In the law of delict, compensation is designed to restore the injured party to the position which would have existed, but for the accident. In the law of contract, compensation is aimed at placing the innocent party in the position in which he would have been, had the contract been performed.

There are sound reasons for this distinction. The victim of a delict has no opportunity to determine the damages for which the wrongdoer should be responsible. A pedestrian cannot negotiate with a car driver before he is knocked down. He should receive an award which is intended to compensate him for all consequences reasonably foreseeable by the defender. The same is not true in

---

[22] *The Heron II* [1969] 1 A.C. 350, *per* Lord Upjohn at p. 425.
[23] *Ibid. per* Lord Wright at p. 18.
[24] (1898) 25 R. 661; (affd. on this point (1899) 1 F. (H.L.) 39).

contract. A party knows the background against which a contract is made. Accordingly, he can have an idea of what loss is likely to result if a breach occurs. Should a party (1) expect special loss to occur as a result of breach, and (2) wish to receive indemnification for that loss from the other party, then he should notify the other party at the time the contract is made. In the absence of such stipulation the assessment of damages is that which naturally and directly flows from the breach.

The theoretical distinction between damages in contract and delict cases may be more apparent than real. In both, the pursuer will normally point to some concrete loss which he has sustained. That is the sum in respect of which compensation will be sought.

Remoteness

There are two brakes on the amount of damages to which the innocent party is entitled. First, there is the restriction imposed by the principle of remoteness. Every breach of contract gives rise to a multiplicity of consequences. The contract-breaker will not be held liable for all the consequences which flow from the breach:

> *Example*: Pedestrian A hires a taxi to go to the airport. The taxi fails to turn up, A misses his plane and loses the opportunity to make an important business deal at his proposed destination. Subsequently A's business goes bankrupt, his wife leaves him and so on.

The policy decision for the law to answer is, how far should the contract-breaker be responsible for the consequences of his breach? In general, a defender is not liable when the loss is "too remote". What is remoteness? Bankton said compensation was payable in respect of loss which "proceeds immediately from the thing itself."[25] But the *locus classicus* on this matter is the statement by Alderson B., in *Hadley* v. *Baxendale*, which is frequently referred to by the Scottish courts:

> "The damages . . . should be such as may fairly and reasonably be considered either arising naturally, i.e. according to the usual course of things, from such breach of contract itself, or such as may reasonably be supposed to have been in the contemplation of both parties at the time they made the contract as the probable result of the breach."[26]

---

[25] I.xi.15.
[26] (1854) 9 Exch. 341 at p. 354.

Note the two branches of the test:
1. It was a normal result, one involving knowledge imputed to everyone.
2. The parties were aware of special circumstances which made it a probable result.

Although the test itself is clear, it is not always easy to apply. A case which clearly illustrates the two branches of the test is *Victoria Laundry (Windsor) Ltd.* v. *Newman Industries Ltd.*[27]:

> A boiler was ordered by the plaintiffs who operated a laundering and cleaning business. It was delivered 20 weeks late. The plaintiffs sought to recover damages in respect of lost business profits for the period during which they should have had the use of the boiler. The defendants knew the purpose for which the boiler was to be used. They also knew it was required as soon as possible. They were not informed specifically, however, regarding the loss of profits which might occur if there was a delay in delivery. These comprised (a) a large amount of profits drawn from the new business "the demand for laundry services at that time being insatiable", valued at £16 per week, and (b) highly lucrative government dyeing contracts valued at £262 per week.

The trial judge accepted the argument for the defendants that under the rule in *Hadley* v. *Baxendale* the loss of profits was not recoverable as it had not been notified. In the Court of Appeal it was felt that this was too wide a view. It was held that damages would be recoverable for what a reasonable person would see as "likely" to result from the breach. Asquith L.J., delivering the judgment of the court, made a number of propositions regarding the award of damages including the following:

> "The aggrieved party is only entitled to recover such part of the loss actually resulting as was at the time of the contract reasonably foreseeable as liable to result from breach."

Reasonable foreseeability is the test used in the law of delict. Accordingly, implicit in Asquith L.J.'s statement was the notion that the cut-off point, the point beyond which damages are not recoverable because they are too "remote", was the same in contract and delict. The House of Lords considered this question in

---

[27] [1949] 2 K.B. 528; [1949] 1 All E.R. 997.

The Heron II (*Czarnikow Ltd.* v. *Koufos*).[28] A delay in the delivery of a shipment of sugar resulted in the charterers achieving a lower price for the sugar at market. The charterers argued, following *Victoria Laundry*, that this loss was reasonably foreseeable, whereas the shipowners claimed that the loss was too remote. All the Lords disagreed with Asquith L.J.'s approach, insofar as it appeared to suggest that the test for remoteness in delict and contract was the same. Lord Reid suggested rather that the proper test of remoteness in contract should be "not unlikely". Others of their Lordships took different approaches. Lord Morris suggested that the phrases "liable to result", "likely to result" or "not unlikely to result" could be used interchangeably. Lord Hodson thought "liable to result" could not be improved upon and Lord Pearce agreed. Lord Upjohn adopted the test of "real danger" or "serious possibility". This plethora of tests all arrived at the same result, namely that the shipowners were liable, as they should have contemplated that their breach—the delay in delivering the sugar—could cause the type of loss which actually occurred.

It did not, however, leave the law in a settled form. If anything, the speeches in *The Heron II* muddied the waters further. A reading of the subsequent case of *H. Parsons (Livestock) Ltd.* v. *Uttley Ingham & Co. Ltd.* confirms this suspicion.[29] Orr and Scarman L.JJ. held in that case that it must have been within the contemplation of the parties as a serious possibility that a defective feeding device for pigs might occasion injury to the pigs. Lord Denning M.R. on the other hand, believed that where physical damage was concerned the test was the same in contract and tort, despite the dicta in *The Heron II*. A recent Scottish example of remoteness is provided by *Balfour Beatty* v. *Scottish Power plc*[30]:

> In 1985 Balfour Beatty were engaged in constructing a bypass road to the west of Edinburgh. The works included the construction of an aqueduct to carry the Union canal across the bypass. Both the roadway and the aqueduct were made of concrete. In order to mix the concrete a site was obtained nearby at a quarry near Ratho. The site was supplied by the predecessors of Scottish Power, the South of Scotland Electricity Board. The aqueduct required a long continuous supply of concrete for the first stage of its construction. When the

---

[28] [1969] 1 A.C. 350.
[29] [1978] Q.B. 791; [1978] 1 All E.R. 525.
[30] 1992 S.L.T. 810; 1993 SLT 1011. This case is on appeal to the House of Lords.

stage was almost complete, the electricity supply was interrupted. In consequence, the first stage had to be demolished and reconstructed. Balfour Beatty sued for breach of contract and concluded for payment of damages of £229,102.53. Lord Clyde held (a) that S.S.E.B. were in breach of contract; but (b) that the loss claimed was too remote. S.S.E.B. were not informed nor could they have been otherwise aware that a continuous pour of concrete was required for a particular operation and that reconstruction would be required if the electricity supply failed. Lord Clyde therefore made no award. On appeal that decision was revered by the Second Division. They held that it was not necessary for S.S.E.B. to forsee the precise damage which occurred. It was enough that the type of consequence was within their contemplation.

Damages for non-pecuniary loss

Breach of contract normally involves loss measurable in money terms. The innocent party is hit in the pocket. As contracts are concerned with economic transactions, it was for a long time impossible to obtain damages for non-pecuniary loss. So if an employee was wrongfully dismissed in humiliating circumstances he could not recover compensation in respect of the injured feelings which he suffered.[31] Such loss was too remote. He could only recover in respect of his lost wages.

In some contracts, however, the only or main loss which results is non-pecuniary. Authority is now available that such loss can be recovered. A wedding photographer who fails to turn up at the wedding to take the official photographs is thus liable in damages for the disappointment this causes.[32] Likewise when a holiday completely fails to live up to the claims made for it in the brochure and ruins the pleasure of the holidaymaker.[33] The proposition to be derived from these cases is that where the main purpose of the contract is to raise expectations of a non-pecuniary nature and breach occurs, damages are recoverable for the disappointment and injured feelings which result.

The principle has been extended to cover situations where it is a direct consequence of the breach that the innocent party will suffer trouble, distress and inconvenience. Most cases for professional negligence brought against solicitors are based upon delict and breach of an implied term. In many such cases, one head of damage will relate to trouble, distress and inconvenience.[34]

[31] *Addis* v. *Gramophone Co. Ltd.* [1909] A.C. 488.
[32] *Diesen* v. *Samson*, 1971 S.L.T. (Sh.Ct.) 49.
[33] *Jarvis* v. *Swan's Tours Ltd.* [1973] 2 Q.B. 233; [1973] 1 All E.R. 71.
[34] *Cf. Hayes* v. *Charles Dodd* [1990] 2 All E.R. 815.

Mitigation of loss

A second brake on the award of full compensation is the principle of mitigation of loss. Faced by a breach of contract, the innocent party is expected to take whatever steps are available to him to reduce or minimise the loss. He is expected to act like a prudent person following the dictates of common sense. If possible he must attempt to stem the dimensions of the loss. He does not have to go to great or extraordinary lengths to minimise; the onus of proof is on the contract-breaker to show that the other party has not mitigated. So a person who breached a contract to ship goods to Canada was liable to pay the costs of shipping by another route at four times the cost unless he could show that another, cheaper method was available.[35] The legal principle is that the innocent party cannot recover a greater sum by way of damages than if he had taken those steps. In a contract for sale of goods, for example, if a buyer wrongfully refuses the goods then the measure of damages is *prima facie* to be ascertained by the difference between the contract price and the market or current price at the time or times when the goods ought to have been accepted.[36] So a grain merchant must attempt to sell the goods to another buyer if the original buyer under the contract refuses to pay for the goods and, if the price he achieves is the same or higher, only nominal damages are recoverable.

The Measure of Damages Seen from a Different Viewpoint

Some writers believe that damages can be more appropriately analysed by breaking down a party's loss into three types: restitution, reliance and expectation of loss. One case, *McRae* v. *Commonwealth Disposals Commission*, graphically illustrates these three types of loss.[37]

> After the Second World War, McRae bought from the defendants the wreck of an oil tanker which was said to lie beside the Jourmaund Reef. He fitted out a vessel to salvage the wreck, hired a crew and proceeded to the supposed location of the wreck. No wreck was found. McRae sought damages in respect of the following losses he had sustained.
> 1. The cost of purchasing the wreck from the defendants—£285 (*Restitution loss*).

---

[35] *Connal Connal & Co.* v. *Fisher Renwick & Co.* (1883) 10 R. 824.
[36] Sale of Goods Act 1979, s. 50 (3).
[37] (1951) 84 C.L.R. 377.

2. The cost of arranging a vessel and crew for salvage—
   c. £10,000 (*Reliance loss*).
3. The profit he would have made if the wreck had been there
   and he had successfully salvaged it—c. £250,000 (*Expectation loss*).

The court decided that the expectation loss was too speculative. Instead, it awarded McRae compensation in respect of his restitution and reliance interests. On the evidence, it decided that his actual expenditure was in the region of £3,000 rather than £10,000, and he received £3,285. Accordingly, he was not being put in the position which he would have been if the contract had been performed—only expectation loss would have done that. Instead, he was to be compensated for the loss to his pocket—the financial outlay he had sustained on the faith of the bargain. There has been no judicial recognition of this analysis in the Scottish courts, but it does perhaps provide a cross check against which the conventional method can be tested.

Contractually Stipulated Remedies

The parties may insert terms into the contract expressly providing what should happen in the event of breach. This provides much more certainty about the consequences of breach of contract. For example, an arbitration clause may be present, referring any disputes which arise to an arbiter. One party may seek to limit his liability by means of an exemption clause. A third device which is commonly used by contracting parties is to stipulate that a determinate amount should be payable by way of damages in the event of breach. Such clauses are perfectly legitimate and enforceable so long as they constitute a genuine pre-estimate of loss. They are then referred to as liquidate damage clauses. But if the clause is intended to punish the party in breach then it is invalid and unenforceable. A clause of that type is known as a penalty clause. The general tendency of the court is not to find that the clause is penal unless it is clearly exorbitant.

Penalty and Liquidate Damage Clauses

In distinguishing between penalty clauses and liquidate damage clauses, the courts have recourse to principles which were authoritatively set out in the leading case of *Dunlop Pneumatic Tyre Co.* v. *New Garage & Motor Co.* by Lord Dunedin.[38] The principles can be summarised as follows:

---

[38] [1915] A.C. 79 at p. 86.

1. The use of the term "penalty" or "liquidated damages" is not conclusive. In each case the court must determine whether the payment stipulated is in truth a penalty or liquidated damages.

2. A penalty is in essence designed to punish the offending party; the essence of liquidated damages is that the sum payable is a genuine pre-estimate of loss.

3. Whether a sum stipulated is a penalty or liquidated damages is a question judged at the time of the making of the contract, not at the time of the breach.

4. Various tests of interpretation are used by the courts in their task:

   (a) A clause will be held to be penal if the sum in question is extravagant and unconscionable.

   (b) A clause will be penal if the breach consists only in not paying a sum of money, and the clause stipulates for a sum greater than the sum which ought to have been paid.

   (c) A clause is presumed penal when "a single lump sum is made payable by way of compensation, on the occurrence of one or more or all of several events, some of which may occasion serious and other, but trifling, damage."

   (d) A sum will not be penal simply because the consequences of the breach cannot be estimated. Indeed "that is just the situation when it is probable that pre-estimated damage was the true bargain between the parties."

A useful illustration of the application of these principles is provided by the case of *Clydebank Engineering & Shipbuilding Co. Ltd.* v. *Castaneda*[39]:

Four torpedo boat destroyers were ordered by the Spanish government from a Scottish shipyard. Substantial sums were to be paid by way of damages in the event of the vessels being delivered late. The ships were delivered many months late but the shipyard declined to pay the sum stipulated. It alleged that the sum was penal and unenforceable because (a) Navy ships were not profit-making assets and accordingly there was no loss to the Spanish government, and (b) the remainder of the fleet had been sunk by the American Navy off Cuba shortly

[39] (1904) 7 F. (H.L.) 77; (1903) 5 F. 1016.

after the delivery date set in the contract. Accordingly, it was contended, no loss had been suffered.

Both these arguments were swiftly despatched by the court and the Spanish government awarded the sums claimed. It was noted that the yard had itself inserted the sums as a way of attracting the order for the vessels, that the clause had been inserted precisely because the quantification of loss was so difficult. It was also stated that if the destroyers had been delivered on time, the fleet might not have been sunk.

Liquidate damage clauses may operate in some instances to limit the liability of one party. This happens where the actual loss suffered is greater than that stipulated for in the contract. But there is a difference in the two types of clause. In a limitation clause the sum specified operates as a ceiling on damages. If the actual loss is lower, the sum recoverable is lower. Where there is a liquidate damage clause, the same amount is recoverable irrespective of whether the actual loss is greater or less than the sum specified in the clause.

Where a clause is held to be a penalty, there is Scottish authority to the effect that the actual loss is recoverable even when it is greater than the sum stipulated for in the penalty.[40] Here, the paradox is that the penalty clause is invalid because it "terrorises" the other party, yet the loss suffered is greater than that sum.

Irritancies

A common clause in leases is an irritancy clause. It provides that the landlord is entitled to irritate (i.e., terminate) the lease in the event of specified breaches by the other party. In a lease for a term of years, for example, it might be provided that if the tenant should default in his payment of the rent, the landlord should be able to irritate the lease. It is now provided by statute that the landlord's right to terminate depends upon his issuing a notice of default to the tenant.[41]

Other Clauses

Several other devices can be used to provide in advance what the remedy should be on the occurrence of a certain event. Examples are (1) acceleration clauses, where if one instalment is not paid time, the whole price becomes immediately payable; (2) forfeiture clauses, where if there is a breach the injured party forfeits his

---

[40] *Dingwall* v. *Burnett*, 1912 S.C. 1097.
[41] Law Reform (Miscellaneous Provisions) (Scotland) Act 1985, ss. 4–7.

deposit;[42] (3) non-breach clauses, where sums are stipulated to be payable otherwise than on the occurrence of breach;[43] and (4) retention clauses, where a percentage of the price is retained for a specified period to cover the cost of remedying any defective performance. In these cases, neither the rules as to penalty clauses nor the provisions of the Unfair Contract Terms Act 1977 apply. Accordingly, the parties will be bound by the terms of the clause.

Mutuality

The principle of mutuality means that the obligations under the contract are reciprocal in nature. Either both the parties are bound or neither is bound. Lord Justice Clerk Moncrieff provided the classic statement on this branch of the law:

> "I understand the law of Scotland in regard to mutual contracts to be quite clear—first, that the stipulations on either side are the counterparts and the consideration given for each other; second, that a failure to perform any material or substantial part of the contract on the part of one will prevent him from suing the other for performance; and, third, that where one party has refused or failed to perform his part of the contract in any material respect the other is entitled either to insist for implement, claiming damages for the breach, or to rescind the contract altogether—except so far as it has been performed."[44]

It is therefore necessary for the party seeking a contractual remedy to demonstrate that he himself is not in breach. He can only insist on performance by the other party if he himself has fulfilled his side of the bargain. In the case of *Graham* v. *United Turkey Red Company Ltd.*[45]:

> Graham entered into an agency contract in 1914, in terms of which he was to sell cotton goods manufactured by the United Turkey Red Company Ltd. Payment for his services was to be made on a commission basis. It was stipulated in the contract that he was not to sell other manufacturers' goods. From 1916 onwards, Graham was in breach of that term. In 1918, after a dispute, Graham terminated the agreement and sued for the balance of his commission for the whole period of the contract.

---

[42] *Cf. Zemhunt Holdings Ltd.* v. *Control Securities plc*, 1991 S.L.T. 653.
[43] *E.F.T. Commercial Ltd.* v. *Security Change Ltd.*, 1992 S.C.L.R. 706.
[44] *Turnbull* v. *McLean & Co.* (1874) 1 R. 730 at p. 738.
[45] 1922 S.C. 533.

The court held that he was only entitled to commission up to the time when he himself was still keeping faith with the agreement. The moment he began selling goods for other manufacturers, he lost his right to insist on performance by the United Turkey Red Company. After 1916 he was not fulfilling his side of the bargain so he could not require them to fulfil theirs. The mutuality of their bargain had ceased.

CHAPTER 9

TITLE TO SUE

EACH party to a contract acquires legal rights against the other. Persons who are not parties to the contract do not acquire rights or duties under it. In this respect a contract can be regarded as a private legislative arrangement between the parties. And this indeed is the general principle of the law—*res inter alios acta aliis nec nocet nec prodest* (a transaction between certain parties cannot advantage or injure those who are not parties to that transaction). Let us take an example: A is owed £100 by B who in turn is owed £100 by C; A cannot sue C for the £100 because he has no rights under the contract between B and C. It is not possible to sue one's debtor's debtor.[1] There are several important exceptions to this principle, *viz.* agency, assignation and *jus quaesitum tertio*.

AGENCY

Agency describes the relationship which arises when one person (the agent) is appointed to act as the representative of another (the principal). A variety of examples come to mind. The owners of a house instruct a solicitor to sell their house for them. A woman going abroad for a long time appoints her son to conduct her affairs for her during her absence. A foreign manufacturer retains a Scottish firm to sell its goods in the U.K.: in each of these cases, two different aspects of agency arise. First, it creates the contract of agency between the principal and the agent. Secondly, the agent can make contracts which bind his principal. This second aspect means that the principal acquires rights and duties under the contract. In other words, he becomes a party to the contract, even though he took no direct part in its formation. For this to occur, the agent must act within the four corners of the authority vested in him. If he acts without authority, then he alone is liable on the contract, unless the principal subsequently ratifies his act.

Example: Joe, Don and Fay are partners in an architects' firm. Fay agrees to purchase three sports cars for herself and her

---

[1] see *Henderson* v. *Robb* (1889) 16 R. 341.

partners. If the partnership deed grants Fay authority to do this, then the partnership must pay for the cars. Otherwise Fay alone is liable to pay the purchase price of the cars unless Joe and Don are prepared to ratify the purchase, in which case the firm must pay for the cars.

Where the agent is acting with authority, then normally only the principal acquires rights and duties under the contract. It is presumed that the other party intends to contract with the principal rather than the agent. The seller of a house intends to contract with the person who wishes to purchase the house, not the solicitor who has drafted and sent the formal offer. If the purchaser defaults in paying the price, the seller will sue him, not his solicitor. In two situations, however, the agent himself may be bound by the contract. This occurs where the agent either (a) does not disclose that he has a principal, or (b) does not divulge his principal's identity. In both cases the third party has a right of election—to sue the agent personally or to sue the principal (assuming that the latter's identity is disclosed). A bidder at an auction, for example, might refuse to state the identity of the client for whom he is bidding. If the bid is successful but the price is not paid within a reasonable time, the seller might opt to sue the bidder. The bidder will be personally liable on the contract of sale, although he has a right of recourse against his principal.

ASSIGNATION

Assignation is the process by which contractual rights are transferred to a third party. For instance, a person who orders a boat to be built might assign the right to receive the boat to another person. The transferor is known as the assignor (or cedent), while the transferee is known as the assignee. Most contractual rights are assignable when consent is given. The question of whether or not one party can assign his rights without the consent of the other party is more difficult. It depends to a large extent on the nature of the rights. Simple debts are assignable. Debt collection companies rely on this principle. It enables them to purchase bad debts from other businesses to pursue against the debtors. In other contracts, a distinction must be drawn between executed and executory contracts.

Executed contracts are those transactions where all that remains is for one party to pay the price or to transfer property. Such obligations are in general assignable.

Executory contracts are contracts where performance is yet to take place. Here, assignation can only take place either with consent of the other party or where no element of *delectus personae* (choice of person) is involved.

Suppose CV commissions a bust from RL, a sculptor: RL cannot arrange for someone else to do the work and demand the price. In the case of manufactured articles, assignability will depend upon whether or not the reputation and expertise of a particular manufacturer is relied upon. In one case, Lord President Dunedin instanced a contract for the purchase of a gun manufactured by Purdie.[2] He said this would not be satisfied by supplying a gun bought in the ordinary market at Birmingham. Each case will turn on its own merits. Where the goods can be made or the services supplied by anyone, the contractual rights are clearly assignable. Special rules apply to leases. Usually the lease itself will prohibit the tenant from assigning the lease. If the lease is silent, then there is a presumption against assignation, except in the case of urban leases for a term of years.

No particular form of words is required to assign a right.[3] It is enough that words are used which show that the assignor intended to transfer his particular rights under the contract to another person. Although assignation takes place between the assignor and assignee, intimation to the other party to the contract may be extremely important in perfecting the assignee's right. If, for example, a debtor pays his debt to the original creditor because he has not been informed that the debt has been assigned, he will be held to have discharged his obligation.

What is the assignee's right? He stands in the shoes of the cedent. All pleas available against the assignor are thus available against the assignee. The relevant Latin tag here is *assignatur utitur jure auctoris*—(an assignee exercises the right of his cedent). Where an insured allegedly made false statements in his proposal form for life assurance and then assigned the benefit of the policy, the insurance company was entitled to seek to reduce the insurance contract.[4] The assignees had no better right to the proceeds of the policy than the insured himself. If his statements were false, he (and in consequence the assignees) had no entitlement to benefit under the policy.

> "It appears to me to be long ago settled in the law of Scotland—and I have never heard of any attempt to disturb the

[2] *Cole* v. *Handasyde & Co.*, 1910 S.C. 68, 74.
[3] *Brownlee* v. *Robb*, 1907 S.C. 1302.
[4] *Scottish Widows' Fund* v. *Buist* (1876) 3 R. 1078.

doctrine—that in a personal obligation, whether contained in a unilateral deed or in a mutual contract, if the creditor's right is sold to an assignee for value, and the assignee purchases in good faith, he is nevertheless subject to all the exceptions and pleas pleadable against the original creditor."[5]

One of the legal effects of death and bankruptcy is to transfer all assignable rights and duties automatically to the executor or the permanent trustee in bankruptcy respectively. Accordingly, when a party to a contract dies, his rights pass to his representatives.

JUS QUAESITUM TERTIO

Jus quaesitum tertio is a right required by a third party literally, "the third party has acquired a right". Unlike English law, Scots law allows two parties to confer an enforceable right upon a third party who is not a party to the contract. The basis of the doctrine is to be found in a passage in Stair's *Institutions*:

> "It is likewise the opinion of Molina, cap. 263 and it quadrats to our Customs, that when Parties Contract, if there be any Article in favour of a third Party, at any time, *est jus quaesitum tertio*, which cannot be recalled by both the Contractors, but he may compel either of them to exhibit the Contract, and thereupon the obliged may be compelled to perform."[6]

Read literally, this passage implies that the third party's right is complete as soon as there is a provision in his favour in the contract. He can sue upon the contract as soon as it is made. It will also be seen that Stair identifies three aspects to this right:
1. the contracting parties cannot revoke the agreement;
2. the third party can compel the contracting parties to display the contract to him; and
3. the third party can enforce the provision in his favour.

The courts have been somewhat reluctant to allow the third party such extensive rights. They will only do so where that is the manifest intention of the contracting parties. This reluctance is understandable. In most instances of *jus quaesitum tertio*, the third party will be receiving a gift and there is a strong presumption

---

[5] *Ibid. per* L.P. Inglis at p. 1082.
[6] I.x.5.

against donation. The leading case is *Carmichael* v. *Carmichael's Executor*[7]:

> A father took out an insurance policy for £1,000 on the life of his eight-year-old son. The policy provided that the sum assured was to be paid on death to the son's executor's, providing he attained the age of 21 years and continued to pay the premiums. If the son died before attaining 21, however, the premiums were to be repaid by the insurance company to the father. Alternatively, he could surrender the policy for whatever value it had. The father duly paid the premiums and kept the policy in his possession, never delivering it to the son. Between his 21st and 22nd birthday and before the first premium payable by him was due, the son was killed in an air accident. He left a will leaving all his property to his aunt. In an action to determine whether the father or the aunt was entitled to the benefit of the policy, the father claimed that the son had not acquired a right to the proceeds of the policy. The contract, he said, was between him and the insurance company. The son would only acquire a right after he had paid the first premium due by him, or if the father had delivered or formally intimated that policy to the son. None of these things had happened. Despite these considerations, the House of Lords found in favour of the aunt.

The decision might suggest that the court adopted a broad view of the doctrine. Nothing could be further from the truth. The speech of Lord Dunedin considerably narrowed the doctrine. He suggested that in Stair's statement, the phrase *"est jus quaesitum tertio"* should be transposed with the words "which cannot be recalled by both the contractors." In other words, the insertion of the clause in the third party's favour was of itself not enough. In addition, it had to be shown that the contracting parties could not revoke their agreement. Delivery or intimation to the other party would be ways of evincing this intention, but in other cases it would be a question of interpretation. Here, the whole circumstances of the case pointed to an irrevocable intention having been formed. The terms of the policy clearly envisaged that the father's rights ceased after the son reached majority. Thereafter, the son could elect to continue the policy, or convert it into a different type of policy, or receive a cash benefit. Irrevocability, however, was no

[7] 1920 S.C. (H.L.) 195.

longer a consequence of the agreement, as Stair had stipulated, but rather a condition of the establishment of the right.

The right to revoke may not be an absolute bar to establishing the existence of a *jus quaesitum tertio*. In *Love* v. *Amalgamated Society of Lithographic Printers of Great Britain & Ireland*, a widow claimed sickness benefit in terms of her husband's trade union membership.[8] Although the right to benefit was revocable (the union rules could be altered at any time) it had not been so revoked at the time of his death. The widow was successful in her claim. This case is difficult to reconcile with *Carmichael* and is perhaps an apt illustration of the saying that hard cases make bad law, or at least law which is more difficult to state in a clear and rational way. In any event it does seem just to hold that the wife's right would only have been defeated if the union rules had been altered before her entitlement arose.

What, then, are the criteria to be satisfied to establish a *jus quaesitum tertio*? The parties must expressly state that the third party is to benefit. In *Morton's Trs.* v. *The Aged Christian Friend Society of Scotland*, the agreement was made between a benefactor and a provisional committee charged with the duty of setting up a charitable society.[9] The contract specifically stipulated that the benefactor was to pay annual instalments to the society, rather than to the provisional committee. This was described as "a clear instance of our doctrine of *jus quaesitum tertio*." Accordingly, the society was entitled to enforce its right to payment of the instalments outstanding on the benefactor's death.

It is not enough for the third party to show merely that a benefit was incidentally conferred upon him. There must be an express provision in favour of a third party (*pactum in favorem tertii*). In *Finnie* v. *Glasgow & South-Western Rly. Co.*, two railway companies agreed to fix the freight rate for the carriage of coal along a certain railway line.[10] When the railway companies varied the rate upwards, a person who transported freight along the line sought to enforce the companies' agreement. The action was unsuccessful. It was not a contract made for his benefit so he had no *jus quaesitum tertio*. Whether the requisite intention is present or not can be evinced in several ways:

1. by the nature of the original contract;
2. by the whole circumstances of the case;
3. by intimation or delivery of the contract.

[8] 1912 S.C. 1078.
[9] (1899) 2 F. 82.
[10] (1857) 3 Macq. 75.

In *Carmichael*, the son and indeed the whole family knew of the policy. Before joining the air force, he had contacted the insurers to check that military service was not inconsistent with the policy and he had spoken to his lawyer about it in relation to his will. An example of intimation is provided by the case of *Burr* v. *Commissioners of Bo'ness*.[11] A sanitary inspector had his salary raised at one council meeting. At the next meeting of the council this decision was revoked. As the original decision was never intimated to the inspector, it was held he had no right to receive the salary increase.

Rights of Enforcement

A *jus quaesitum tertio* can be enforced even if the original contracting parties no longer have an interest to sue. In *Morton's Trs.*, the provisional committee had become defunct once the charitable society had been founded. The third party may enforce the right even where one of the contracting parties can also sue on the contract. In *Lamont* v. *Burnett*, the purchaser of a hotel in Crieff, in addition to the purchase price of £7,000, offered to pay to the seller's wife "not less than one hundred pounds as some compensation for the annoyance and worry of the past few days, and for her kindness and attention to me on my several visits to Crieff."[12] This was accepted by the seller. It was held that this extra provision could be enforced by the wife and the view was expressed that the husband might also enforce the provision.

A doubt existed as to whether the *tertius* could sue for defective performance or only for total failure to perform.[13] That question has recently been considered in *Scott Lithgow* v. *G.E.C. Electrical Products Ltd.*[14]:

The Ministry of Defence commissioned Scott Lithgow's predecessors to build a new naval vessel, *H.M.S. Challenger*. The electrical work was sub-contracted to G.E.C. Electrical Products Ltd., which in turn sub-contracted some of the work to other sub-contractors. Defects developed in the wiring of the electrical equipment. The Ministry claimed that they had a *jus quaesitum tertio* arising out of the contracts between G.E.C. and the sub-contractors as they were expressly mentioned in

[11] (1896) 24 R. 148.
[12] (1901) 3 F. 797.
[13] see Gloag on *Contract* (2nd ed.) p. 239; *cf. Cullen* v. *McMenamin*, 1928 S.L.T. (Sh.Ct.) 2.
[14] 1992 S.L.T. 244.

those sub-contracts. They also claimed that they were entitled to seek damages from the "sub-sub-contractors" for defective performance.

After debate, Lord Clyde held that such a claim could exist and allowed the averments on this branch of the case to go to proof before answer. He stated:

> "In general I can see no reason why a third party should not be entitled to sue for damages for negligent performance of a contract under the principle of *jus quaesitum tertio*, but whether he is so entitled must be a matter of the intention of the contracting parties. That has to be ascertained from the terms of the contract."

The Status of *Jus Quaestium Tertio*

There have been relatively few cases of late dealing with *jus quaesitum tertio*. However, that does not mean it is without significance in Scots law. There is good sense in giving effect to contracting parties' intention to benefit a third party, if they make that intention sufficiently clear. For example, should a Building Society document contain a disclaimer which is intended to exclude liability on the part of a firm of surveyors, the surveyors should in principle be entitled to the benefit of that notice.[15] In England, there has been agitation since before World War II to have a similar principle adopted into their legal system. At present, English lawyers have to make elaborate use of artificial approaches based on trust law and collateral contracts to cover third party situations which arise.

JOINT AND SEVERAL LIABILITY

We have been examining circumstances where someone other than the parties themselves can sue upon the contract. It is convenient to discuss here the principles to be applied where more than one party is liable under a contract. A contract may involve undertakings by more than two parties. For example, if a man and woman jointly contract to purchase a flat, they will both be liable to the seller. In the event of default, the seller may choose to sue both prospective purchasers. However, suppose that the man has gone missing and

---

[15] *Melrose* v. *Davidson & Robertson*, 1992 S.L.T. 611, 614 (the provision was subject to the Unfair Contract Terms Act 1977).

cannot be traced. The seller is entitled to sue the woman alone for the whole account. This is referred to as joint and several liability. The liability is joint, in the sense that each obligant is liable for the whole amount to the creditor. It is several, in the sense that each has a right to seek to recover the contribution from the co-obligant. Accordingly, should the woman in the example pay the whole purchase price, she has a right of action against the man for his share, should he re-appear.[16]

In many situations in Scots law, joint and several liability will be expressed by the parties or be implied by law.[17] This occurs where, for example, the words "joint and several liability" are actually used, in guarantees, in partnership obligations, and in relation to bills of exchange.

> *Example*: Lender X lends money to Y after receiving an undertaking that Z will guarantee the sum. Should Y default in payment, Z is bound to repay the whole £100 to X and Z would then be entitled to recover any such payment from Y.

If the liability of the obligants is not joint and several, each co-obligant is only bound to the extent of his own proportionate (*pro rata*) share.

---

[16] *Moss* v. *Penman*, 1993 S.C.L.R. 374; *McGillivray* v. *Davidson*, 1993 S.L.T. 693.

[17] see *Wright* v. *Tennant Caledonian Breweries Ltd.*, 1991 S.L.T. 823.

CHAPTER 10

THE REQUIREMENT OF LEGALITY

A CONTRACT must be lawful both in its object and in its mode of performance. If either of these requirements is not satisfied, then the courts will decline to enforce the contract. Such contracts are referred to as illegal contracts (*pacta illicita*). The reference to illegality is misleading as it tends to suggest the commission of a crime, whereas the principle of contractual legality extends over a much wider field. A contract of slavery would not be enforced by the courts, but the mere making of the agreement is not a criminal offence. Indeed one of the curiosities of contract law is that the most important type of agreement classified under this heading, restrictive covenants, is one which is frequently seen as laudable and enforced rather than illegal and invalid.

The general principle is that no action arises out of an immoral situation (*ex turpi causa non oritur actio*). Neither party can enforce or claim damages for breach of an unlawful agreement. The unlawfulness does not need to be plead by the parties; it is the duty of the judge to take notice of an unlawful transaction.

> *Example*: A householder engages a plumber to carry out the replacement of the lead pipes and tank in his house. The works are eligible for grant assistance from the local authority. The parties agree that the plumber shall carry out various other repair works at the house and that he will artificially inflate the estimate for the lead replacement work in order to attract the maximum council grant. If a dispute arises and either party seeks to enforce the contract, they run the risk that the court will refuse to adjudicate on the matter. Both parties seek to defraud the local authority. Accordingly their contract is tainted by illegality. The Sheriff may even direct that the papers be sent to the Procurator Fiscal's office to consider whether a prosecution should be brought.

What Constitutes Unlawfulness?

Some contracts are forbidden by statute. Others are illegal at common law. It is possible for a particular agreement to be enforce-

167

able under both heads. The most important categories of unlawful contracts are as follows:

Contracts to commit a crime or delict

An agreement to commit a crime is not enforceable. It may also amount to conspiracy and be punishable under the provisions of the criminal law. Contracts to commit a delict are likewise unenforceable. It is clearly against public policy to uphold such bargains.

Contracts promoting sexual immorality

Contracts tending to promote sexual immorality are not upheld. It is thought undesirable to associate the law with such transactions. This can be illustrated by reference to a case beloved of generations of law students, *Hamilton* v. *Main*[1]:

> Hamilton sought to set aside a promissory note for £60 which he had granted to Main. Hamilton gave the note in payment of his account in respect of his sojourn at Main's public house. The evidence disclosed that Hamilton had resided there for seven days, together with a prostitute. During his stay they had purchased 113 bottles of "port and Madeira, besides a large quantity of spiritous and malt liquors".Hamilton claimed that he had granted the promissory note when he was intoxicated and that it had been induced by fraud and circumvention.

The First Division held that the promissory note could not be enforced. No reasons for the decision are given in the somewhat cryptic report of the case. It is probable that the bill was not enforced because such transactions were not to receive the approbation of the court. By depriving the landlord of his normal right to enforce the bill, the decision of the court deterred other landlords from countenancing such immoral arrangements. The dignity of the law should not be soiled by adjudicating upon disputes of this nature.

If there is an immoral purpose known to both parties, the courts will refuse to allow the parties to sue on the contract even where the bargain itself is perfectly legitimate. In *Pearce* v. *Brooks*[2]:

> A firm of coachbuilders agreed to hire a brougham carriage of "intriguing design" to a prostitute. They knew she was going to

---

[1] (1823) 2 S. 356.
[2] (1866) L.R. 1 Ex. 213.

use the carriage to ply her trade. She failed to pay the hire and the firm sued on the contract.

It was held that they could not succeed. The contract indirectly promoted sexual immorality and was therefore illegal. What constitutes immorality is changing. In older times, marriage broking contracts fell under this heading. Today, it is likely that the contracts which dating and marriage agencies enter into with their clients are enforceable, although the prudent broker might be wise to ask for the money in advance.

Contingency fees

It has always been the law of Scotland that lawyers are not entitled to accept contingency fees (*pacta de quota litis*) for their services. In other words, lawyers cannot agree to act in a case in return for a percentage of any sums successfully recovered for their clients. It is, however, possible to agree to act on the basis that the fees will be paid only if there is a successful outcome to the case. Such cases are referred to as speculative actions. Contingency fees are allowed in several other countries including the United States, where such feeling is a well-established practice. There is a perennial debate about contingency fees. Proponents argue that it enables lawyers to take the cases they would not otherwise handle. Opponents point to the high level of claims such fees engender. Stair said that the reason why contingency fees were prohibited in Scotland was to prevent "the stirring up, and too much eagerness in pleas."[3] In other words, contingency fees may lead a solicitor or advocate to become too personally involved in a case. This would remove the disinterested perspective which is of vital importance if the lawyer is to honour the paramount duty to justice.[4]

Contracts against public arrangements and justice

Arrangements which involve any element of corruption will be held unlawful. These include the purchase of honours such as knighthoods, together with contracts attempting to interfere with the processes of justice, such as an agreement to bribe a witness. When war breaks out, contracts with individuals or companies in the opposing state are in general invalidated. The foreign national is

---

[3] *Institutions*, I.x.8.

[4] In the only recent case on this matter, decree was granted finding that such arrangements were void. (*The Law Society of Scotland* v. *Quantum Claims Compensation Specialists and Frank Lefevre*, unreported ((1991) 36 J.L.S. 462)).

then deemed to be an enemy alien and it is against public policy to assist such persons.

Contracts in restraint of trade

This is the most important type of contract presumed to be unlawful. It will be discussed later in the chapter.

Declaring Contracts Unlawful

The courts have long asserted a power to declare contracts illegal at common law. Underlying the courts' intervention in this area is the notion of public policy. Is it in the interest of the community that a particular contract be struck down? Obviously, the greater the intervention of the courts, the more they will be seen to be legislating and thereby usurping the function of Parliament. After a lengthy period of judicial creativity, particularly in the nineteenth century, there has been a tendency for the courts to avoid inventing new heads of public policy. But, as always, there are supporters and opponents of this view. For those who believe that there are no new grounds on which courts can declare contracts to be against public policy and hence unlawful, the following quotation of Burroughs J. is apt:

> "Public policy is a very unruly horse and when you once get astride it you never know where it will carry you."[5]

But with typical bravado, Lord Denning adopted a more adventurous approach:

> "With a good man in the saddle, the unruly horse can be kept in control. He can jump over obstacles."[6]

Perhaps the most important statement on the matter is, however, found in the words of Sir George Jessel M.R.[7]:

> "It must not be forgotten that you are not to extend arbitrarily those rules which say that a given contract is void as being against public policy, because if there is one thing more than another public policy requires it is that men of full age and competent understanding shall have the utmost liberty of

[5] *Richardson* v. *Mellish* (1824) 2 Bing. 229 at p. 252.
[6] *Enderby Town F.C.* v. *F.A.* [1971] Ch. 591 at p. 606.
[7] *Printing and Numerical Registering Co.* v. *Sampson* (1875) L.R. 19 Eq. 462 at p. 465.

contracting and that when their contracts are entered into freely and voluntarily shall be held sacred and shall be enforced by Courts of Justice. Therefore, you have this permanent public policy to consider—that you are not lightly to interfere with this freedom of contract."

This statement is often cited as the embodiment of the doctrine of freedom of contract. That doctrine accepts that public policy requires that certain contracts should not be enforced, but indicates that it is of the first importance that these powers be exercised sparingly. Accordingly, it is the legislature which has had a more important role in relation to unlawful contracts in recent times.

Many statutes contain provisions affecting the validity of particular contracts. Thus early Scottish statutes provided that contracts of usury, where the interest stipulated was above the legal rate, were annulled. Unfortunately the parliamentary draftsmen have not adhered to a consistent nomenclature in proscribing contracts. Here are some examples of the terms that have been used: "Illegal null and void";[8] "null and void";[9] "unlawful";[10] and "not be lawful".[11] When applying these provisions to individual circumstances the judges have emphasised that their task is to construe the provision in the context of the whole Act and the mischief at which it was directed. "[A] . . . presumption of legality . . . exists where a contract is reasonably susceptible of two meanings."[12]

Where a contract is not directly prohibited by statute, it may still be alleged that it is illegal because the statute imposes a penalty for the type of conduct which has occurred. This can occur where a contract is performed in an illegal manner. In *St. John Shipping Corp.* v. *Joseph Rank*[13]:

A charterparty was entered into for the carriage of grain from America to Britain. Contrary to the Merchant Shipping Acts, the master overloaded the ship 11 inches beyond what was legal on the "Plimsoll marks". He was fined £1,200 for the offence. The charterer refused to pay part of the costs of carriage, claiming that it should not be bound when its cargo had been put at risk. So when the shipowners brought action

---

[8] Truck Act 1831, s. 2 (now repealed by the Wages Act 1986).
[9] Life Assurance Act 1774, s. 1.
[10] Resale Prices Act 1976, ss. 1 and 2.
[11] Road Traffic Act 1972, s. 60.
[12] *Neilson* v. *Stewart*, 1991 S.L.T. 523, *per* Lord Jauncey at p. 525.
[13] [1957] 1 Q.B. 267.

for recovery of these sums, the defence was that the contract was illegal.

Devlin J. held that the sums were recoverable. Upon a true construction, he said that the statute was directed toward the prevention of overloading, not the prohibition of contracts. Accordingly, the mere fact that there had been an illegal manner of performance did not debar the shipowners from recovering. The intention of the legislature was to create a statutory offence for overloading, not to declare particular types of contract illegal.

The Consequences of Illegality

If an action could never be brought on an illegal contract, injustice could result. A rogue could engage in an unlawful contract with an innocent party and thereby obtain money or property. If no action were allowed, then he would reap the advantage of his own pernicious dealings.

> *Example*: X agrees to supply Mongolian widgets to Y. After Y pays the price, X discloses that it is illegal to import Mongolian widgets into this country. If no action for recovery of the price was available to Y—as suggested by the maxim *ex turpi causa non oritur actio*—the rogue X would have successfully duped Y.

Accordingly, the law has devised a series of principles to deal with the consequences of illegal contracts. The difficulty is that these principles have never been fitted into a coherent scheme and that the two leading cases on the topic are conflicting. Let us begin by trying to identify the general approach of the law.

Parties Equally Blameworthy

If the parties are equally at fault (*in pari delicto*), the principle is that the position of the possessor is the better one (*in turpi causa melior est conditio possidentis*). To put it another way, the loss is allowed to lie where it falls. So if a person pays money for an illegal drug, he cannot recover the money from the supplier, even if the drugs were never given to him. An illustration of this point is provided by *Barr* v. *Crawford*[14]:

A woman was informed that her chances of taking over the

---

[14] 1983 S.L.T. 481.

licence of a public house from her deceased husband were slender. On the strength of certain representations made to her, she made an initial payment of £8,000 to two individuals. She understood that a payment of £10,000 would secure the transfer of the licence at the next meeting of the district licensing board. Later, she sought to recover the money from the two individuals.

It was held that the payment was a bribe and the transaction was an illegal one. The pursuer did not offer to prove that she was not *in pari delicto* and accordingly the judge dismissed the action.

Parties not Equally Blameworthy

Where parties are not equally blameworthy, a distinction is drawn between the rights of the guilty party and the rights of the innocent party. By "innocent party" in this context we mean a person who has been induced to enter the unlawful contract as the result of some unfair advantage having been taken of him by the other party. The courts do not weigh the relative turpitude of two guilty parties against one another.

(a) The Guilty Party

The guilty party can never sue on the contract. "No court will lend its aid to a man who founds his cause of action upon an immoral or an illegal act," said Lord Mansfield. It should, however, be remembered that where there has been an illegality in performance and not in the object of the contract, the party who has transgressed the statute may recover.

(b) The Innocent Party

The innocent party can enforce the contract if he has made a mistake regarding the illegality alleged to taint it. In *Archbolds (Freightage) Ltd.* v. *Spanglett Ltd.*[15]:

> The defendants contracted to carry the plaintiff's whisky in their van. Unknown to the plaintiffs, the van was not licensed to carry goods by the defendants and the carriage therefore amounted to an offence. The whisky was stolen. The plaintiff's action for recovery of the value of the whisky was defended on the ground of illegality. The Court of Appeal held the plaintiffs entitled to recover the value of the whisky as the measure of damages for breach of contract. A mistake as to the existence of the licence did not deprive the plaintiffs of the right to

---

[15] [1961] 1 Q.B. 374; [1961] 1 All E.R. 417.

enforce the contract. It was only the method of performance which was illegal rather than the making of the contract itself.

The mistake will operate if it is one of fact but not where it is one of law, for as we all know, ignorance of the law excuses no one (*ignorantia juris neminem excusat*). Apart from mistake, two other grounds which may entitle the innocent party to enforce the contract have been developed in English law.

(1) If the contract itself is illegal the innocent party may enforce a collateral warranty.

(2) If there has been fraud then even though the contract cannot be enforced there may be damages for fraud.

It is difficult to know how far such grounds might be accepted in Scotland. Scots law has a more fully developed concept of unjust enrichment than English law. There are, accordingly, circumstances where a party may recover when a contract has failed through illegality. In addition, there may be recovery upon a *quantum meruit* basis (payment for work done). If it is shown that a statute was designed to protect a particular class, and an innocent party has been prejudiced as a result of an illegal contract, then he may be granted a remedy. Accordingly, where a contract of loan was made with an unregistered moneylender, the borrower could recover property deposited with the moneylender. This was because the Act which required the moneylender to be registered was for the benefit of borrowers as a class.[16]

There are two leading Scottish authorities on the consequences of statutory illegality. In *Cuthbertson* v. *Lowes*[17]:

> Two fields of potatoes, were sold by the Scots acre. This was contrary to the Weights and Measure Act, which declared null and void any contract using local or customary measures. It was held that the seller was entitled to recover the market value of the potatoes.

Lord President Inglis said that the seller was not suing upon the contract but was in effect pursuing a claim for recompense under the principles of unjust enrichment. The decision was distinguished in the subsequent case of *Jamieson* v. *Watt's Trs*,[18] where a joiner did work in excess of the amount he was authorised to do by licence under the Defence Regulations. It was held that the proprietor did

---

[16] *Phillips* v. *Blackhurst*, 1912 2 S.L.T. 254.
[17] (1870) 8 M. 1073.
[18] 1950 S.C. 265.

not have to pay for the excess. There has been a tendency to regard *Cuthbertson* as wrongly decided or, at best, to be binding only on its own special facts. For instance, Gloag draws a distinction between agreements which the law will not allow to operate as contracts and contracts which are contrary to law.[19] That is a difficult distinction to understand or apply. It seems rather that the consequences of illegality depend on two factors: the degree of turpitude involved and the requirements of public policy. It was not particularly heinous to sell potatoes according to an old measure. But there were strong grounds of public policy for preventing joiners from doing work without a licence shortly after the Second World War, when a variety of economic restrictions were in force.

It may be the case that the courts reserve the right to deal with illegality on an equitable basis depending on the particular circumstances which have occurred. An example is provided by a recent decision of the Court of Appeal in England.[20]

> S agreed to pay H £25,000 to remove an aircraft from Nigerian airspace. The sum was to be paid in two instalments. In Nigeria, H feared there was a threat to his life. Without obtaining the necessary permission, he flew the aircraft to the Ivory Coast chased by a Nigerian fighter. The aircraft was impounded and returned to Nigeria. S sought the return of the first instalment of £12,500 which had been paid. H sought payment of the balance. He was held entitled to the full sum. His side of the bargain was fulfilled when he flew the plane out of Nigeria. The breach of air traffic control regulations was committed to escape imminent danger. It was therefore not against public policy to allow him to recover the sum from S.

RESTRICTIVE COVENANTS

Restrictive covenants are clauses which aim to limit a party's liberty to practice his or her trade or profession. They are sometimes referred to as clauses in restraint of trade. Such clauses are frequently found in contracts of employment, partnership, and sale.
Examples
1. Chop agrees to buy Loin's butcher shop. In terms of the

---

[19] at p. 550.
[20] *Howard* v. *Shirlstar Container Transport* [1990] 1 W.L.R. 1292.

> agreement, Loin undertakes not to set up in business as a butcher within five miles of the shop for a three-year period.

2. Amp works for the Plug Electric Co. His contract of employment stipulates that if Amp leaves the company he shall not join a rival company within the U.K. for 12 months after his employment with Plug ceases.

Courts dealing with restrictive covenants have a difficult balance to strike. On the one hand, they wish to uphold contracts. They are reluctant to release a party from an obligation freely entered into. To do so destroys the security of contractual engagements. It tends to make parties less likely to abide by their contracts in future. However, the courts also wish to uphold individual liberty. A person ought to have the right to earn a livelihood. It is in the public interest that competition be encouraged. Persons should not be allowed to abuse a superior bargaining position to secure an unfair trading advantage. Accordingly, the balance is between:

Freedom of Contract v. Freedom of Trade

The Right to Bargain v. the Right to Work or Trade

The Ground Rules

Over the years, a number of principles have been developed to determine whether or not a restrictive covenant is valid. The principles are essentially five in number:

1. Restrictive covenants are *prima facie* void and unenforceable.
2. Restrictive covenants will only be upheld if they are reasonable (i) as between the parties, and (ii) in the public interest.
3. Restrictive covenants are most readily enforced in contracts of sale of a business.
4. In employment cases, an employer cannot protect himself against competition alone. He must demonstrate some exceptional proprietorial interest, *e.g.* a trade connection or trade secret.
5. The restriction must go no further than is reasonably required.

The classic statement of the law occurs in the speech of Lord Macnaghten in *Nordenfelt* v. *Maxim Nordenfelt Guns and Ammunition Co. Ltd.*[21]

> "The public have an interest in every person's carrying on his trade freely: so has the individual. All interference with individual liberty of action in trading, and all restraints of trade of

---

[21] [1894] A.C. 535.

themselves, if there is nothing more, are contrary to public policy, and therefore void. That is the general rule. But there are exceptions: restraints of trade and interference with individual liberty of action may be justified by the special circumstances of a particular case. It is sufficient justification, and indeed it is the only justification, if the restriction is reasonable—reasonable, that is, in reference to the interests of the parties concerned and reasonable in reference to the interests of the public, so framed and so guarded as to afford adequate protection to the party in whose favour it is imposed, while at the same time it is in no way injurious to the public."

In determining reasonableness, regard will be had to a number of factors, including the nature of the restriction imposed, its duration, and the spatial area over which it is imposed. At one time it was thought that a general restraint, which prevented a person from working anywhere in the world, was unenforceable. This was considered in *Nordenfelt*:

In 1886, Nordenfelt sold his arms business to a limited company which was formed for the purpose of purchasing it. He received a large sum for the sale and it was agreed he would act as the new company's managing director for five years after its formation. Two years later, the company amalgamated with another company. At the time of the transfer Nordenfelt entered into a restrictive covenant with the company similar in terms to one he had agreed to on the sale of the business in 1886. It was stipulated that for a 25-year period he should not "engage except on behalf of the company either directly or indirectly in the trade or business of a manufacturer of guns, gun-mountings or gun powder explosives or ammunition."

When he attempted to breach this undertaking, the company sought to enforce the covenant by way of injunction. Nordenfelt contended that the restraint was wider than was required to protect the company's legitimate interests and that: "It cannot be the law that a man should be prevented from earning his living in any part of the wide world." The House of Lords rejected this contention and upheld the covenant. In view of the fact that it was a worldwide business ("He had upon his books almost every monarch and almost every State of any note in the habitable globe") and that he had received a very good price for his transfer, the restraint was reasonable.

Contracts of Sale of a Business

When a business is sold as a going concern, one part of the purchase price will be in respect of the goodwill of the business. The goodwill comprises the customers and reputation of the seller, in other words, the seller's trade connection. If the purchaser could not insert a restrictive covenant into the contract to restrict competition by the seller, the goodwill would be valueless. The seller could immediately set up in the same business again and attract his customers to the new premises. Accordingly, such restrictions will be enforced when they provide protection to the purchaser's legitimate interests. Recently, the Privy Council has stated that such clauses do not come within the operation of the doctrine of restraint of trade "provided that the degree of interference does not exceed the accepted standard."[22] This is another way of saying that in contracts of sale of a business, the presumption has shifted in favour of such covenants being upheld. The power of the court to intervene is still present, but it will only be exercised when the restraint is demonstrably excessive or against the public interest.[23]

While it is open to the purchaser to restrict competition by the seller, the converse proposition probably does not hold. In one case, the seller of a men's hairdressing business sought to prevent the buyer from engaging in ladies' hairdressing in competition with the seller.[24] The restriction sought was refused. The reason given by the sheriff in this novel situation was that the restraint was not designed to protect the seller's legitimate interest, but simply to stifle competition.

Contracts of Partnership

Where a restrictive covenant is inserted in a partnership deed, the question will again turn on the legitimate interests of those who rely upon the term for protection. In the first reported Scots decision on restrictive covenants, the Court upheld a covenant involving a bookselling partnership in Glasgow.[25] If all the partners have accepted the same restriction there is a definite presumption that the term is enforceable. Otherwise it is impossible to give a precise guide to which covenants will and which will not be enforced. Two cases will suffice as illustrations. Interdict has been granted to prevent a doctor from exercising the profession of a general

---

[22] *Deacons* v. *Bridge* [1984] 2 All E.R. 19.
[23] see *George Walker & Co.* v. *Jann*, 1991 S.L.T. 771.
[24] *Giblin* v. *Murdoch*, 1979 S.L.T. (Sh.Ct.) 5.
[25] *Stalker* v. *Carmichael* (1735) Mor. 9455.

practitioner in a small country town on the basis of covenant. No argument seems to have been led regarding the public interest in securing the best possible medical provision in the particular area.[26] But public interest was a factor of some importance when a large Hong Kong firm of solicitors sought to enforce a covenant against a partner who had left the firm.[27] The firm was departmentalised, which meant that the covenant went well beyond the individual partner's role in the firm. Nevertheless, the public interest in facilitating the assumption of new partners by established solicitors' firms was accepted by the Privy Council. If a partner was not bound by such a provision, it would deter firms from assuming partners, because once the partner had acquired clients through the firm, he might set up on his own taking the clients with him. However, if the restriction sought is too wide, it will be struck down. A covenant which sought to prevent a solicitor from practising within twenty miles of Glasgow Cross was thought to be excessive and interim interdict refused.[28] Council for the respondent had submitted that the area probably included about half the law firms in Scotland.

"Solus" Agreements

A more recent category of restrictive covenants involves contracts whereby oil companies attempt to regulate the trading of petrol stations. These are known as "solus" agreements and usually involve three elements:
(1) an obligation upon the retailer to purchase all his products from the company;
(2) an obligation to keep the garage open during stipulated hours; and
(3) an obligation to ensure that any subsequent purchaser enters a similar agreement with the oil company.

The novelty of such agreements is that they restrict the trading use of a particular piece of land, rather than the future exercise of a trade or profession by an individual. On that basis, it was argued that the doctrine of restraint of trade did not apply. That approach has been rejected by the House of Lords. In the leading case on the issue, a solus agreement of four years, five months was held reasonable, but one for 26 years

---

[26] *Anthony v. Rennie*, 1981 S.L.T. (Notes) 11.
[27] *Deacons v. Bridge* [1984] 2 All E.R. 19.
[28] *Dallas McMillan & Sinclair v. Simpson*, 1989 S.L.T. 454.

unreasonable. The latter restriction was held to be too long and against the public interest.[29]

Cartels etc.

Apart from covenants involving individuals, freedom of trade can also be prejudiced where manufacturers or traders combine together to regulate the availability of certain commodities, or to fix prices. Suppose, for example, all the manufacturers of widgets agreed together to fix a price for widgets well in excess of production costs. That would greatly enhance their profits to the detriment of the public interest. This area is now largely covered by statute which provides extensive controls for, amongst others, the Director-General of Fair Trading, the Monopolies and Mergers Commission and the Restrictive Practices Court, to regulate such practices.[30]

Employment

In contracts for the sale of a business, the seller receives something in return for his agreement to the restrictive covenant, *viz.* the value of the goodwill. This is not true in the case of an employee. He or she might only be persuaded to sign a contract containing a covenant to ensure that they obtain the job and therefore a means of livelihood. In employment cases, a restrictive covenant is "a *pactum illicitum* only if the restriction imposed is wider than is necessary to protect the legitimate interests of the master."[31] Plainly, the two crucial phrases in this passage are "wider than is necessary" and "legitimate interests." What do they mean? Let us begin by looking at the term "legitimate interests." It unpacks into two separate but overlapping categories: (a) trade secrets and confidential information, and (b) preservation of business connection.

Trade Secrets and Confidential Information

With good reason the area covered by trade secrets and confidential information has been described as "somewhat nebulous and ill-defined." This is because true trade secrets will normally be

---

[29] *Esso Petroleum Co. Ltd.* v. *Harpers Garage (Stourport) Ltd.* [1968] A.C. 269; [1967] 1 All E.R. 699.
[30] see, *e.g.* Fair Trading Act 1973, Resale Prices Act 1976, Restrictive Trade Practices Act 1976.
[31] *Scottish Farmers' Dairy Co. (Glasgow) Ltd.* v. *McGhee*, 1933 S.L.T. 142, 145 *per* L.P. Clyde.

protected by intellectual property rights such as patents and copy-rights. Moreover, independent of any express contractual term, there is an implied term in contracts of employment that an employee will not disclose confidential information to other parties.[32] The relevant principles are as follows:

1. The parties' obligations are *prima facie* determined by the contract of employment.
2. The question of the use and disclosure of information is the subject of implied terms.
3. The duty of good faith and fidelity during the employment which is implied by law depends upon the nature of the employment. The duty is broken if the employee copies or memorises customer lists.
4. After the employment ceases, the duty of good faith is more restricted in scope. It only covers information of a type amounting to a trade secret.

Whether or not information is so confidential as to amount to a trade secret depends upon the whole circumstances of the case. Relevant factors are (a) the nature of the employment; (b) the nature of the information; (c) whether the employer impressed the confidentiality of the information upon the employee; and (d) whether the information can be easily isolated from other information which the employee possesses. Prices and customer lists can constitute trade secrets. Restrictive covenants cannot extend the employer's rights to protect information which would otherwise be the subject of implied terms.

A difficult issue concerns the employers' general business methods and organisation. Does this constitute a trade secret or confidential information? In *S.O.S. Bureau* v. *Payne*, which involved an employee who sought to leave an employment agency where she had worked, the sheriff upheld a covenant in order to prevent disclosure of the employers' "system of work, presentation of the service to the customer and in particular fee charging policy."[33] This statement would effectively cover most employees. If an employee does not know about the employer's system of work, he is more likely to be looking down the wrong end of an unfair dismissal barrel than worrying about the validity of a restrictive covenant. The more persuasive line of authority can be traced back to Lord Atkinson. He accepted that information about business organisation and methods was naturally acquired by the employee

---

[32] *Faccenda Chicken Ltd.* v. *Fowler* [1987] Ch. 117; *Harben Pumps (Scotland) Ltd.* v. *Lafferty*, 1989 S.L.T. 752.
[33] 1982 S.L.T. (Sh.Ct.) 33.

and stated that "he violates no obligation express or implied arising from the relation in which he stood to the [employers] by using in service of some persons other than them the general knowledge he has acquired of their scheme of organisation and methods of business."[34] His words were echoed in a later case by Lord Pearson, who stated that the employer's scheme of organisation and methods of business are not to be counted as trade secrets.[35] Lord Ross has accepted Lord Pearson's view as a correct statement of the law.

But an illustration of the continuing importance of restrictive covenants where issues of trade secrets and confidential information are concerned is provided by *Bluebell Apparel* v. *Dickinson*[36]:

> In January 1977, D was taken on as a management trainee by B.A., manufacturers of "Wrangler" jeans. By June 1977, D was in sole charge of their Kilwinning factory but in August he intimated that he was leaving to take up a position with Levi Strauss and Co. B.A. sought an interdict to prevent this on the basis of an agreement which D had signed when he joined them. It provided that except with the written permission of the employers, D would not, for a period of two years after the end of his employment with them, perform any services, either as owner, partner, employee, or consultant for any person or business entity in competition with B.A.

The First Division upheld the covenant on the basis that D possessed confidential information about B.A. Accordingly, D was prevented from working for a competitor anywhere in the world in any capacity for a period of two years. It may be that, even without resorting to industrial espionage, there is little that D knew about the actual products which competitors could not have found out by buying, ripping asunder and examining a few pairs of Wranglers. Nevertheless, such knowledge as he had after only eight months regarding pricing policy and customers was thought sufficient to justify a two-year long, worldwide restraint.

Preservation of Business Connection

Employers are not entitled to protection against competition alone. Competition is the very essence of the market. Where there are no trade secrets or confidential information to protect, the presumption is that the employee is entitled to freely practise her trade or

---

[34] *Herbert Morris Ltd.* v. *Saxelby* [1916] 1 A.C. 688.
[35] *Commercial Plastics Ltd.* v. *Vincent* [1964] 3 All E.R. 546 at p. 551.
[36] 1980 S.L.T. 157.

profession. However, there are certain qualifications to that general approach. An employer does have a legitimate interest in preserving his business connection, which be enforced in certain circumstances.

Let us first deal with non-solicitation of clients. Prohibitions against active attempts to poach clients for a limited period are frequently upheld. It is thought reasonable by both sides that the employee will not seek to undermine the employer's business in this manner. After all, what reasonable employer intends to train "fifth columnists" to steal business out from under his nose? But when it is simply a case of competition, either by joining a competitor, or by setting up in business on one's own, the general principle is that the employee cannot be shackled.

Secondly, a reasonable restraint will be enforced when there is some intimate relationship between the employee and the customers of the business such that he acquires a degree of influence over them. In *Scottish Farmers Dairy Co. (Glasgow) Ltd.*, a milk-roundsman was the only contact between the business and the customers. His contract contained a covenant which prevented him from setting up in competition with the company for a period of two years within a one-mile radius of his employers' place of business.[37] It was held that he should not be allowed to take advantage of the position his job gave him *vis-à-vis* the customers. This would be unfair competition with the employer. Accordingly, the covenant was upheld:

" . . . the preservation of his business connection is a legitimate interest of every trader; and if, to protect that interest, a prohibition against competition by the servant is made necessary by the particular nature and circumstances of the master's business, the law of Scotland recognises the prohibition as an enforceable term of the contract of employment."[38]

If the employee did not have an opportunity to exercise influence over clients or customers, it is difficult to see why he should be prevented from competing under this head.[39]

---

[37] 1933 S.C. 148; 1933 S.L.T. 133.

[38] *Scottish Farmers Dairy Co. (Glasgow) Ltd.* v. *McGhee*, 1933 S.C. 148, 153 *per* L.P. Clyde.

[39] *Hinton and Higgs* v. *Murphy*, 1989 S.L.T. 450; *Office Angels Ltd.* v. *Rainer Thomas* [1991] I.R.L.R. 214.

Wider than is necessary

On the following page are some examples of spatial and temporal restrictions which have been held to be valid. It will be seen that a great range of different restrictions have been enforced, from a quarter of a mile to the world in extent, from six months to life in duration. Where trade secrets are concerned, then the ambit of the restriction can be very wide as in the "Wrangler" case. In employment contracts, however, area covenants are in general looked upon with disfavour. This is because they appear to be simply an attempt to stifle competition. There is now Court of Appeal authority in England to the effect that they will not be enforced where a lesser, more precise restriction would have adequately protected the employer's interests.[40]

The covenant should be directed at the job which the employee did. In *Rentokil* v. *Hampton* the restrictive covenant sought to prevent the employee from being involved with the "marketing, sale or supply of products or services" in competition with Rentokil.[41] As he was a timber infestation surveyor, the restraint was held to be wider than was required and declared invalid. It prevented him from competing, not only in respect of his own area of work, but in respect of new areas. Similarly there was no legitimate interest in preventing him from dealing with persons with whom he had no connexion during the period of his employment. However, there can be exceptions to that rule where confidential information is at stake and it is thought that employment in any capacity for a rival business will give the competitor an unfair advantage by securing insider knowledge from the employee. Accordingly, the manager of a Wrangler jeans factory could not take employment even as a doorman in Nicaragua for Levis or Lee Cooper.[42]

Severability

Frequently, a restrictive covenant will consist of several separate restrictions. If each restriction is truly independent of the others, then the invalidity of each will not affect the validity of the others. Accordingly, a reasonable restriction will be enforced even where the unreasonable restriction falls. So where a salesman agreed not to canvass his employer's customers and also not to carry on business as a traveller in a particular area, the former provision was

---

[40] *Office Angels Ltd.* v. *Rainer Thomas, supra.*
[41] 1982 S.L.T. 422.
[42] *Bluebell Apparel (supra).*

Examples of Spatial Restrictions

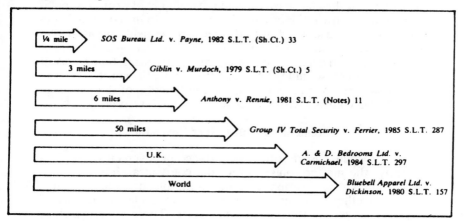

Examples of Temporal Restrictions

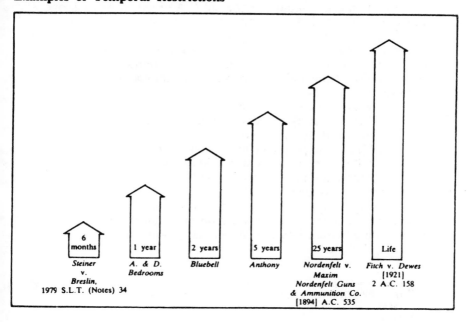

upheld but the latter rejected as too wide and too vague.[43] The divisibility of the clause can provide the subject of express stipulation in the contract.[44] However, it is not open to the court to delete parts of the clause which would otherwise be held unreasonable, unless there is an express power to do so. The parties cannot exclude the jurisidiction of the courts by declaring that terms of covenant are reasonable.[45] Nor can they invite the court to rewrite their contract, for that is to confuse the function of the parties in making the contract with that of the courts in interpreting it.[46]

Remedies for Breach of Covenant

Court procedure is of critical importance in covenant cases. Frequently, the matter comes before the court at an interim stage. Accordingly, the decision is made on the pleadings as they then stand, together with such statements as are made by the parties' representatives at the bar of the court. There is a two-stage approach. First, the petitioner must make out a *prima facie* case. Secondly, he must demonstrate that on the balance of convenience, the interim interdict should be granted.[47] A *prima facie* case is one which has a seeming congency. It is sometimes said that the pleadings disclose a case to try. The balance of convenience broadly speaking relates to the relative prejudice which will be suffered by the parties if the interim interdict is granted or refused. Among the considerations which the court will take into account are the following:

> When was the action brought?
> How long does the covenant have to run?
> What is the prejudice to the employer?
> What is the prejudice to the employee?
> Will the employee be deprived of his livelihood?
> Is there a remedy in damages?[48]
> Is the loss quantifiable?[49]
> Is the employee being paid for covenant?[50]

There are two other remedies which may be available to employers faced with apparent loss of confidential information. First, if the

---

[43] *Mulvein* v. *Murray*, 1908 S.C. 528.
[44] *Hinton & Higgs (U.K.) Ltd.* v. *Murphy*, 1989 S.L.T. 450.
[45] *Ibid.*
[46] *Ibid.*
[47] *Toynar* v. *Whitbread*, 1988 S.L.T. 433, *per* L.J.C. Ross.
[48] *Group 4 Total Security* v. *Ferrier*, 1985 S.L.T. 287; 1985 S.C. 70.
[49] *Rentokil* v. *Kramer*, 1986 S.L.T. 116.
[50] *Agma Chemical Co.* v. *Hart*, 1984 S.L.T. 246.

information is truly a secret, such as a trade process, it may be covered by intellectual property rights under the law relating to patents and copyrights. Secondly, if it is reasonably thought that the employee has removed trade items, customer lists, schedules of prices and the like, these may be recovered by a "dawn raid" carried out by a commissioner under section 1 of the Administration of Justice (Scotland) Act 1972. This can be an effective-—but very expensive—manner of proceeding.

Chapter 11

THE EXTINCTION OF OBLIGATIONS

WHEN does a contract come to an end? In most instances, contractual obligations are extinguished when both parties have fully performed their respective sides of the bargain. A contract for the sale of goods, for example, is normally terminated when the item is delivered in return for the correct price. The parties owe no further duties to one another under the contract. Similarly, in unilateral obligations, once the person who has made the promise fulfils his undertaking, the obligation is at an end. So if a businessman promises to pay a law student £100 if she comes first in an essay competition, the obligation will be discharged on his paying her the money if she wins the competition. Apart from performance, however, there are several other methods by which contractual obligations can come to an end.

Discharge by consent

The parties may agree to release each other from their respective contractual obligations without performance. Put simply, the contract is cancelled by mutual agreement. Where a creditor agrees to release the debtor, this is known as "acceptilation". If, for example, A owes B £50 in respect of a quantity of towels which B has delivered to him, B may agree to waive the debt because A has done him a favour. This gratuitous renunciation of rights by B can only be proved by writ or oath, so A must ensure that he obtains a signed discharge from B.

Novation and delegation

An obligation is extinguished when it is agreed that a fresh obligation by the debtor be substituted for it (novation) or when a new obligation by another debtor is substituted for it (delegation).

Example: Ben owes Sid £50. Ben suggests that if Sid lends him a further £50 he will give him a new receipt for £100 (novation). Alternatively, Ben may suggest that as Alf owes him (Ben) £50, a new obligation should be entered into under which Alf owes Sid £50 (delegation). If Sid accepts either proposal, the original obligation by Ben will be extinguished.

There is a presumption that a new obligation is additional to an existing obligation. Accordingly, a debtor should always ensure that he obtains an express discharge of the original debt.

Compensation

Where each party owes the other a sum of money, the one debt can be compensated or set off against the other.

> *Example*: Ralph and Zeke are grain merchants who have constant dealings with each other. Ralph owes £50,000 in respect of a wheat consignment he bought from Zeke yesterday. Zeke in turn owes Ralph £120,000 for oats which he bought from him a week ago.

The two debts can be set off against each other resulting in an obligation by Zeke to pay Ralph the difference, that is £70,000. The effect of compensation is accordingly to cancel Ralph's obligation. There are some conditions which must be satisfied before the right of set-off can be used. First, both claims must be liquid, which means they must be readily ascertainable in money terms. If one of the claims is illiquid, then no right of set-off exists. A claim for damages is illiquid because until a precise figure is put upon the claim by a court, the sum is not ascertained. Secondly, the debts must be presently due. There is no right of set-off in respect of future debts. Finally, both parties must be creditor and debtor to each other in the same legal capacity. Suppose a solicitor is owed £2,000 by a client in respect of professional fees. The client cannot claim set-off on the basis that the solicitor is the trustee of an estate which is due to pay him a sum of money. But the client could claim a right of set-off if he was a joiner who had done work for the solicitor which had not been paid for.

Set-off must be distinguised from retention. The aim of set-off is to extinguish part or all of the obligation. Retention, on the other hand, is about securing performance by the other party by withholding one's own obligations under the contract.

Confusion

A person cannot be under an obligation to himself. If company A owes company B money and subsequently B takes over A, then the obligation has been "confused" and the debt is extinguished.

Two further methods by which contractual obligations are extinguished require more detailed discussion. The first is prescription, the second frustration.

PRESCRIPTION

The doctrine of prescription concerns the extinction of rights and obligations by the lapse of time. Before looking at the doctrine in detail, it is worth making a few general points about the effect of time on contracts. Some contracts, such as those of hire, lease and employment, continue over a period of time. If the contract in question is stated to be for a fixed period, then it will expire at the end of that period. Of course, the parties can consent to the contract being renewed or extended beyond the original period if they so choose. In the case of leases, there is a special rule. If no notice is given by either party before the period of the lease terminates, then it is extended by operation of law. This is known as "tacit relocation". Leases originally for a year or more will be extended by one year. Those for a shorter period, for the same duration again. This process of tacit relocation can go on indefinitely. Is it possible to have a contract of indefinite duration? In one English case a contract was entered into in 1919 for the supply of water at a fixed rate "at all times hereafter."[1] It was held that such a contract could not have been intended to endure forever and that it should be terminable on the giving of reasonable notice.

The principle of prescription governs the length of time for which obligations subsist. The need for such a rule is clear. Rights cannot exist forever. A creditor must exercise his right within a reasonable time. It would be unfair if someone were to live year after year under the threat that action might be taken against him by the other party. Further, as time elapses, it becomes increasingly likely that evidence will be lost. Witnesses' memories will be dimmed. They may go abroad or die. Accordingly, the law presumes that after a period of time has elapsed without a claim having been pursued, the creditor must be deemed to have abandoned that right. The right is then said to have "prescribed."

Before 1973 the law regarding prescription was in a confused and chaotic state. On the basis, however, of work done by the Scottish Law Commission, the Prescription and Limitation (Scotland) Act 1973 was enacted, which signally improved and simplified this branch of the law. It deals with three different categories: positive prescription, negative prescription and limitation. Our main interest lies with the second of these categories, but it is worth giving a brief idea of the other two.

Positive prescription involves the situation where a person holds

---

[1] *Staffordshire Area Health Authority* v. *South Staffordshire Waterworks Co.* [1978] 1 W.L.R. 1387; 3 All E.R. 769.

heritable property on a defective title.[2] By defective title, we mean that for some reason full ownership was not transferred. Perhaps the seller has purported to convey a parcel of land which he did not own. If the purchaser possesses the property for a 10-year period "openly peaceably and without any judicial interruption" then his title is fortified. In other words, his right to the property is perfected.

Limitation of actions requires a person who claims damages in respect of death or personal injuries to bring an action within a 10-year period from the date that the injury was sustained.[3]

Negative Prescription

There are two periods of negative prescription, (a) a short negative prescription of five years, and (b) a long negative prescription of twenty years. Most contractual obligations are extinguished at the end of five years.[4] So if a car is sold and the price not paid within five years, the debt is thereafter extinguished. The main exceptions concern those obligations which relate to land and to obligations contained in probative writing. In such cases, the 20-year period applies.[5] So the price of a flat can be pursued, for example, ten or sixteen years after the agreement is made, assuming it is in probative form. However, it is not always possible to extend the prescriptive period for contractual obligations by incorporating them in probative writing. The 1973 Act specifically disallows parties such an option in, for example, cautionary obligations and obligations to pay rent.[6]

Computation of Prescriptive Period

The prescriptive period commences running on the date on which the obligation becomes enforceable.[7] In respect of a claim for breach of contract, the action must be brought within five years of the date of the loss, injury or damage which occurred as a result of the breach.[8] In *Greater Glasgow Health Board* v. *Baxter Clark & Paul* the following circumstances occurred[9]:

---

[2] Prescription and Limitation (Scotland) Act 1973 (hereafter "1973 Act"), ss. 1–5.
[3] 1973 Act, Pt. II.
[4] 1973 Act, s. 6.
[5] 1973 Act, s.7.
[6] 1973 Act, Sched. 1, para. 2.
[7] 1973 Act, s. 6 (3).
[8] 1973 Act, s. 11 (1).
[9] 1992 S.L.T. 35.

Between 1969 and 1972, a firm of architects supervised works which were undertaken at Yorkhill hospital in Glasgow. Some physical damage in the form of cracks manifested in 1972. In 1978 a document was signed between the parties where the architects accepted that there were faults but not that they were liable. No action was raised until 1982. It was held that the action had prescribed. The prescriptive clock had commenced ticking in 1972. Accordingly, by the time the action was raised the prescriptive period had elapsed.

Where there is a series of transactions between the parties, the prescriptive period commences on the date on which payment for the goods last supplied or the services last rendered became due.[10] In the case of a loan or deposit of a sum of money, the period commences on the date stipulated for repayment in the contract or, if no such stipulation is made, the date on which a written demand for repayment is made.[11] So far as obligations to pay money or execute work by instalments are concerned, the date of commencement is that on which the last of the instalments is to be paid or executed respectively.[12]

Prescription stops running when a relevant claim is made by the creditor or a relevant acknowledgment is given by the debtor. What does this mean? A relevant claim is made if the creditor has taken steps to pursue his right, either by raising a court action or referring the matter to arbitration.[13] Both courses of action clearly indicate that he has not abandoned his claim. The same principle applies if he contests any claim inconsistent with his own alleged right, for example, if he stated his right as a defence to an action brought against him by the admission that the obligation is still due.[14] Alternatively, a person's actions may amount to acknowledgment if they clearly indicate that he regards the claim as still subsisting. This might occur, for example, if he made part-payment of a debt allegedly owed by him.

Mora, Taciturnity and Acquiescence

There is an older, common law principle by which a claim may be time-barred. This is known as mora, taciturnity and acquiescence. Translated into modern language, this means delay, silence and

---

[10] 1973 Act, Sched. 2, para. 1 (4).
[11] 1973 Act, Sched. 2, para. 2 (2).
[12] 1973 Act, Sched. 2, para. 4 (2).
[13] 1973 Act, s. 9.
[14] 1973 Act, s. 10.

consent. Even if a right has not prescribed, a person may nevertheless be personally barred because he has taken an unreasonable length of time to vindicate the right.

> *Example*: Ted and Alice sign a probative agreement regarding the sale of widgets. Nothing follows on from the agreement but 16 years after it is concluded, Ted seeks to enforce it. Although the prescriptive period has not yet elapsed, Alice may argue mora, taciturnity and acquiescence. If the plea is successful, Ted's claim will fail.

FRUSTRATION

After the parties have contracted, an event may occur which renders performance of the contract either impossible or radically different from that which the parties originally envisaged. The parties' original purpose may then be said to have been "frustrated." Should they be released from their contract or are they bound to go through with it? In other words, is the risk of the event which has occurred thrown on one party, or is the risk to be allocated by discharging both parties from their obligations? Two questions of importance in determining this issue are:

(a) How did the event arise? It is important to ensure that the event occurred without fault on either side; and

(b) What did the parties intend? The parties may already have provided for the contingency which has occurred. If so, the doctrine of frustration is not brought into play. It is only when the parties have not provided for the contingency that the doctrine operates.

Suppose that A is commissioned to paint B's portrait. Before the portrait is begun, A dies. Clearly, performance of the contract is now impossible. Scots law has always taken a common sense view of such circumstances. If neither party is responsible for the event and it is not provided for in the contract then the contract is at an end. Bankton mentions contracts being "void by supervening accident."[15] However, the Institutional writers did not discuss the issue in detail. It seems to have been assumed that certain types of event discharged the parties from further obligations under the contract. Their subsequent relations were then governed by the

---

[15] I.xi. 7.

principle of unjust enrichment, which ensured that the termination of the contract did not enrich one of the parties at the expense of the other.

Apart from situations where one of the parties died or fell ill and was thus unable to render performance, the most common event considered in the early Scottish legal decisions was destruction of the subject matter of the contract (*rei interitus*). In *Morison's Dictionary* the cases on this subject are collected together under the title of "*Periculum*". In each case the question asked was: on whom should the risk fall? So if a horse was hired and then stolen whilst in the possession of the hirer the question was: who should bear the loss of the horse, the owner or the hirer.[16] Similarly, if goods were damaged in transit, should the owner or the carrier be liable? Out of these cases, certain rules were established regarding the passing of risk in the most common contract—sale. In a contract for the sale of goods, risk is presumed to pass when property in the goods passes, unless the parties have agreed otherwise.[17] In a sale of heritage it has been established that risk passes when the missives are completed. In *Sloans' Dairies* v. *Glasgow Corporation*, premises were sold under missives.[18] Before the disposition had been delivered, the subjects were badly damaged by fire and had to be demolished. It was held that the risk was the purchasers' and they therefore had to bear the loss which had occurred.[19]

The operation of these rules regarding the passing of risk in sale reduces considerably the problem of supervening events. In such cases, it is up to the person who bears the risk to take whatever steps he can to minimise or insure against the risk. So as soon as missives are completed for the sale of a house, the purchaser's solicitor should immediately arrange insurance cover for the property.

The concept of frustration is applied to situations where neither the law nor the parties themselves have allocated the risk of an unforeseen event. The concept was developed in English law as a qualification to the rule that contracts were absolute. This rule is usually traced to the case of *Paradine* v. *Jane*:[20]

During the English Civil War, a tenant was dispossessed of his

---

[16] see *Trotter* v. *Buchanan* (1688) Mor. 10080.
[17] Sale of Goods Act 1979, s. 20.
[18] 1977 S.C. 223.
[19] In *Report on the Passing of Risk in Contracts for the Sale of Heritable Property* (Scot. Law Com. No. 127), a change in the law is recommended.
[20] (1647) Aleyn 26.

lands by an army commanded by Prince Rupert. It was held that he still had to pay the rent for the period during which he did not have the enjoyment of the lands.

To illustrate the entirely different approach of Scots law, *Paradine* can be contrasted with a case decided in 1612, *Lindsay* v. *Home*.[21] There it was held that where property was overblown by sand, the landlord was compelled either to take the land back or to accept a reduced rent.

The idea of releasing parties because of a supervening event was first discussed in England in the case of *Taylor* v. *Caldwell*:[22]

> The Surrey Garden and Music Hall was hired on four dates for the purpose of holding a "series of four grand concerts and day and night fêtes." The gardens and hall were accidentally damaged by fire before the concerts were due to be held. An action was brought by the persons who had hired the hall against the owners for breach of contract. Their action was unsuccessful. It was held that the fire excused both parties from performance of their respective obligations under the contract. In arriving at their decision, the court had somehow to overcome the principle that contracts must be performed no matter what supervening events had occurred. The court achieved this result by holding that there must be read into the contract an implied term "that the parties shall be excused in case, before breach, performance becomes impossible from the perishing of the thing without default of the contractor."

A number of points can be made about this decision. First, it bases the discharge of the parties on an implied term. Secondly, it requires that neither party shall be responsible for the event. Thirdly it purports to deal exclusively with the issue of destruction of the subject-matter of the contract.

The first case actually to use the term "frustration" was *Jackson* v. *Union Marine Insurance Co.*[23] It heralded a significant extension in the scope of the doctrine:

> A charterparty was entered into for the carriage of iron rails from Newport to San Francisco. It was stipulated that the ship was to proceed to Newport "with all possible dispatch (dangers

[21] (1612) Mor. 10120.
[22] (1863) 3 B. & S. 826.
[23] (1874) L.R. 10 C.P. 125.

and accidents of navigation excepted)." The ship went aground on its way to Newport and it took several months to effect the necessary repairs. Meantime, the charterer had arranged for the rails to be transported on another ship. An action was brought by the owner of the ship to receive compensation under an insurance policy.

The court accepted the finding of the jury that "the time necessary to get the ship off and [repair] her so as to be a cargo-carrying ship was so long as to put an end in a commercial sense to the commercial speculation entered into by the shipowner and charterer." In other words, as the ship would have arrived in August instead of January, it made the contract an entirely different venture to that originally contemplated by the parties. So the clause "dangers and accidents of navigation excepted" did not cover this situation, as the whole substance of the contract had changed. Potentially, this approach was capable of very wide application indeed. Let us now examine the circumstances required for frustration to operate.

The Event must be Unforeseen

If the parties have foreseen a particular event and have provided for the event in their contract, then the doctrine of frustration is not brought into play. So if there is a danger that war will break out and the parties make provision for such a contingency in their contract, the term of the contract will govern the legal relations of the parties if war does indeed break out. This requirement that the event is unforeseen gives the lie to the implied term theory. How can the courts imply a term on the basis of giving effect to the parties' intentions when the event is one to which, by definition, they have not directed their minds? A graphic refutation of the implied term theory was provided as long ago as 1922 by Lord Sands:

> "A tiger has escaped from a travelling menagerie. The milkgirl fails to deliver the milk. Possibly the milkman may be exonerated from any breach of contract; but, even so, it would seem hardly reasonable to base that exoneration on the ground that "tiger days excepted" must be held as if written into the milk contract."[24]

---

[24] *Scott* v. *Del Sel*, 1922 S.C. 592; affd. 1923 S.C. (H.L.) 37.

Neither Party at Fault

As frustration is an equitable doctrine, it has no role to play if the circumstances disclose that one of the parties was at fault. Where, for example, it was known that there was a war zone and one of the parties caused a ship to enter that zone, he could not thereafter plead frustration.[25] It was his act which caused the detention of the ship. So it was not possible to claim that a supervening event had occurred without fault of either of the parties. Accordingly, the obligation was not discharged. Self-induced frustration is, in fact, no more than breach.

> *Example*: An opera singer is engaged to appear with Scottish Opera for five weeks. If she loses her voice accidentally through illness, the contract is frustrated. But if she negligently or deliberately stands out in inclement weather and thereby catches pneumonia so that she cannot perform, that is breach of contract.[26]

Types of Frustrating Event

Impossibility is the primary ground on which the doctrine of frustration proceeds. So if one party dies and a degree of *delectus personae* is present, then frustration operates. Likewise if there is destruction of the subject-matter. Changed circumstances can make performance impossible. A modern example is provided by the closure of the *Shatt el Arab* waterway on the outbreak of the Iran-Iraq war. Ships which had contracted to go up the waterway could no longer do so without extreme risk to life and property and the charterparties were frustrated (those, that is, which did not provide for such a contingency in the contract terms).

Apart from actual impossibility, there is also legal impossibility:

> *Example*: A makes a contract with B to deliver rare Scottish heather to Liberia. After the contract is made, the government passes a law forbidding the export of Scottish heather.

Clearly, A can no longer perform the contract. Otherwise he would be guilty of an offence. Accordingly, the parties are discharged

---

[25] *The Eugenia* [1964] 2 Q.B. 226; [1964] 1 All E.R. 161.
[26] *Cf. Poussard* v. *Spiers* (1876) 1 Q.B.D. 410.

from their respective obligations. The leading case on this branch of the law is *Fraser* v. *Denny Mott and Dickson*[27]:

> In 1929 a timber yard was let and it was agreed that the lessor should purchase all his timber from the lessee and that the lessor should have an option to purchase. On the outbreak of war, certain legislation was passed which meant that further trading between the parties could not continue. The lessor sought to exercise the option to purchase the yard.

It was held by the House of Lords that the whole agreement, including the option clause, was terminated when the relevant legislation was passed. The legislation had effectively frustrated the agreement. Another example of legal impossibility occurs when war breaks out between two countries. If a contract exists between two persons in two states, that contract automatically falls on the outbreak of war. Thus in a contract for the supply of marine engines between an Austrian and Scottish company, the outbreak of the First World War terminated the contract.[28] Thereafter, the Austrian company was an enemy alien with whom it was illegal to do business.

There remains for consideration a third type of supervening event which we might loosely call "commercial impossibility." In such cases, performance of the contract is not physically or legally impossible, but circumstances have changed to such a marked extent that the venture is no longer that which the parties originally envisaged. In *Jackson* it was still possible for the ship to transport the goods to San Francisco, but the delay of seven months made it in effect a new contract. But it is firmly established that frustration does not occur simply because performance has become more onerous or expensive for one of the parties. In *Tsakiroglou & Co. Ltd.* v. *Noblee Thorl GmbH*[29]:

> A charterparty was entered into to carry freight to Britain. It was assumed by the parties that the ship would proceed through the Suez Canal although nothing was expressly stated in the contract. The Suez crisis of 1956 intervened and the canal was closed and the ship would have had to undertake its voyage round the Cape of Good Hope.

[27] 1944 S.C. (H.L.) 35; [1944] A.C. 265.
[28] *Cantiere San Rocco S.A.* v. *Clyde Shipbuilding & Engineering Co.*, 1923 S.C. (H.L.) 105; [1923] A.C. 226.
[29] [1962] A.C. 93.

It was held that the charterparty was not frustrated. Although the voyage was longer and more expensive to perform than envisaged at the time the contract was made, that was not a ground for discharging the parties from their obligations. The court indicated, however, that if the freight had been perishable and if it were to be damaged or to perish as a result of the longer voyage, then the contract probably would be frustrated. Another example is provided by *Davis Contractors Ltd.* v. *Fareham U.D.C.*, where inflation had caused the cost of a particular building contract to increase dramatically.[30] This would have meant the contractor would have made no profit on the contract price as originally agreed. Nevertheless he was held bound to his contract. The extra cost was no reason to invoke the doctrine of frustration. Today, building contracts are usually drawn up on special standard forms which contain provisions designed to deal with this contingency of escalating costs.

The most radical example of "commercial frustration" is provided by the English case of *Krell* v. *Henry*[31]:

> Rooms overlooking Pall Mall were hired at a high price to view the processions which were to take place in connection with Edward VII's coronation. Because the King had appendicitis, the coronation had to be postponed.

It was held that the contract for the hire of the rooms was terminated by frustration. The basis for the claim was that the whole rationale or purpose of the contract, the bedrock on which it was founded, had disappeared. The hirers did not want to see the Mall in its usual livery with its usual assemblage. They had paid a high price to see the procession.

It has been suggested that *Krell* would not be followed in Scotland. Lord Cooper, founding on Professor Gloag, doubted whether it is good authority north of the border.[32] Even south of the border its authority is in some doubt. It was decided only a few weeks apart from another "Coronation case," *Herne Bay Steamboat Co.* v. *Hutton*[33]:

> A pleasure boat was hired to view the naval review which was to take place off Spithead in connection with the coronation

---

[30] [1956] A.C. 696; [1956] 2 All E.R. 145.
[31] [1903] 2 K.B. 740.
[32] Cooper, (1946) 28. J.Comp.L. 1.
[33] [1903] 2 K.B. 683.

celebrations. When the review was cancelled, it was argued that the contract for the hire of the boat was frustrated.

The same court which decided *Krell* held in this case that the contract was not frustrated. What are the distinctions between the two cases? Clearly, there is very little to choose between them. The operative distinctions appear to be first, that the owners of the pleasure steamer were in the business of hiring out their craft. It was not their purpose to inquire into the reasons for the hire. Just as a taxi driver might know his vehicle was being hired to go to Musselburgh, but did not know that it was to see the races, so the boat owner could not be expected to inquire into the motives for every contract of hire into which they entered. By contrast the owner of the flat in Pall Mall was hiring it out on a "one-off" basis.

Secondly, there was actually something to see in *Herne*. The distinguished jurist, Sir Frederick Pollock, went to view the British fleet assembled at Spithead and declared it to be a very impressive spectacle.[34] There was unlikely to be any special attraction in watching the usual pedestrian and vehicular traffic in Pall Mall.

It remains true, however, that distinguishing between the two cases is decidedly tricky. In Scotland, it is more likely that the presumption would be in favour of the contract being upheld if, as here, all that had occurred was the non-occurrence of an expected event as opposed to the occurrence of an unexpected event. In *Hong Kong and Whampoa Dock Co. Ltd.* v. *Netherton Shipping Ltd*[35]:

> Shipowners sought to cancel a contract which they had made with a Hong Kong company to repair one of their ships. The shipowners claimed that it was "commercially impossible" for them to deliver the ship at Hong Kong within a reasonable time. This was because the ship lay at Singapore and the authorities there had stipulated that extensive preliminary repairs had to be carried out. Accordingly, the ship would not be ready to set out before the typhoon season, when it was dangerous for her to be at sea. Nevertheless the contract was upheld. All three judges in the Inner House expressed their unease over extending the width of the concept of commercial impossibility.

---

[34] Pollock, 20 L.Q.R. 4.
[35] 1909 S.C. 34.

The Position of Leases

From earliest times, Scots law has taken the view that a lease, like any other contract, can be frustrated. In English law this is not the case, partly because a lease constitutes a separate estate in land, partly because of the belief that a person who enters a contract for a period of years must assume the risk of whatever contingencies occur in those years. Not everything can be foreseen, but it is at least likely that a variety of incidents will occur in the course of a long time. It has been stated that while it is untrue to say that a lease can *never* be frustrated in English law it is true to say that such a situation will hardly *ever* occur.[36]

Scots law is so far different in this respect that not only do we allow frustration of a lease in the event of actual destruction of the subject (*rei interitus*), but we also hold a lease frustrated in the event of constructive destruction. So where the tenants in a 19-year lease of salmon fishings were unable to take advantage of the lease when the area came to be used by the Royal Air Force as an aerial gunnery and bombing range, the lease was held to have terminated.[37] A similar decision was reached in *Mackeson* v. *Boyd*, where a mansion which had been let was requisitioned by the authorities during the war, 14 years into a 19-year lease.[38] Despite the relatively short proportion of the lease still to run and the uncertainty, in 1940, of how long the requisition would last, the lease was nevertheless held terminated by constructive total destruction of the subject-matter. Lord President Normand said in the course of his opinion:

> "In the chapter of leases of heritage, and I think also in the chapter of *rei interitus*, our law is by no means the same as the law of England, and, to quote Lord Justice-Clerk Hope, if we were to attempt to apply that law in these cases, we should run the greatest risk of spoiling our own by mistaking theirs."[39]

---

[36] *National Carriers Ltd.* v. *Panalpina (Northern) Ltd.* [1981] A.C. 675; [1981] 1 All E.R. 161 (emphasis added).
[37] *Tay Salmon Fisheries Co.* v. *Speedie*, 1929 S.C. 593.
[38] *Mackeson* v. *Boyd*, 1942 S.C. 56.
[39] *Ibid.* at p. 63.

BIBLIOGRAPHY

This is a small selection from the extensive literature on contract law.

1. WORKS OF REFERENCE

Gloag, W.M., *The Law of Contract* (2nd ed., Edinburgh 1929).
McBryde, W.W., *The Law of Contract in Scotland* (Edinburgh 1987).
Walker, D.M., *The Law of Contracts and Related Obligations in Scotland* (2nd ed., London 1985).
[Professor McBryde's work provides an illuminating guide to the modern law. Read together with Gloag, it will yield great assistance in solving most contract problems.]

2. OTHER BOOKS

Gow, J.J., *The Mercantile and Industrial Law of Scotland* (Edinburgh 1964).
Smith, T.B., *A Short Commentary on the Law of Scotland* (Edinburgh 1962).
Stein, P.G., *Fault in the Formation of Contract in Roman and Scots Law* (Edinburgh 1958).
Wilson, W.A., *The Law of Scotland Relating to Debt* (Edinburgh 1982).

3. ARTICLES, ETC.

Atiyah, P.S., "Contract, Promises and the Law of Obligations" (1978) 94 L.Q.R. 193 [reprinted in *Essays on Contract* (Oxford 1986) Chap. 2].
Cameron, J.T., "The True Meaing of Stair I, x, 5," 1961 J.R. 103.
Clarke, M.G., "The Buyer's Right of Rejection," 1978 S.L.T. (News) 1.
"The Unfair Contract Terms Act, a Revolution in the Law of Contract, " 1978 S.L.T. (News) 26, 33.
Cooper, T.M., "Frustration of Contract in Scots Law," (1946) 28 Jo. of Comp. Leg. 1.

Cusine, D.J., "Manufacturers' Guarantees and the Unfair Contract Terms Act, " 1980 J.R. 185.

Forte, A. D. M., "Economic Frustration of Commercial Contracts," 1986 J.R. 1.

Forte, A. D. M. and MacQueen, H.L., "Contract Procedure, Contract Formation and the Battle of the Forms," (1986) 31 J.L.S. 224.

Huntley, J., "Commercial Practice and the Formation of Contract," 1988 S.L.T. 221.

Huntley, J., "Quotations, Business Practice and the Law, " 1989 S.L.T. 121.

Huntley, J., "Conditional Acceptances and Letters of Intent," 1990 S.L.T. 121.

McBryde, W.W., "The Intention to Create Legal Relations," 1992 J.R. 274.

MacCormack, G., "Some Problems of Contractual Theory," 1976 J.R. 20.

"A Note on Stair's Use of the Term Pollicitatio," 1976 J.R. 121.

MacCormick, D.N., "Jus Quaesitum Tertio—Stair v. Dunedin," 1970 J.R. 228.

McKendrick, E., "Economic Duress—A Reply," 1985 S.L.T. (News) 277.

"Specific Implement and Specific Performance," 1986 S.L.T. (News) 249.

MacKenzie Stuart, A.J., "Contract and Quasi Contract," Stair Society, Vol. 20, Chap. 19.

MacQueen, H.L., "Promoters' Contracts, Agency and the Jus Quaesitum Tertio," 1982 S.L.T. (News) 257.

"Constitution and Proof of Gratuitous Obligations," 1986 S.L.T. 1.

Murray, J., "Potestative Conditions," 1991 S.L.T. 185.

Reid, K.G.C., "Unintimated Assignations," 1989 S.L.T. 267.

Rodger, A.F., "Potestative Conditions," 1991 S.L.T. 253.

Rodger, A.F., "Molina, Stair and the Jus Quaesitum Tertio," 1969 J.R. 34, 128.

Scottish Law Commissioin Memoranda:
No. 35: "Unilateral Promises."
No. 36: "Formation of Contract."
No. 37: "Abortive Constitution."
No. 38: "Stipulations in Favour of Third Parties."
No. 39: "Formalities of Constitution and Restrictions of Proof."
No. 42: (2 vols.): "Defective Consent and Consequential Matters."

No. 65: "Legal Capacity and Responsibility of Minors and Pupils."

No. 66: "Constitution and Proof of Voluntary Obligations and the Authentication of Writings."

Stein, P.G., "The General Notions of Contract and Property in 18th Century Scottish Thought," 1963 J.R. 1.

Stewart, A.L., "Rei Interventus Reconsidered," (1966) 11 J.L.S. 263.

Stewart, W.J., "10 years of Fair Contracts in Scotland?," 1987 S.L.T. 361.

Stewart, W.J., "Of Purpose to Oblige. A Note on Stair 1.x.13," 1991 J.R. 216.

Stewart, W.J., "Stair 1.x.13. A Rejoinder," 1993 J.R. 83.

Thomson, J., "Error Revised," 1992 S.L.T. 215.

Wilson, W.A., *Essays in Honour of T.B. Smith.*

Woolman, S.E., "Restrictive Covenants—the Case for Review," 1985 S.L.T. (News) 253.

"Error Revisited," 1986 S.L.T. (News) 317.

INDEX